# THE TERRORISTS

# THE TERRORISTS

## THEIR WEAPONS, LEADERS AND TACTICS

by Christopher Dobson
and Ronald Payne

## Facts On File

119 West 57th Street, New York, N.Y. 10019

# THE TERRORISTS

Simultaneously published in the United Kingdom by
Macmillan Press Ltd., London and Basingstoke under
the title *Weapons of Terror*.

**Library of Congress Cataloging in Publication Data**

Dobson, Christopher.
    The terrorists.

    Bibliography:   p.
    Includes index.
    1.  Terrorism.   I.   Payne, Ronald, joint author.
II.   Title.
HV6431.D62      1979      364.1'35      79-797
ISBN 0-87196-406-6


9 8 7 6 5 4 3

# Contents

# 1

# Terror: How it Came to the Seventies

An india-rubber ball that, when squeezed in his trouser pocket, detonated a glass flask of dynamite concealed in his jacket 20 seconds later was the primitive yet effective device carried by the archetypal terrorist of literature, "The Professor." In Joseph Conrad's novel *The Secret Agent,* written at the turn of the century, this clever university dropout was pitted against the head of England's anti-terrorist squad, Chief Inspector Heat. It was entirely appropriate that he should have used an academic title; for then as today the feeling of power enjoyed by a terrorist held strong attraction for intellectuals who turned to the gun and the bomb when their political arguments failed to convince. As he himself boasted, The Professor had no future—yet his philosophy goes marching on.

The terrorist with the elaborately contrived weapon in his pocket spoke the truth when he said of England:

It is this country which is dangerous, with her idealistic conceptions of legality . . . to break up the superstition and worship of legality should be our aim. Nothing would please me more than to see Inspector Heat and his likes take to shooting us down in broad daylight with the approval of the public. Half our battle would be won then; the disintegration of the old morality would have set in its very temple.

He might well have been thinking out loud as the spokesman for a terrorist group today; his descendants are still intent upon making a violent clean sweep of the "old morality," the same battle still rages, and it is fought under the same principles of terrorist war by similar people with similar aims. Only the weapons have changed, and they have changed in spectacular style.

The aim of this book is to show how the development of military technology, producing ever-smaller and more deadly weapons, has affected the skills of terror and altered its tactics. Although the forces of order also benefit from improved weapons, that is not really the point; for the more often they have to use these weapons, the more propaganda they provide for the terrorist cause. The Professor's modern counterparts still want to provoke shooting in the street. Security forces want above all else to avoid it, and in this battle their improved weapons are psychological rather than military. Former Commissioner Michael Codd of the New York City police department, which used to be known as a "shoot-first force," now says:

There can be no precipitate use of firepower, considering the carrying strength of the average bullet. It can travel further than the limits of where the problem exists, and is a serious danger in the crowded urban conditions under which we live.

Thus, the up-to-date bullets of law and order, when used without care, not only travel farther, but strike in the cause of the terrorists they are seeking to overcome. That is why a new squad is in action in New York City— the hostage negotiating squad under Capt. Frank Bolz, who has talked out 90 hostage-takers with the slogan, "We aim to bore them to death." This technique was used in Chicago on August 18, 1978 when two Croatian nationalist gunmen were talked into surrender after holding six hostages at gunpoint throughout 10 hours of talk.

Modern weapons help the terrorists more than they help security forces, whether they be police or soldiers. By the time the British Army in Northern Ireland was issued U.S.-made Armalite rifles in July 1977, this same highly efficient weapon had been in the arsenal of the Provisional Irish Republican Army (IRA) for several years. The rifles were issued in limited numbers to the anti-terrorist military squads, and then only for specific sniping tasks, even though Mr. Robert Brown, a British Defense Ministry official, described them as being "the best available against terrorism." The Armalite is light and easy to handle, yet its high muzzle velocity gives its .223 caliber bullet devastating penetration power. It is this power which makes it such an effective weapon of terror, but makes the British Army so cautious about its use. A bullet that killed a soldier in August 1977 passed through him and seriously wounded a young girl.

Ironically, at about the time these rifles went into service with the British Army, the Ministry of Defense gave orders for the standard infantry weapon, the self-loading rifle, to be modified by the addition of a cam to the selective fire switch so that this automatic weapon could fire only single shots.

Although it is a great advantage for the terrorists to fire rapid bursts because they do not care how many people they injure, counterfire by security forces must be restricted so that, if possible, only terrorists are hit. Whenever British soldiers wound or kill nonterrorists, the IRA reaps a rich harvest of propaganda. Even when a gunman is hit, his weapon is spirited away, and the terrorists claim him to be an innocent victim. When American soldiers used their Armalites on full automatic fire in Vietnam, the effect was so destructive that men hit by the hail of bullets were said to be "blown away." There can be no blowing away in Northern Ireland, even of an established terrorist, because of the sympathy it would evoke for his cause.

One of the main aims of terror is to make murderers into heroes and so persuade opponents and neutrals that the terrorists' cause is righteous and their actions are justified. Their tactic is to make the authorities appear guilty of brutality and in the wrong. In a topsy-turvy way weapons that are too deadly help to promote this tactic.

The equipment of the terrorist during the nineteenth century was the revolver and the bomb. The revolver was usually bulky and woefully inaccurate except at point-blank range—the KGB, the Soviet intelligence agency, still teaches its assassins not to fire until they can almost touch their victims. The bomb was an elaborate affair with a fuse that was often difficult to manage; not until the end of the century were efficient hand grenades in use.

This basic equipment did not change radically until World War II when, during the Nazi occupation of Europe, resistance groups were set up throughout the occupied territories with the support of the Allied governments operating from Britain. We have in our possession an official manual composed by the renowned Sir Colin Gubbins, K.C.M.G., D.S.O., M.C., who ran Special Operations Executive (SOE) from his headquarters in Baker Street, London. This illustrated pamphlet describes in a variety of languages how to sabotage railway lines and how to carry out attacks on the army of occupation. It was parachuted by the thousands to resistance groups in Europe. With the pamphlets the Royal Air Force (RAF) dropped supplies of easily assembled Sten sub-machine guns and the new and very adaptable plastic explosives with instantaneous fuses and simple detonators.

Even before the war Gubbins, who had seen service in Ireland and in Russia in 1919, composed several manuals on the practice of guerilla warfare. The first was a common-sense guide pointing out the need for a friendly population and daring leadership. "Guerilla actions," he wrote, "will usually take place at point blank range as the result of an ambush or raid . . . Undoubtedly, therefore, the most effective weapon for the guerilla is the sub-machine gun."

He then put together the *Partisan Leader's Handbook* for a more popular readership, explaining how to prepare an ambush or blow up a railway engine. He also recommended giving short shrift to informers—kill them. Later he produced a clearly written pamphlet on how to use high explosives, and it was this work that developed into the airlifted guide we have already quoted. Significantly, British soldiers on the eve of World War II were already developing such expertise and were running a number of training courses in forms of subversive warfare for selected civilians—explorers, linguists, mountaineers and those with extensive foreign contacts. The skills of guerilla warfare were learned by respectable citizens, and modern weapons became virtually household utensils.

The practice of terrorism became not only respectable but honorable, and above all, an everyday affair.

There was no American equivalent of SOE until June 1942, when the Office of Strategic Services (OSS) was set up by "Wild Bill" Donovan, who had many friends in the British command and had visited their training camps as early as March 1941. After Pearl Harbor, Americans began attending courses in Britain, and under an agreement made between U.S. and British chiefs of staff, the special operations branch of OSS was practically fused with SOE in northwestern Europe. M.R.D. Foot, the official historian of SOE, has commented on the American officers, "Their intelligence, enthusiasm, and originality made up for their lack of equipment, training or experience."

Since the war much more reliable, smaller and more deadly automatic weapons have been developed. They are compact, easy to conceal and have greater killing power. Smaller amounts of explosives can do greater damage. The great advantage of these developments to those who indulge in terrorism is that one man can carry a great deal of hidden death with him. Paradoxically, a result of this increased ability to kill is that the threat of death has overtaken actual assassination as the prime weapon in the terrorists' arsenal.

When Czar Alexander II was bombed to death by a revolutionary group, the process set in motion led directly to the Russian Revolution and the killing of the Russian Royal family at Ekaterinenburg. When Gavril Princip mortally wounded the Archduke Franz Ferdinand at Sarajevo, he did so on the grounds of nationalism. His shots brought about World War I, destroyed empires and dynasties and led to the formation of the world as we know it.

But when John F. Kennedy, leader of the world's most powerful nation was shot down by Lee Harvey Oswald— who until conclusive evidence is produced to the contrary must be judged to have acted alone for his own reasons— the world wept but continued on its course. The truth of the matter is that in modern states with an efficient bureaucracy working in a settled infrastructure, the fate of the world does not depend on the life of a single individual. President Lyndon B. Johnson was a very different individual than Kennedy, but was he any worse as a President? Would Kennedy have been better able to cope with Vietnam? It is at least debatable.

The recent assassinations of Wasfi Tell, Prime Minister of Jordan, King Feisal of Saudi Arabia and Christopher Ewart-Biggs, the United Kingdom's ambassador to Dublin, were carried out for a variety of reasons: Tell's was for revenge by Black September, Feisal's by a deranged member of his family and Ewart-Biggs' by the Provisional IRA (Provos) trying to prove that they could strike in the Irish Republic as well as in Northern Ireland. None was motivated by old-fashioned revolutionary reasons. None has changed the face of the world. The only recent political assassination carried out for true revolutionary reasons by a terrorist group was the killing of the Spanish Prime Minister Luis Carrera Blanco. But even that killing was superfluous, for after the death of Generalissimo Francisco Franco, Spain was set firmly on the path towards democratic liberty. Carrera Blanco's death neither hastened nor retarded its progress.

Over the past 25 years the threat of the deed has become a more effective weapon than the deed itself—especially when the potential victim is not a replaceable politician but a group of people that includes women and children whose plight can be displayed on television in the most poignant fashion.

It is here that technical advances play into the terrorists' hands. The developments in weapons enable one terrorist to carry the firepower of a platoon, and the advent of the jumbo jet has provided the terrorists with the ideal target. The jumbo is totally under the control of the captain and a handful of men in the cockpit who are responsible for the lives of several hundred passengers confined within a vulnerable cell flying several miles high. Once terrorists are able to threaten the flight crew, they have virtually achieved victory. For unless the authorities give in to the hijackers' demands, the terrorists must be overcome either physically or mentally. The dangers of a shoot-out are apparent—within an aircraft someone is bound to get hurt. On the other hand, the inevitably long, drawn-out process to break down the hijacker's will involves mounting psychological stress for the hostages as well as the hijacker, with the danger that one of the terrorists may crack and blow everybody to pieces.

It is this element of the unknown, of inherent danger that makes hijacking so much more effective a tool of terror than assassination. And as aircraft become bigger and more complicated to operate, armed takeover becomes more dangerous, and therefore more spectacular. The seizure of a jumbo jet with 400 people on board attracts greater attention than that of a smaller plane with fewer passengers in danger. Experience has proved that despite increased security precautions, it is still possible to smuggle arms and explosives on board these giant aircraft. Indeed the more people being processed before a flight, the more likely it is that terrorists can evade the security checks. There have also been instances of ground crew—cleaners and caterers—planting weapons on board aircraft so that their comrades, who pass the security checks "clean," have their guns and grenades waiting for them. This is precisely what happened when a Palestinian group hijacked an Olympic Airways plane over Rhodes in order to secure the release of fellow terrorists jailed in Greece. The weapons were smuggled on board by cleaners at Beirut.

From an analysis of two decades of hijackings it appears that the ideal terror group for the purpose consists of a leader and four or five accomplices. The leader plus one, both armed with automatic pistols and grenades, make their way to the cockpit, usually from the first-class compartment. It is their responsibility to threaten the captain and flight crew and then give them orders for radio transmission. English is the standard international language for airline operations, so the leader must at least speak understandable English. Somewhere in the main cabin one of the hijackers places explosive charges at prearranged positions after careful examination of the type of aircraft before the raid—modern hijackers know their aircraft well. The charges must be in position before the aircraft lands at the fuel stop or destination ordered by the leader. The role of the other three or four men and women in the team is to intimidate the passengers and cabin crew by ostentatiously displaying automatic weapons and grenades, while the explosives operator goes about his business. They must create an atmosphere of fear.

Most of the early hijackings were regarded sympathetically in the West, for these acts in the years just after World War II were the work of desperate political refugees intent on flight from the new tyranny in Soviet-controlled Eastern Europe. All but a handful of the 21 hijackings reported fell into this category in the years 1945–52.

The armed seizure of aircraft for political terror aims was first organized by Raul Castro, brother of Fidel. In 1958 Cuban revolutionaries pirated a Cuban airliner flying from Miami and crashed it in the Oriente province killing 17 people. From that modest beginning developed the methodical seizure of more and bigger aircraft, and it was Castro who had the dubious honor of welcoming to Cuba the first jumbo jet ever to be hijacked. To mark the occasion in August 1970 he went to Havana airport to inspect the plane. In the two-year period before that there had been no less than 121 hijackings to Cuba, more than half of them from the United States. Not all were acts of political terrorism; many were carried out by criminals, the mentally unbalanced and political refugees. Partly because of the criminal involvement, Castro became disillusioned by hijacking: by 1973 cooperation between Cuba and the United States had become so customary that the two governments signed a five-year agreement to return seized aircraft and ships and hijackers for trial and severe punishment. The agreement ended the frantic period of air piracy in that part of the world.

But by that time the Cuban technique of air piracy was being actively exploited and perfected in the Middle East by Arab terrorists. The most notable exponents were members of the Popular Front for the Liberation of Palestine (PFLP), the most extreme of the Palestinian movements. Marxist in outlook, the PFLP is quasi-

Maoist and honors Kim I' Sung, the extraordinary communist dictator of North Korea, as one of its heroes. Defeated in its attempts to raid effectively across the Israeli border, its bases in Gaza and on the West Bank destroyed after the Six Day War in 1967, and thrown out of Jordan by King Hussein, the PFLP adopted hijacking as the modern equivalent of raiding, the traditional form of tribal warfare in the countries of Arabia.

For the Arabs, hijacking appeared on the scene when they were desperately searching for some way to strike at Israel. The Israeli Army had defeated and humiliated the armies of the Arab states and had then mopped up the guerillas. The Palestinian cause was being lost by default. Terrorism, and particularly hijacking, provided the answer. All that was needed was money and arms. And they had plenty of both. Money was flowing into their coffers from the newly prospering oil states, and the Arabs had the resources to equip themselves with new weapons for the continuing struggle.

During the 1950s stocks of up-to-date arms and ammunition had fallen into Arab hands when, at the end of the ill-fated Suez campaign of 1956, the Anglo-French forces withdrew from the canal and the British abandoned their bases in the zone. Before Egyptian nationalization of the canal, the British had come to an agreement with President Gamal Abdul Nasser that these bases would remain after a withdrawal of troops from Egypt so that in the event of a major international conflict, they could be reactivated to supply the British Army. At the end of 1956 when the last troops left after the so-called police action, the Egyptians took over the installations and found themselves in possession of a huge store of weapons, equipment and ammunition. Small arms and ammunition, Sten guns, short-magazine Lee Enfield rifles and grenades soon found their way into the arsenals of Arab independence and terrorist movements all over the Middle East. Quantities were passed over to the Algerian National Liberation Front fighting against the French in Algeria, and other supplies went to the Palestinians. For the first time these groups had the military hardware needed to establish training camps and set up guerilla forces on a lavish scale. It is one of the ironies of the Middle East's continuing wars that these arms, planned for use by the British to keep the peace, came to form the armory of those groups dedicated to making war.

However, these weapons from the British bases were not the latest in design. More modern equipment obtained through another act of power politics quickly superseded them. For in the course of his quarrel with the British, and stung by the refusal of John Foster Dulles to finance the building of the Aswan High Dam, President Nasser began flirting with the Russians. Military aid from the Soviets included for the first time the highly sophisticated weapons being produced for the Soviet Union by the efficient arms factories of Czechoslovakia. It was the time of the Kalashnikov, AK 47, rifle. A new generation of weapons was suddenly available in Egypt, and by way of Egypt to the terrorist groups and liberation movements, so that guerillas no longer needed to make do with second-hand equipment.

So, frustrated in their attempts to raid into Israel, but with gold in their war chests and modern Russian weapons in their arsenals, the Palestinians moved into the field of terrorism taking the Cuban and Latin American revolutionaries as a model. And what could be more obvious than to strike internationally? The Israelis were international people with Jewish friends and relations in communities in every country of the world. The Arab terrorists, descendants of warriors who had raided across the deserts to attack the caravans of their enemies, began using their new weapons to attack the airline routes of the twentieth-century world.

The first Palestinian hijacking was on July 23, 1968, when PFLP terrorists boarded an El Al Boeing 707 at Rome airport and forced it to land in Algiers. This was followed by a number of other attacks on Israeli airliners in Europe, and the campaign continued successfully until El Al began placing guards armed with high–velocity .22 pistols on all flights and installing locked bullet-proof doors to the cockpits of their aircraft. These precautions proved their value in September 1970 when Leila Khaled and Patrick Arguello, a Latin American working for the

PFLP, tried to hijack an El Al aircraft they had boarded in Amsterdam. They were overpowered by armed Israeli sky marshals and Arguello was fatally wounded. Leila Khaled did not press home the attack, failing at the critical moment to take the pin from the grenade she was holding. Arguello did pull the pin from his grenade, but it had a weak spring and failed to explode.

Despite this failure other similarly equipped terrorist squads forced a TWA 707 and a Swissair DC-8 to land at Dawson's Field, a runway carved in the desert by the RAF at the end of World War II, 40 miles north of Amman in Jordan. A British VC-10 en route from London to Bahrain was also forced down there and held hostage for the release of Leila Khaled, who was now being detained at Ealing police station after the El Al flight had made an emergency landing at Heathrow airport. Finally in this biggest of all series of hijacks, a TWA jumbo jet flying out of Amsterdam was seized, taken to Cairo and blown up.

Five governments became involved in lengthy negotiations with the Palestinians, who were of course then able to claim that they were operating on a nation-to-nation basis and that their cause had been officially recognized. But as in so many acts of terrorism, the very success of the act brought about a violent reaction. King Hussein of Jordan decided to rid himself of his dangerous guests and unleashed his Bedouin army on the Palestinian guerilla bases. In sharp fighting the guerillas, who provided the terrorist groups with their men, weapons and sanctuaries, were either wiped out or forced to retreat into Syria and Lebanon. It was then that Al Fatah, the Palestinian group led by Yasser Arafat, formed Black September to seek revenge against Hussein and to carry on the war against Israel by terror. Black September was responsible for the massacre at the Munich Olympic Games in which 11 Israeli athletes were murdered; the same organization then mounted an elaborate hijack of a Lufthansa flight to secure the release of their imprisoned comrades. So terrorism bred a terrible retribution and then yet more terrorism.

Although the mass hijackings practiced in 1970 have

not been repeated, it is none the less true that the big jet aircraft in use all over the world remain extremely vulnerable to attack in the air. A jumbo with more than 400 people aboard and worth over $20 million can still be held at the mercy of terrorists equipped with simple weapons.

In almost every case two weapons have been used for air piracy—the pistol, easily concealed about the person of the hijacker, and the hand grenade. The grenade is the backup weapon. As long as the terrorist has the courage to remove the pin and hold the lever in his hand, all he has to do if guards threaten to shoot or overpower him is to release his grip. Then everyone dies.

Grenades were an important part of the arsenal carried in suitcases by a suicide squad of the Japanese Red Army working with the PFLP who carried out a murderous raid at Israel's Lod airport, in 1972. Their bags were not searched by Air France, and when they disembarked in Israel they simply opened up the suitcases, took out grenades and Czech VZT 58 automatic rifles, and opened fire on the people in the airport, killing 24 and wounding 72 others.

Hijacking of aircraft is just one method of terrorist warfare now used extensively. Kidnapping of prominent figures either for a ransom or to score some political propaganda point is just as common, if less spectacular. It is an ancient technique that again was revived by the Cubans. They set the fashion for the political use of kidnapping when, in 1958, Castro supporters grabbed the racing driver Juan Fangio. Other Latin American groups of terrorists began to pick on foreign diplomats. When, in 1970, the Guatemalan government refused to accede to the demands of terrorists who had seized the West German ambassador, Count Karl von Spreti, the terrorists murdered him.

Inspiration for the Latin American terrorists came from Carlos Marighella, who was a Communist Party veteran already in his sixties when he abandoned rigid party methods in favor of real revolution. "The only way out for Brazil," he wrote, is "through armed struggle and preparation for the armed insurrection of the people."

The chapter "Handbook of Urban Guerilla Warfare" in Marighella's book *For the Liberation of Brazil* rapidly became the textbook for terrorists operating far away from Brazil—in Japan, the Middle East and Europe. Marighella explained:

> The urban guerilla does have one enormous advantage over the conventional soldier and the policeman: he is defending a just cause, the cause of the people—whereas they are on the side of an enemy the people hate.
> Though his arms are inferior to those of his enemy, his moral superiority is incontestable, and it is this which enables him to carry out his major tasks: to attack and to survive.

Of course, when Marighella speaks of the terrorists' arms being inferior, he is thinking in terms of heavy weapons, for it is usually true that in conventional military terms the forces of law and order can outgun the terrorists. The point is that with the range of weapons—including hand-held rockets with the explosive power of an artillery shell—now available to terrorists who have the funds or influence to acquire them, they can develop their own tactics. This makes them formidable opponents who cannot easily be defeated.

No particularly complicated weapons are needed for political kidnapping: anything will do—a pistol, a knife, a bludgeon, even a mere threat—as long as it is strong enough to overcome a person's mental or physical resistance. What is new in the technique is the kidnappers' exploitation of the act through television. Terrorism enjoys high ratings among the world's TV viewers and the terrorists revel in massive exposure—a far cry from the old days of secret cells and passwords where exposure usually meant death and was to be avoided at all costs.

During the bargaining phase—or as it is now more grandly called, the negotiation phase—of a kidnapping, a vast audience is involved as well as the principals, and the kidnappers' temporary importance is elevated in direct ratio to the number of viewers. The best example of the use of publicity by urban guerillas was the Olympic Games massacre at Munich in September 1972. International attention was already concentrated on the games when the Palestinians struck, and television cameras transmitting to almost every country in the world were on the spot to register this cruel assault. Through the wonders of satellite television, the murderers had an audience of 500 million people. The fact that they hardly could have believed that Israel would give in to their demands did not matter. They achieved what they had really set out to do: they had made the rest of the world aware of the Palestinian cause.

Much less publicized is the urban guerilla tactic of bank robbery, favored in Latin America and imitated elsewhere. Almost every group in the terrorist movement has resorted to it—the Algerian FLN, the IRA, the Baader-Meinhof gang in West Germany. Josef Stalin was a renowned bank robber in his terrorist days. For the revolutionary with a pistol or two in the armory, bank robbery has several appealing features: it can be carried out swiftly, it supplies funds for the movement, and it gives the terrorist the ideological satisfaction of believing that he or she is striking a blow against the capitalist system. Marighella wrote in "Handbook of Urban Guerilla Warfare": "Bank raids are the most popular form of action . . . we have almost made them a kind of entrance exam for apprenticeship in the technique of revolutionary war." The only drawback, according to the Brazilian, was that they might confuse ordinary customers who lost their money and possessions. For this reason, the instructor advised his followers not to behave like bandits—not always easy advice to follow.

Because it carries little risk for the terrorist, bombing is a popular tactic. However, the disadvantage is that innocent people are often killed by indiscriminate use of the shopping bag bomb and the even more lethal car bomb, arousing the wrath of the public against the bomber. It is after bomb outrages that calls for executions are most frequently heard, but even that can serve the terrorists' purpose of creating martyrs.

The making of bombs is one craft that has greatly advanced since the beginning of the twentieth century, and terrorists have made full use of improved methods to employ bombs for political purposes. There is no mystery about the components of any kind of bomb—a high–explosive charge weighing anything from a few ounces for a letter bomb to hundreds of pounds for a car bomb. Modern explosives in good condition are easy to handle and safe until they are set off by a detonator, usually a metal tube containing a more sensitive explosive such as fulminate of mercury. The detonator explodes if crushed, but the heat of a flash can also set it off, and a flash can easily be produced in several ways. Chemical action, or an electric current passed through a filament, or a percussion cap like those used in firearms can all serve the purpose. These basic methods place a wide range of possible bomb devices at the disposal of terrorists skilled in their use. In a later chapter we shall go into details about the workings of various kinds of bomb devices and explain how difficult it is for antibomb squads to disarm such devices. The importance of these technical developments is that they have affected the operational methods of urban guerillas by giving them a wider range of action and a greater choice of targets. A skilled explosives operator can send a letter bomb through the mail to kill one person. He can just as easily destroy an aircraft when it reaches a selected height by using an altitude fuse that detonates a bomb at that point. In November 1974 the Provisional IRA placed two time bombs using cheap watches as timers in two crowded Birmingham pubs. They killed 20 people and wounded 180.

Bombs, even the most sophisticated kind, are well established in the terrorist armory. Now there are signs that the same terrorists who have made unscrupulous use of them are graduating to even more powerful weapons. In 1975 "Carlos," Ilich Ramirez Sanchez, the most notorious of all present-day terrorists, unsuccessfully fired a Russian rocket launcher on an El Al plane at Orly airport near Paris. In a similar operation a few days later at the same airport, another unsuccessful attempt was made to destroy an aircraft. There can be no doubt that heavier modern weapons are already in the arsenal of urban guerillas for their war on society.

Italian police—tipped off by the Israelis—raided an

apartment leased by a group of Arabs at Ostia, near Rome, in September 1973, and there they made a most alarming discovery. For not only were the Arabs members of PFLP, they were armed with two SAM 7s, the Russian hand-held antiaircraft missiles, with which they intended to shoot down an El Al airliner as it approached Leonardo da Vinci Airport: the apartment was directly beneath the flight path to the airport. It would have been a simple target for a weapon designed to shoot down supersonic fighters and proven capable of doing so many times during the Yom Kippur War. Later, British police made raids near London Airport, and the army was called out in search of similar weapons following a tip-off that the Palestinians had smuggled SAMs into England. Other SAMs were captured near Nairobi airport when the Kenyan police arrested a joint PFLP-Baader-Meinhof commando group who were again planning to shoot down an El Al airliner.

Weapons such as the SAM are made available to terrorists by friendly governments, particularly the Libyan government of Colonel Muammar El-Qaddafi—the SAMs found in Rome came from his armory, where massive stocks of modern Russian weapons are stored. Before the advent of SAM-type weapons, it would have been very difficult for terrorists to set up antiaircraft guns powerful enough to shoot down a jumbo. But now hand-held missiles guided by infra-red devices can be brought to an airfield perimeter on the backseat of a hired car or set up on the roof of a strategically sited apartment to shoot down a $20 million airliner carrying hundreds of passengers.

What of the future? Will terrorists eventually turn to the use of even more devastating weapons in order to blackmail world governments and to make their propaganda points? The science of mass killing has made great progress since The Professor invented his rubber ball and flask device in the Conrad novel. Chemical weapons capable of poisoning a city's water supply are available in most countries. Nuclear materials can be found, bought or captured in the ever-increasing number of countries with atomic weapons or power generators. It sounds melodramatic to suggest that a determined terrorist group might make its own nuclear bomb and threaten to detonate it unless its political demands were met. Yet it is perfectly possible for a physicist to make such a device—in fact, a Princeton University student already has produced the plans of a workable nuclear device. We shall examine the possibilities in a later chapter, but first, in order to appreciate the dangers of terrorists' weapons, it is necessary to examine the kind of people who use them.

# 2

# Terrorism: The Reasons Why

What really makes a terrorist? Some come to it by chance, some by design, for "wide is the gate and broad is the way" that leads to this particular form of destruction. The ranks of the urban guerilla armies include many types, idealists as well as criminals and psychopaths. And yet, despite their differences, all terrorists share a common heritage: they have all come under the influence of those political thinkers who preach that violence is essential to make the world a better place "for the masses." The criminals and psychopaths use the philosophers to provide them with a glib rationalization for their actions, while the idealists are deluded by their gurus into thinking that violence provides the only true road to salvation.

As the anti-colonialist wars in several parts of the world came to an end in the 1950s and 1960s, the concept of a Third World composed of the poor and miserable countries evolved and acted as a magnet for the interest and compassion of young people in the Western world and in Japan, the only truly industrialized nation in the East, who identified with Third World struggles and with the poverty of less-fortunate people in their own countries. The feeling grew among young intellectuals that rich countries should do more for the poor and that we in the West should feel guilt for our past colonial exploitation and pay for that guilt through massive aid programs.

It was in this atmosphere of revulsion against the luxuries of life brought by capitalism to the middle classes of the developed world that the philosophers of terror be-

19

gan writing their volumes of theory—and in some cases of practice—about the efficacy and morality of guerilla and urban guerilla warfare. The inspiration came from Latin America, for Fidel Castro's triumph in Cuba had impressed everyone; he had shown how a small band of guerillas could overthrow the regular army of a dictator. He and his companions became immediate heroes in the universities. Before long the students of Europe and America began devouring the new literature of subversion.

Among the earliest and most influential of the new wave philosophers was Frantz Fanon, a black doctor born in Martinique who took over as head of the psychiatric department of Blida Hospital in Algeria as the war between the Arabs and French began there in 1952. He became a supporter of the Algerian National Liberation Front but died of leukemia shortly before independence was achieved in 1962. Although not a violent man himself, Fanon was consumed with hatred for colonialism and racial oppression, and he raised violence to a mystique. "Violence alone, violence committed by the people and educated by its leaders, makes it possible for the masses to understand social truths and gives the key to them," he wrote in a book entitled *The Wretched of the Earth*.

Not only was violence a means of ending colonial rule, he argued, but was also beneficial for its own sake, "a cleansing force." "It frees the native from his inferiority complex and from his despair and inaction; it makes him fearless and restores his self-respect."

Fanon justified such beliefs with the premise that European affluence was in itself scandalous because it was derived from robbery of the very soil of the Third World and from slavery. An immense debt had therefore been built up that must now be repaid, and it justified the armed struggle by the wretched of the earth against deportations, massacres, forced labor and slavery, "the principal means used by capitalism to augment its reserves of gold and diamonds, its wealth . . ."

A Marxist in theory, Fanon felt nothing but scorn for the working class in the West, for it had simply accepted

the benefits of latter-day colonialism. During the Algerian war he even had harsh words for Jean-Paul Sartre,
whom he otherwise admired. Simone de Beauvoir reported: "He could not forget that Sartre was French and he
blamed him for not having expiated that crime sufficiently."

The violent preachings of Fanon were important because they set a pattern of thought among leftward-lean-
ing intellectuals in the Western world, especially in the
United States among civil rights activists. This helps to
explain the process by which students turned to terrorism. His books instilled that sense of guilt, that feeling
that the Third World of the ex-colonies had right on its
side, which has provided so much support for international terrorists. The West Germans of the Baader-Meinhof groups and before them the French students, whose
revolt in Paris in 1968 coincided with a climax of anti-
Americanism over the war in Vietnam, drew inspiration
from Fanon's impassioned pleading on behalf of the colo-
nially exploited and oppressed. He helped set the scene
for international terrorism by justifying it as a legitimate way of attacking injustice.

If the inspiration for latter-day terrorism came from
Fanon and his Algerian experiences, its modern tactics
were perfected in Latin America. The founding father of
this school of violence was Carlos Marighella, who practiced what he preached, running a revolutionary group in
Brazil. In his chapter "Handbook of Urban Guerilla Warfare" in *For the Liberation of Brazil* he wrote:

Bank raids are the most popular form of action. In Brazil they
are very common; we have almost made them a kind of entrance exam for apprenticeship in the technique of revolutionary war . . . In this particular activity, revolutionaries have
two types of competitors—bandits and right-wing counter-
revolutionaries. This to some extent confuses ordinary people,
and therefore the guerilla will try to make clear the purpose of
his action, in two ways: he will refuse to behave like a bandit,
either by misguided violence, or by taking money or personal
possessions from customers who may be in the bank; and he
will back up his expropriation by some form of propaganda—
writing slogans attacking the ruling classes and imperialism

on the walls, handing out pamphlets, or giving people leaflets explaining the political purpose of what he is doing.

This passage gives the flavor of the naive and extraordinary advice handed out by the master. Yet it was taken seriously not only in Latin America but by European terrorist bands. The Baader-Meinhof gang, who on several occasions left copies of the Marighella handbook in their abandoned cars, specialized in bank robberies. Moreover, on one occasion in West Berlin in July 1975, they attempted to placate the customers of banks under attack as Marighella advised, by offering them chocolate-covered cakes known as "Negro kisses." They even left behind a box of these delicacies for the bank employees they had been threatening to kill only a few minutes before. The armed raiders, two men and two women, then made off with 100,000 deutsche marks, or nearly $35,000 at the time. It is not surprising that Andreas Baader once remarked that he found the gathering of money stolen from banks "a particularly pleasing experience." The terrified customers at the Berlin bank did not comment on their feelings.

In Great Britain, the Angry Brigade, a much less effective group that shared many ideas in common with Baader-Meinhof and was by no means unacquainted with the works of Marighella, made their money more modestly by stealing check books and credit cards. But shortly before the ringleaders were arrested, they began planning raids on post offices and banks, justifying their actions with the thought that respect for the law should never be more than a tactical consideration.

Although terrorist groups that formed in the United States had common origins with those in other countries their operational style was different. The Symbionese Liberation Army, though it never achieved any great support, was typical of the "cult" movements popular among young people in the early 1970s. The secret society nature of this movement drew in a number of immature intellectuals. But the SLA made its mark through a notable propaganda coup, the kidnapping of Patricia Hearst, the 19-year-old daughter of newspaper publisher William Randolph Hearst. This was a piece of terrorist theater designed to get the headlines and television coverage. Later Patricia Hearst was convicted in March 1976 of robbing a bank on the orders of SLA members and using a gun. Even so the strong suspicion remains that in robbing banks the SLA was more intent upon getting itself talked about than on training its supporters in revolutionary warfare.

In Brazil, Marighella's suggestion was carried through by his followers more ruthlessly, and in less than a year they lifted the best part of $1 million from banks in Rio and Sao Paulo. But in the course of their "entrance exams," a number of Brazilian comrades were taken by the police. In order to rescue 15 of them from prison, Marighella's group in September 1969 kidnapped the United States ambassador to Brazil, Charles Burke Elbrick, and held him hostage. The government gave in to their demands in order to avoid bloodshed and diplomatic embarrassment. Encouraged by this victory the terrorists went on to other acts, gradually escalating their demands for the release of more prisoners. Five were handed over for the life of the kidnapped Japanese consul, 40 more for the West German ambassador and finally 70 for the Swiss ambassador. In the end the government of Brazil learned that it did not pay to give in to terrorist blackmail. But the successes of the hostage-takers also showed that from their point of view the advice of Carlos Marighella was sound. In "Handbook of Urban Guerilla Warfare" he wrote:

We can kidnap and hide policemen, North American spies, political figures, or notorious enemies who are a danger to the revolution . . . To kidnap figures known for their artistic, sporting or other activities who have not expressed any political views may possibly provide a form of propaganda favorable to revolutionaries, but should only be done in very special circumstances, and in such a way as to be sure people will accept it sympathetically.

Kidnapping American personalities who live in Brazil, or who have come to visit here, is a most powerful form of protest against the penetration of U.S. imperialism into our country.

That the tactical precepts of Marighella were taken seriously by followers throughout the world is proved by a glance at the subsequent activities of the international groups. The Palestinians turned to hostage–taking and the murder of diplomats and distinguished foreigners; Baader-Meinhof and the Moluccans in Holland kidnapped and demanded either the freeing of prisoners or the publication of political communiques in return for their lives. "Carlos" went so far as to hold hostage the entire ministerial strength of OPEC, the international oil body and possibly the most powerful group of men in the world. In every case the terrorists accepted the dictum of Carlos Marighella that the duty of a revolutionary is to make the revolution. They were no doubt flattered by his outline of the personal qualities of an urban guerilla—courage and initiative, good tactics and a good aim with a gun, and skill and cunning. They amount to what used to be called in the British Army OLQ—officer-like qualities.

Although Marighella was killed in 1969 in the wave of repression the actions of his supporters had provoked, his ghost is still with us through the influence of his teachings. His book became the standard work for ambitious terrorist leaders, and when it was translated into French in 1970, the French government forbade its distribution and sale. About the same time it was published in Berlin, and later a West German terrorist said about it, "You find quite concrete instructions: the urban guerilla must be fit, and must read this and that, and learn to do this and that."

Marighella's military theories are neither sensational nor very new, but his book did help to popularize the term "urban guerilla." He declared that urban guerilla warfare started in Brazil in 1968. But the theories are heavily derived from Chairman Mao Tse-tung's instructions to the Communists on how to take over China from the Nationalists.

When such tactics were applied in Latin America by people like Che Guevara, they met with far less success. Conditions in the various republics of that continent were different from those in the Far East. Because Mao had formulated the principle that Communist guerillas could strangle the cities from the countryside and had, moreover, proved it in battle, the "encirclement of the city by the countryside" became holy writ. But in Western industrialized societies, and in many parts of Latin America, the great majority of people live in cities. In such places it is hardly possible for the country minority to "strangle" the city majority.

Even at the time when Marighella was first putting his theories into practice, counterinsurgency forces with new techniques and good training were in the process of destroying rural guerillas in Latin America. Guevara, who planned to provoke U.S. military intervention in Bolivia and so create a perpetual war like that in Vietnam, had over-reached himself. Rural guerillas had also failed in Brazil.

The rural *foco*, or focus, advocated by Guevara was a guerilla-occupied base for activity in the countryside into which recruits theoretically poured to form a miniature revolutionary state. In Latin America the rural guerillas were unable to win the support that theorists believed would be forthcoming from farmers and peasants. What Marighella did was to adapt the *foco* principle to urban activities, and so the terrorists came to town. It was in the cities and towns that enthusiastic converts such as students and intellectuals were most at home, and there they stood a better chance of survival.

In Latin America the turning point in the terrorist campaigns came with the death of Che Guevara in Bolivia in 1967. In the early 1960s insurgent movements had spread rapidly in Guatemala, Brazil, Peru and other countries in the hemisphere. Their inspiration came from Cuba, where Fidel Castro set about using his island base to encourage revolutionary movements on the continent. As well as providing the know-how and the weapons, Castro furnished the example. Tyranny and capitalist imperialism symbolized by the United States were the enemy. "I was born in Argentina, I fought in Cuba, and I began to be a revolutionary in Guatemala," was how Che Guevara summed up his autobiography. It was this Spanish Irishman who became not only the theorist but the wandering missionary of revolution in Latin America. He was an occasional student and perpetual traveler who learned the theory of subversive warfare and in

1960 became famous by writing *Guerilla War*. Cuba was his only successful campaign in the field. Despite his meticulous writing on the subject, his advice was derivative, and in action he made mistake after mistake. What he managed to do was to provide the fashionable trimmings of political theory and philosophy.

As the Guevara cult grew he exerted great influence on more capable guerilla leaders and on the terrorists as well, although he himself favored guerilla war as opposed to terror raids. He once warned against the dangers of terrorism that hindered "contact with the masses and makes impossible unification for actions that will be necessary at the critical moment." He saw the need to win the support of local populations in order to get recruits, and there was about him a knightly aura of the social reformer in arms who fought only with the support of the oppressed people.

The Guevara cult and the ideas of the man were spread to Western Europe and, to a lesser extent, to the U.S. by his admirer Regis Debray, the French intellectual and philosopher. What was attractive for Europeans in the Guevara theory was the adapted doctrine of proletarian internationalism. Parties and political programs seemed less important to the revolutionary than the fighting itself, for from the armed clash political beliefs would eventually emerge. The message was: destroy first, see what happens later. And that message caught on among the European students and intellectuals.

When Guevara went off searching for more action once Cuba had been liberated, it was already too late for him in Latin America. The guerillas were being outfought and outmaneuvred by counterinsurgency forces who had learned well the Cuban lesson. An enthusiastic though blundering commander, Guevara fought his forlorn battles in Bolivia until the autumn of 1967 when the Bolivian Eighth Division, some of its troops disguised as peasants, surrounded Guevara and his band in the Santa Cruz district. Guevara, who had been wounded, was finally captured leaning against a tree. The soldiers took him to the tiny village of La Higuera, and it was there that General Joaquin Zentano Anaya, then a colonel, received orders from La Paz to shoot the captured guerilla leader.

His death in such romantic circumstances generated a whole new mythology, and soon "Che Guevara lives" became the rallying call for leftist rebels throughout the world. His name still lived in 1976 when the ill-fated Entebbe hijackers announced that they were called the Che Guevara-Gaza Group, deriving the name from a Palestinian terrorist who styled himself the Che Guevara of Gaza.

The face on the tee shirt is now known everywhere. The worry is that Guevara has now been adopted as an unofficial hero by the rigid old Communist Parties he hated and that he is now idolized by them as well as by the fringe revolutionaries.

Dashing posters of Che in full guerilla regalia appeared everywhere, and it almost seemed as though everybody under the age of 25 wanted to be a guerilla. What was less obvious at the time was that irregular forces, defeated in Latin America, were already transforming themselves into urban guerillas, that is to say town-terrorists. It was not long before like-minded groups in different parts of the world, and in Europe particularly, turned from national to international targets. It was a natural development for these terrorists to strike first against soft American targets, diplomats and advisers and then businessmen, in reaction against the strength of U.S. influence in Latin America. It was the U.S. Army and the CIA who had helped to train the counter-insurgency forces that destroyed revolutionary hopes.

The new radicals in U.S. and European universities found it easy enough to identify with the man in the beret who died for a cause in the Bolivian mountains. Emotionally at least, students who occupied buildings in London and Berlin or who fought the Chicago police at the Democratic Party Convention there, were the spiritual followers of Che. In one way or another they were intent on using different degrees of violence to change the established order.

A new nihilism based on rash, though high-minded,

principles was emerging. Regis Debray, the French disciple of Che Guevara who made Guevara more famous after his death than he had been in life, was jailed in Bolivia for aiding the guerillas. His lengthy defense of his own actions and of guerilla war were widely read. He served only three years of a 30-year sentence.

Debray posed the question, who should lead the revolution. "The irony of history has willed . . . the assignment of precisely this vanguard role to students and revolutionary intellectuals, who have to unleash, or rather initiate, the highest forms of class struggle." And he continually stressed the need for armed struggle. Such statements spread the idea among the young radicals that they should take up arms against the system. In his introduction to Debray's *Strategy for Revolution*, Robin Blackburn summed it all up:

Along with other guides to guerilla strategy, Debray's writings have helped a new style of revolutionary politics to spread from the Third World back to the metropolitan heartlands of imperialism. The sort of immediacy which the *foco* strategy can achieve has also been attained in the actions of the revolutionary movement of Europe and North America—in factory and university occupations, black uprisings, squatters' movements and so forth.

The other philosopher who inspired similar thoughts in the universities was Herbert Marcuse, born in Berlin in 1898, also a theoretician and sociologist who had become Professor of Political Thought at the University of California. He belonged to the Frankfurt school of philosophy whose supporters had already made the connection between Western prosperity and Third World misery. On the one hand, they said, there was material plenty and "choice" which gave an illusion of freedom; on the other was the war in Vietnam, black ghettos in America and the sufferings of peasants in Bolivia and Uruguay. To shorthand this contrast they spoke of "consumption terror" or sometimes "consumption fascism," which was already halfway to justifying the use of terror to overthrow the system that brought it about.

The   Frankfurt   philosophers   busied   themselves

confirming and justifying feelings abroad in the tumultuous 1960s. Moreover the Marcusian argument that Western power elites had provided a surfeit of material needs by creating artificial demand for a superfluity of goods appealed most to the radical chic groups (known in Germany as the *Schili*) as well as to students. Most of them were middle- and upper-class people feeling guilty because they in particular were so well provided with worldly goods. Nowhere did this take hold so firmly as in West Germany, where the economic miracle had brought such a cornucopia to people who less than 25 years before had been so impoverished by war that a woman could be bought for a carton of cigarettes.

Marcuse also preached that the scientific and technological revolution had changed the structure of the working class, thus altering classic Marxist assumptions. A new technologically based society had emerged in the West, creating an alliance between big business and the working class, which was no longer revolutionary or intent on overthrowing the established order. "The people, previously the ferment of social change have moved up to become the ferment of social cohesion . . ." This development created a situation in which only what he called the "outsiders" comprised the true revolutionaries. The outsiders were those forced out of the system because they were unemployable; those persecuted for their color; the exploited masses of the Third World; and the students disgusted by comfortable consumerism in the West.

Marcuse had observed that in the 1960s many young people were already in revolt against their elders and their ways. He encouraged them in what he called the "great refusal" to take part in the rat race. He codified and explained their discontent, indeed flattering them by describing them as the vanguard, "the most advanced consciousness of humanity." Their mission was to lead the powerless and ignorant substratum of society in revolutionary uprisings. They were urged to reject a society whose interests required the peaceful continuance of its ways and, when legal methods failed, to resort to illegal ones. In Europe the California-based German philosopher provided a complete though devious justification for student aggression by telling them that they were no more free than those who lived in totalitarian states east of the Berlin Wall. They enjoyed only an illusion of freedom because the consumer society foisted upon them comfort and luxury.

Marcuse had as great a following in America as he later won in Europe. In the U.S. the student movement concentrated on the Vietnam War and its consequences, while also attacking the universities because they were used both for military research and for military recruitment. Racial discrimination and big business were also targets in student attacks on ostentatious wealth and exploitation. The same themes were obvious as student revolt spread to Europe. Nowhere was the movement more active than in the Free University of West Berlin, whose students went through the whole range of fashionable war cries as the SDS—the Socialist Student Union—gave its support to every campaign from "ban the bomb" to "Americans, get out of Vietnam," "racial equality" and "help the Third World." The proximity of East Berlin and its climate of oppression originally drove East Germans to seek freedom in the West to demonstrate against their Communist masters, but when the flow dried up after the building of the Berlin Wall, the students, lacking the experience of the refugees, moved to the left.

The German universities were still stuffy, crowded and old-fashioned places. Though the Free University, established after World War II, was the most modern of them, this did not prevent it from becoming a focus for trouble. It was the place for demonstrations, sit-ins, talk-ins and all the other "happenings" familiar in the 1960s. All these events became indelibly stamped upon the personalities of those who later took to terrorism in West Germany.

One event in particular had a powerful effect. In 1967 the Shah of Iran made a state visit to West Germany and undertook the ritual pilgrimage to its beleaguered outpost, West Berlin. The students seized upon him as a natural enemy, the representative of oppression in the Third World. The police handled the demonstration clumsily, and one officer opened fire on the crowd and killed a mild-mannered demonstrator named Benno Ohnesorg, a 26-year-old student from Hanover. This killing horrified the demonstrators and left its mark on the whole student movement.

A comparable incident took place in 1970 when National Guardsmen opened fire without warning on students demonstrating at Kent State University in Ohio against President Richard M. Nixon's invasion of Cambodia. They killed four students and wounded 10. While Nixon dismissed the incident as an inevitable consequence of "the resort to violence"—violence of the young that is—it provided young people throughout the Western world with a perfect example of violence by the state.

Both the Berlin affair and the Kent State tragedy convinced student radicals that the state and the authorities were the violent oppressors and that they were justified in answering state violence with revolutionary violence.

Coincidentally it was while Marcuse was visiting the Free University on May 13, 1968 that a dramatic protest movement similar to the Berlin incident was at its climax in Paris. There thousands of students were marching behind the red flags of Communism and the black flags of anarchy. The revolution had begun in protest against the overcrowded and archaic universities of France. But as the barricades went up on the boulevards and clashes with riot police developed, it became obvious that French students were determined to follow through on the idea that they should inspire the sluggish workers in marching to overthrow capitalism.

For a short while the ecstasy and the excitement of that revolution did spread to the workers, who, although they resented the students and their ways, went on strike and in many cases occupied their workplaces. It began to look as though General Charles de Gaulle's Fifth Republic would be destroyed. Then, largely through de Gaulle's extraordinary energy and the countermagic of his personality, the Republic was saved. The terrified bourgeoisie rallied to his cause, troop reinforcements were brought back from West Germany, and, significantly, the workers abandoned their occupations of factories and offices in return for more money and better working conditions.

May 1968 was the high water mark of student revolt. The red strongholds that had been set up in the Sorbonne and at Nanterre, the new branch of the University of Paris, failed to make a successful revolution, but they had created a new mythology. The French students had briefly united the new radical themes: the violence preached by Fanon; the *foco* theory of Guevara and Debray, tried out in the streets rather than in the jungles; and the student vanguard of Marcuse's outsiders. Yet, when the end came the world did not seem to have changed all that much. The predictions of Marcuse had come to pass. After ritual strikes and noises of revolution, the workers returned to the pleasures of "terror consumption." Perhaps they really were apathetic toward revolution and were in league with the capitalists. After the heady excitement of the barricades, the young revolutionaries tasted bitterness and disappointment. There was no further point in supporting the classic Communist Parties, far less the old-fashioned socialists. They needed something more extreme, and thus justified their turning to terrorism.

This then was the process that transformed young students into terrorists. However, it would be wrong to think that all terrorists are intellectuals fighting for idealistic motives. The ranks of the IRA, for example, are filled with men who are neither intellectual nor idealistic; men like Anthony Clarke, a laborer from Liverpool who was arrested after a crude incendiary bomb he planted in a store exploded prematurely and set him on fire. In court he described his recruitment by the PIRA, the Provisional Irish Republican Army. "Two Belfast men called on me. They asked me if I fancied planting some bombs when they were talking about the Irish troubles. I said I would have a go."

Harry Duggan, a baby-faced PIRA gunman captured in London after being besieged in an apartment on Balcombe Street with three other terrorists in possession of an arsenal of weapons, took his first steps on the road to murder six years before, when he began attending Provisional Sinn Fein meetings. He came from a village called

Feakle, and had become an apprentice in a chipboard factory where his father worked as a carpenter. His father thought he was good at his job and had no idea that he had become a gunnman for the Provos. He was rated by the Provisional Army Council as "a very useful man," and at a time when his mother in Ireland was saying that he had always been a good boy in school, he was selected to go on a terror mission to London. His group killed Ross McWhirter, editor of the *Guinness Book of Records*, and blew up an eminent cancer specialist in a London street.

Duggan started his career at Irish political meetings, where loquacious Provos denounced the British and their evil ways, and before long he was out on the banks of the river Shannon practicing with .22 rifles and specially adapted Webley .38 revolvers. But he was still described by friends as a decent boy who, at the age of 23 looked as if he should be singing in the local church choir.

The IRA gave him money and a smart suit and sent him to kill in London. There he joined up with Hugh Docherty, a 25-year-old brought up in an Irish ghetto called Toryglen, a high-rise development area of Glasgow, Scotland. Raised in bigotry in an isolated community in an alien country, Docherty had moved into terrorism as naturally and easily as he might have fallen into crime.

These three men are typical of the IRA, a world apart from Baader-Meinhof and the Japanese Red Army. Although some of the cliches of international terrorism have entered the limited vocabulary of the IRA and there has been some operational contact between the international groups and the IRA, that organization remains an insular movement, content with its own myths. One of the oldest of the terrorist movements, it has a justified reputation for strict discipline. From 1973 until the end of November 1978, its kangaroo courts ordered no less than 677 "punishment shootings." Ninety-nine percent of these were in fact "kneecappings" in which punishment is inflicted by shooting the victim in the back of the knee. The year 1975 was the worst recorded—at least 189 kneecappings were carried out.

"Kneecappings" are inflicted for a variety of offenses

from trying to keep part of the haul from post office and bank raids to showing reluctance to remain on duty with an Active Service Unit. It is not the only form of punishment—recently there have been cases of fingers cut off with razors, and one case of castration has been reported. Any attempt to work with the British security forces is, of course, rewarded with death, the victim being hooded and shot through the head. Thus, IRA terrorists are kept in line through fear.

But apart from its harshness, the movement depends on the kind of patriotic fervor that inspires some of its "hit" men. Many of its members have moved into the terror business for sentimental reasons. And probably as many Irishmen have gone off gun in hand through the influence of whiskey and black porter, hymned on by the catchy traditional revolutionary songs, as through any hard-headed political conviction or true revolutionary philosophy. As one IRA mother told a television interviewer, speaking of her son who had killed a British soldier, "He is a patriot fighting for his country."

Between the start of the terror campaigns in Northern Ireland in 1969 and the end of November 1978, the IRA killed 490 members of the security forces and 1,400 civilians. It accomplished all this with the active support of only a small percentage of the population, and without achieving any real political aim.

It is not without interest that when intellectuals and middle-class revolutionaries from outside have tried to aid the cause of the IRA, they have been treated with suspicion and contempt. To Irish hit men, the kind of terrorists who would be welcomed by, for example, the West German Red Army Faction are simply an embarrassment. When Dr. Rose Dugdale, an English sympathizer, was arrested for terrorist actions—including bombing a police station with an explosives-filled milk churn from a hijacked helicopter—which both she and the IRA admitted were in support of the Provos, David O'Connell, a senior member of the leadership, showed no sign of enthusiasm in her support. He admitted that some Provos were involved in the operations with Dr. Dugdale, but they had done so without the approval of the Provisional Army Council.

In this respect the IRA by no means typical of present-day terrorist movements, most of which have international support and strong transnational links. The IRA is a much more earthy group, more suspicious of outsiders and unfriendly to the student revolutionaries found in most similar movements. It even keeps at arms' length the Breton nationalist fighters of France who share similar aims.

The only acceptable outsiders giving support to the IRA are Irish Americans. Here again the link is sentimental. Over the last few years, and largely because the government of the Irish Republic has gone out of its way to inform leaders of Irish-American opinion about the true face of Irish terrorism, the number of dollars flowing into IRA funds has fallen. From a total of $600,000 in 1972, donations fell to $150,000 in 1977. William V. Shannon, the U.S. ambassador to Dublin, explained the matter very well in an interview in *The Times* of London early in 1978. He said that Irish Americans like himself and Senator Edward M. Kennedy had come around to the view that if Britain were to give in and withdraw from Northern Ireland, "there might well be more violence."

When it started in 1969 the civil rights issue burst into flames, and Irish Americans tended to think it was the final act of the drama which began in 1916. To start with there was an instinctive desire to rally behind the Irish, to kick the British out and reunite the country . . . But as the guerilla war has ground on, people have become much more conversant with the realities and complexities of the situation in the North.

If Irish-American support for the Provisionals waging urban guerilla warfare in the British Isles continues to decline, the terrorists may eventually have to turn towards the transnational terrorist groups to help provide them with modern weapons and money. But so far the IRA has remained aloof. It has, moreover, never made use of techniques common elsewhere such as hijacking aircraft, though hostages have been taken. Until now the IRA has stuck very much to the old ways.

Because it fights a traditional cause of some antiquity, the Irish Republican Army attracts a higher proportion of mature terrorists to its colors than almost any other such group. For similar historical reasons Irish terrorists tend to be more working class and decidedly less intellectual than is the case with other "liberation" movements.

The original IRA was formed to fight in a patriotic cause against an occupying army. Thus it bore more of a similarity to the Spanish guerillas who fought against Napoleon and to the Algerian National Liberation Front struggling against the French who ruled their country than to the current revolutionary causes.

It is often accepted as fact that the terrorist activities of the old IRA won the establishment of the Irish Republic. The claim is rejected by many Irishmen in the south, including Conor Cruise O'Brien, a former minister in the Dublin government. In a lecture on "Liberty and Terror" at Oxford, England, he argued: "Basically our state owes its existence to the known and attested demand of a majority of its inhabitants for self-government and to the recognition, in Britain and the world, of the legitimacy of that demand. That demand was repeatedly expressed at the polls: it was also expressed by violent means."

Even when the democrats had negotiated the establishment of the new state with British Prime Minister Lloyd George in 1921, they then had to defend it against the pure Republicans and the gunmen who persisted. Michael Collins, who had successfully negotiated with the British, was assassinated the following year by the IRA because he had agreed to compromise over the six largely Protestant counties in the north that remained part of the United Kingdom. From 1922 onwards the IRA was fighting against the government of the Irish Republic and against the Irish Catholics who elected it.

In the 1960s the IRA began to acquire a political flavor of Marxism; that was largely through the influence of one man, David O'Connell, on its leadership. But within a few years it became clear that most members, including those active in terrorism, were not interested in political ideology so much as in the basic nationalism of their cause. The Provisional IRA that took over activities in the north was simpler in its philosophy.

What attracts apprentice killers to the Provo cause is the very simplicity of the movement's basic aims, which may be summed up as "get the army and the British out of Northern Ireland." Their ostensible aim is to allow the Irish government in the south to rule all of Ireland. What they really want is to destroy the democratic government of Dublin, and to sever the connections with the Europe of the Common Market, as well as with England. The Provisional IRA has a rather woolly concept of creating a "new" Ireland. As Dr. Conor Cruise O'Brien remarked in his Oxford lecture: "The achievement of that new Ireland would I think require two rather basic changes for the island of Ireland: a new geographical location and a new population. These may prove difficult either to negotiate or to extort by political force."

The basic aim of the IRA is separatist and nationalist. Here we have an important split in the aspirations of terrorist movements in the modern world. It is important to distinguish between those movements in America, Europe and Japan who use their form of warfare to make international revolution and overthrow the present system; and those who, like the Irish, are concerned with establishing power in their homeland. In this respect the Irish have something in common with the Israelis, who succeeded in setting up their own state through use of the terror weapon: indeed the Israeli Prime Minister, Menachem Begin, was once leader of the 700-strong force of terrorists known as Irgun Zvi Leumi.

The two outstanding examples of what may be called "territorial" terrorists are the IRA and the various branches of Palestinian liberation forces. But the Palestinians, unlike the Irish, are much more willing to accept the aid and support of outsiders and conduct their campaigns worldwide. In fact after Munich, when every Arab in Europe was marked as a potential terrorist, they came to rely on international groups to carry out their missions. In addition, they provided training, weapons and money for these groups of ideological terrorists who at first glance had little reason to be involved in the underground war between Arabs and Jews. Into this category fell members of Baader-Meinhof, the Japanese Red Army and the "Carlos" network.

For all that, the various Palestinian organizations,

which are the best publicized of all guerilla and terrorist groups, remain fundamentally interested in territorial aims. To them Palestine means the whole of Palestine, and they want to recover that land from Israeli possession and to control it themselves. However, their campaign has been a long one, and in the course of it the various brands of revolutionary Marxism have impressed themselves upon individual leaders. A distant aim of world revolution in the minds of numerous Palestinian terrorists gives guerillas from that part of the world something in common with the terrorist groups of Latin America and Europe.

It may well be assumed that if the Arab oil powers and the "confrontation" states financed by them finally accept an international political settlement of the Palestine problem, the radical Palestinian movements will turn their attacks on those countries with the aim of producing revolutionary governments. Already there have been terrorist attacks, sometimes sponsored by Colonel Muammar Qaddafi of Libya, against the Egyptian government. The leadership of this trend, which takes Palestinian terrorism out of its purely territorial role and involves it in international revolution, rests with men like Dr. George Habash and Wadi Hadad, who until his death in April 1978 was his chief of operations. They ran the most active and ruthless group, the Popular Front for the Liberation of Palestine. (PFLP).

The PFLP is fiercely committed not only to the destruction of Israel but to the creation of a Marxist–Leninist revolution throughout the Arab world. And after disposing of the "feudal" Arab states, it intends to terrorize in the cause of world revolution. That is why Dr. Habash's men are so ready to provide bases and training for international movements working in the same cause and to make use of their members. Habash's philosophy is that there is no point in classic military operations against Israel, only terror can be effective. PFLP spokesman Bassam Abu Sherif, himself badly scarred by an Israeli parcel bomb, told one of the authors at PFLP headquarters in Beirut in 1973: "We intend to attack imperialist and

Zionist interests wherever we find them in the world. They are legitimate targets."

There can be little doubt that the effectiveness of PFLP operations led to the birth of Black September, established originally to take revenge for the destruction of the guerilla movement in Jordan by King Hussein. After its success in killing Wasfi Tell, the Jordanian Prime Minister, Black September expanded into an international organization that proved its savagery by carrying out the massacre at the Munich Olympics.

Another Arab terrorist group is a breakaway from PFLP. Known as the Popular Democratic Front for the Liberation of Palestine, it is led by a revolutionary named Naif Hawatmeh. Like several other splinter groups, it comes under the umbrella of the Palestine Liberation Organization (PLO) led by Yasser Arafat, who is recognized at the United Nations as the respectable statesman of the Palestinian cause. But he also leads the politico-military organization known as Al Fatah ("the struggle"), which itself controlled Black September. Arafat, seeing that he was making more headway through the Council Chamber than by terrorism, has ordered Black September to cease operations. He is an excellent example of a nationalist in transition from terrorism to political leadership.

All these leaders are clever and mostly well-educated men. Many have been influenced by the international theorists of terrorism, its aims and methods, whose doctrines we shall outline. If Marighella and Che Guevara are known as the philosophers and writers of revolution by subversive warfare, these men are the terrorist warlords. Through their influence and petrodollar resources, they are in a position to get the most modern weapons for their followers. They also supply supporters in the groups of brother terrorists. From the great arsenal of Soviet weapons bought by Colonel Qaddafi, supplies of advanced and heavy weapons trickle through the hands of Palestinian groups to other terrorists in the West willing to use them in the cause. There is a danger of more antiaircraft missiles, bazookas and new grenades filtering through to guerilla movements worldwide in this way.

In this process yet another warlord of terror, code-named Carlos, still plays a large part. His is an interesting case history, for in his own career he has brought together a number of the threads that weave into the fabric of international terrorism. This plump and affected 29-year-old was born Ilich Ramirez Sanchez, one of the three sons of a Venezuelan communist lawyer who made his millions through property dealing. The father chose as first names for his sons the three names of Nikolai Lenin, and he arranged the education of Carlos with care. The young Ilich was packed off to Cuba to learn the political and martial arts in Fidel Castro's brave new world. One of his instructors was a well-known KGB man, and it seemed only logical that he should progress to complete his studies in Moscow at the Patrice Lumumba University. With such an upbringing it was inevitable that he should make his career in terrorism, after bringing himself up to date with the latest techniques in guerilla warfare under the tuition of Arab instructors at the Palestinian camps in the Middle East.

Carlos worked on behalf of the Palestinians in Europe and elsewhere. He was organizationally in touch with Baader-Meinhof groups in Frankfurt and in Hamburg, but he first came to wide public attention when, in order to escape arrest in Paris, he shot and killed his own fellow terrorist, Michel Moukharbel, and two officers of the French DST. (Defence de la Securite du Territoire), the French internal counter-intelligence organization set up after World War II. He wounded a third inspector of this special police unit. Even before that *Il Gordo* (the fat one), as he was known, had attempted to kill a prominent member of the Jewish community, department store executive Teddy Sieff. But it was not until he led the squad of Arabs and West German Red Army Faction members who seized as hostages the 11 ministers at the Vienna conference of the Organization of Petroleum Exporting Countries (OPEC) and flew them in a getaway plane to Algiers that his full persona emerged publicly. On the aircraft he spent hours in the company of that shrewd judge of character Sheikh Zaki Yamani, the Saudi Arabian minister of petroleum. Carlos by turn threatened to kill him and poured out confidences, clearly anxious to tell somebody the story of his life, or at least his life as he chose to see it.

He was acting out the role of a grand spokesman, a diplomat of terror. But he could not resist using melodramatic language—"You will have heard of me already; I am Carlos. You can tell that to the others," he proclaimed, according to Sheikh Yamani over Saudi radio and in conversation with one of the authors. Carlos dressed dramatically for the occasion in a long trenchcoat with a beret a la Guevara, but tilted threateningly forward. He affected a thin fringe of beard, the badge of the anarchist, which also conveniently hides a double chin. As weapons he carried a Makarov automatic pistol and a submachine gun.

When his German accomplice told him she had just killed two people, he smiled and said, "Quite right, I killed one myself." To Sheikh Yamani he spoke happily of putting pressure on the Austrian government, he boasted of his power and of his sexual exploits, but the political content of his words rang false to Yamani. Carlos claimed mockingly to be a democrat who consulted his fellow terrorists before making any decision. But Yamani noted that Carlos "is not a committed communist . . . does not believe in the Palestinian cause or in Arab nationalism but . . . [considers] them as factors which might be exploited to help spread the international revolutionary movement." Here we have a very precise description of the international terrorist. We are also indebted to Sheikh Yamani, one of the few men who has spent long hours with a talkative terrorist leader and lived to tell the tale, for this summation:

If a criminal were to deserve the admiration of non-criminals, then Carlos would stand high in the list of those who deserve such admiration. For in addition to his intelligence and outstanding ability . . . many of us believe that he was able to combine all sorts of contradictions by grouping enemies in one force, whatever their aims and intentions. In one operation he served them all . . .

That is the picture of a successful terrorist warlord who achieves a measure of fame and fortune by the skill with which he carries out his raids. Such men are ready to use even the most devastating weapons for self-glorification in the ostensible cause of imposing their ill-thought-out philosophies.

# 3

# Terrorists:
# Behind the Mask

"George Washington was a terrorist. To describe a man as a terrorist is a term of honor." So spoke one of the Baader-Meinhof defendants after his arrest in West Germany. The thinking behind this statement is that acts of violence are not criminal when carried out in opposition to the force used by a state that is itself deemed to be criminal by the terrorists concerned. The West German Red Army Faction believed that the war in Vietnam was an "unjust" one, and that in this respect it might be compared to the eighteenth-century English war against the American revolutionaries.

One man's terrorist is another man's freedom fighter. While that may be true with respect to historical movements opposing national tyranny when no other means were available, it is more difficult to sustain considering terrorist movements in the last decade have cut across recognized national and ideological boundaries. In some cases, such as in Ireland and Palestine, there are obvious, though confused, territorial aims for the violent movements involved. But many of today's most active groups kidnap and kill to achieve objectives that are international, doctrinal and revolutionary for revolution's sake. Their campaigns involve guerilla and terrorist leaders who, unlike the guerilla troops of the Irish and the Palestinians, have received better than average educations and often come from prosperous families. They can afford the intellectual luxury of launching themselves into violent politics without the pressures of poverty to drive them on.

In the cases so far considered only the leaders are persons of superior education. Dominant terrorists and the theorists who inspire them have the conviction that they can impose their beliefs on others. But for every revolutionary who goes on to become a leader of a powerful politico-terror movement, for every revolutionary who eventually becomes head of state or prime minister, there are thousands of common soldiers of terrorism who can expect only death, imprisonment or disillusion. They are the infantry of subversive warfare.

Little is recorded of their personalities, or even their fate. Yet only by examining flesh and blood examples is it possible to discover what makes such a terrorist, and to decide why young men and women forsake their studies and abandon their careers in order to take to the political maquis. Fortunately most terror groups, particularly those that operate in Europe and in Japan, are now better known, and their personnel can be examined in greater detail. The best-documented organizations are the Baader-Meinhof, the Japanese Red Army, the Red Brigades of Italy and minor groups of the same sort in Britain and the United States—the Angry Brigade and the Weathermen. All share roughly the same emotive political convictions. "One of our tasks is to lay bare and liberate the type of man who wants revolution, who must have revolution because otherwise he would fall apart," wrote Herbert Marcuse in one of his lectures (in *Five Lectures*). In another context that is our task too, and it is certainly true that some have indeed fallen apart.

Take the case of Hans-Joachim Klein. Born in 1947, he became involved with the Red Army Faction in West Germany by way of friends with whom he lived in a Frankfurt commune. This commune was connected with a revolutionary publishing enterprise called Red Star. There, he met Klaus Croissant, who sympathized with the Baader-Meinhof gang and became one of their defense lawyers. Croissant later fled to France to escape charges of helping the terrorists plan operations even while they were imprisoned. He was extradited in hurried circumstances by France and at the time of this writing is awaiting trial.

In Frankfurt Klein met Carlos, and as one of Carlos' men he took part in the raid on the OPEC conference in Vienna. He was shot in the stomach during the raid, and, although he was badly wounded, the gang took him with them to Libya where he received treatment from a German doctor before disappearing into the terrorist underworld.

Early in 1977 he sent a remarkable letter with a set of his fingerprints to prove the letter's authenticity and a Czech-made pistol and ammunition to the West German magazine *Der Spiegel.* Klein declared that thinking about the Vienna affair during the two months he spent recovering from his wound had brought him to the decision to give up terrorism. His letter told of his disillusion:

What I heard in a month about the way in which revolutionary violence would bring about a fairer and more humane world made me sick. This was a cause for which I would have gone into the streets. Both my own experiences and the plans I heard about at that time gave me food for thought. That was the most important thing that happened to me  . . . I haven't changed from Saul to Paul, but from Saul I have changed back to a person with sensible political thinking and behavior . . . For this I had to pay a hell of a price.

In West Germany, although some have turned aside in horror from the movement they once supported, and although the leaders—Ulrike Meinhof, Andreas Baader and Gudrun Ensslin—have in despair taken their own lives in prison, the movement they launched still exists and kills.

In the beginning it was hope and humanity that inspired the young recruits of the Red Army Faction; they were imbued with the enthusiasms of the New Left for reform of the universities and of society in general. But the movement continued after the universities had effected the reforms for which the students had fought. It was still intellectual and its members were almost all middle class. Indeed, except for one ecstatic moment in the course of the Paris revolution when the masses seemed to be following, the workers had never shared the revolutionary spirit of the movement. In West Germany

most of the early supporters were found in the ranks of
clergymen, doctors, professors and journalists.

Then protest turned to violence, for it was not enough
simply to march and shout slogans. The first stages of violence in West Germany had to do with the Third World
and in particular the war in Vietnam. Andreas Baader
and his "revolutionary bride," Gudrun Ensslin, set fire to
a department store in Frankfurt to show the comfortable
burghers what the horrors of war in Vietnam were really
like. Then they began to acquire revolvers, grenades and
submachine guns for the inevitable confrontation with
the police. They had to buy the weapons, at first from
Palestinians who were well supplied. To pay the Palestinians they robbed banks. And to rob banks they needed
more weapons and getaway cars, and so it went on. Even
those who became involved for high-minded reasons
found themselves gun in hand, shooting at the forces of
law and order—for had not the police killed Benno Ohnesorg in Berlin without any real reason. They began to
feel that they were acting in self-defense. "They'll kill us
all. They have weapons, we haven't. We must arm our-
selves," screamed Ensslin.

As had already happened in other parts of the world
when terrorist groups turned to bank robbing, they soon
attracted recruits drawn more by the idea of easy money
than by idealism. A case in point was Karl-Heinz Ruhland, a motor mechanic, and therefore so far as the Baader crowd was concerned, a genuine member of the working class. He needed money to pay off his debts, and when
they asked him, he agreed—provided that he was properly rewarded—to doctor stolen cars for the gang. He had
not, he said, ever heard of this Marighella that they mentioned, but promised to read a pamphlet and help make
the revolution. Before long he was asked to take part in a
bank robbery. They gave him a submachine gun and
went to rob the bank. Ruhland, who was nervous, hoped
that no one would give the alarm, "All they had to do was
to stay nicely away from their desks so that the police
were not called too soon and I would not have to start
shooting."

After a suitable moral lecture about the propriety of

taking capitalists' money, and an assurance that the "little man" would not lose by their activities, the gang leaders shared out the loot. Ruhland was a bit disappointed with his portion, 1,000 deutsche marks, but optimistically thought he would eventually make a good living out of such activities. Before long the revolutionary mechanic was accompanying Ulrike Meinhof on her first successful urban guerilla raid, the theft of identity cards and passports from municipal offices at Neustadt am Rubenberg and Lang-Gons. Soon he accepted as entirely normal going about armed, with the safety catch off his revolver.

But Ruhland lost heart with the game when it did not produce the money he hoped for, and took the opportunity of being stopped at a police roadblock to surrender and confess all. His experiences illustrate how easily young men and women can become involved in terrorism without any burning faith in revolution.

The German groups provide numerous examples of the many different paths by which people get caught up in political violence. Some of the most ruthless members joined Baader-Meinhof through the influence of Dr. Wolfgang Huber, a Heidelberg psychiatrist, who taught his group therapy patients that only revolutionary change could cure the sick capitalist society of West Germany, which, he said, produced nothing but sick people. The Socialist Patients' Collective (SPK), which he set up, had a 'Working Circle (Explosives)' led by Huber's wife, where the patients learned how to make bombs. One of the therapy patients was Siegfried Hausner who took up bombing on behalf of the Red Army Faction to cure his own mental disorders through therapeutic attacks on the "sick" society. He helped plant bombs at the Hamburg offices of Springer Publications, and he eventually died after blowing himself up with his own bomb during a raid on the West German Embassy in Stockholm in 1975.

Some joined for money, some for therapy, some for excitement. When the Bonnie and Clyde image of Baader-Meinhof had spread, others came into the movement attracted by the combination of excitement and the possibility of sexual indulgence. Others thought of terrorism as a kind of student happening "with arms." Yet the original members remained self-righteous to the end, arrogantly convinced of their own moral and intellectual superiority.

Ulrike Meinhof, the most intriguing figure among the Germans, had more complicated motives for changing her lifestyle to that of a terrorist. Older than most of her accomplices, she had been fashionable for some time as a radical chic journalist-heroine of the New Left. As the star columnist of *Konkret,* a popular mixture of soft porn and radical politics, she had a wide following and she placed a formidable seal of respectability on the Baader-Ensslin arson attack in Frankfurt by praising it as a bold act of criminality.

She had been brought up by a gentle but firm foster mother, Dr. Renate Riemeck, a Christian pacifist, only a little older than Ulrike. As a student Meinhof became a nuclear disarmer and then moved on to condemn the comfortable and prosperous society of the Federal Republic of West Germany. This rather handsome woman, by then married to the playboy publisher and editor of *Konkret,* was successful and well-to-do. She seemed a thoroughly unlikely candidate for service as a terrorist leader. When a relative fired a gun during a walk in the woods, she was so upset that she burst into tears. Yet not long afterwards she boasted of her skill with automatic weapons on the range at an Arab guerilla training camp in the Middle East.

Her marriage to Klaus Rainer Rohl was not a happy one, and after the Frankfurt episode she left their rather grand home in Hamburg taking her twin children with her. She lived for a while in an upper-class commune in a smart section of West Berlin. Plunging into the subculture world and the world of student politics at the Free University, she came into closer contact with Gudrun Ensslin, a clergyman's daughter, brought up as a devout Protestant, who, through pacifism, had proceeded into the antiauthoritarian protest movement. Ensslin and her lover Andreas Baader had already taken to political violence. They argued that there was no longer any point in just writing and talking, it was necessary to do something, and Ulrike Meinhof agreed. When Baader was arrested and imprisoned, she joined with Gudrun Ensslin in plotting and then executing the raid that freed him. She literally leapt into the new life through the window of the library where Baader had been allowed to work. She drove off with him in a silver-painted Alfa Romeo. She had broken the law and was committed to a new life as a terrorist.

Jillian Becker, in her excellent book *Hitler's Children*, brings her novelist's insight to bear on the real reason for Ulrike Meinhof becoming a terrorist. Writing of Baader and Meinhof escaping together she had this to say:

An illusory sense of power and a certainty of victory would make them feel their own capabilities to be great. Each could seek personal relief through acts of violence and blood and terror, and always with a grandiose moral justification. They could call a lust for revenge "a thirst for justice," and terrorism a righteous fury that "society" had called down upon itself. In Ulrike's case "society" was a euphemism (which she could not recognize, her insight into her own motives not having matured with her years) for her own feelings, and for Klaus Rainer Rohl. And her committing of herself to a life outside the law was a venture to overcome not governments, nor systems, but private despair.

Andreas Baader became a terrorist because he was dark, handsome, sexy and a braggadocio. By the time he was 25 he had done nothing but fail at school and make a vague shot at being a potter. He was more interested in getting girls to bed than in getting the world put right, for so far as he was concerned, politics was all "shit." Only by accident had he come to read Marcuse and the other philosophers of terror, and the accident was named Gudrun Ensslin, already a devotee of political action. They found each other highly compatible sexually and set up housekeeping of a sort in Frankfurt. It was there that they celebrated their initiation into terrorism by setting fire to the department store.

Although Andreas Baader learned to parrot the correct slogans, there is little to show that he had any real political convictions. Certainly before he took up with Ensslin, his dislike for the consumer society and its horrors was based on the fact that this spoiled boy had no money to finance his expensive consumer tastes. He took naturally to the rather comfortable life of the West German terrorists. There have always been enough well-heeled sympathizers who could permit themselves the luxury of lending apartments and providing money for those wanting to overthrow the society in which their financial angels flourish. In West Germany, students, teachers and professional people have all given help to the terrorists. "Sheltering a Red Army man on the run is almost as good as setting up your own operation," said one student. Providing refuge for terrorists on the run has been described as both a patriotic duty and a protest against the system. On several occasions Baader-Meinhof members, even those who are known to have murdered and maimed people, have received protection from German clergymen and priests.

An even more remarkable facet of German terrorism is the number of women, most of them young and attractive, who have taken part in operations. No less than half of the 28 most wanted urban guerillas on the police list in West Germany are females; they are obviously much more than just terrorists' molls and providers of safe houses. Why this should be so has puzzled the authorities to the point that in 1977 the West German government set up a committee to try to discover the reasons.

Attention was again drawn to women terrorists during the Red Army Faction's offensive in the summer of 1977. When they raided the opulent home of Juergen Ponto, one of the country's most influential bankers, and killed him, it was his 26-year-old god-daughter who got the killers admitted to his well-defended house. "It's me, Susanne," said Susanne Albrecht, carrying with her a bunch of roses to give to her godfather. The door was opened. There was a struggle—possibly the intention was kidnapping—and Ponto was shot dead. Susanne, aged 26, had been a student at Hamburg University before dropping out to join squatters' groups, graduating to terrorism and becoming instrumental in bringing about the murder of the man who loved her like a daughter.

Another notorious woman terrorist, who led a desperate prison breakout, is Inge Viett, a 33-year-old former children's nurse who, like Susanne, comes from Hamburg. Two other female terrorists were in the group that escaped: Gabriele Rollnik, a sociologist and member of a well-to-do family from Dortmund, and Juliane Plambeck, a 25-year-old student of philology from Munich, who is on the list of 15 people suspected of complicity in the murder of Hans-Martin Schleyer. Plambeck's other claim to fame is that she was known among her male comrades as the "trophy for the erotic challenge cup."

Yet another group of female terrorists is known as the Croissant Group, because, according to the authorities, they were mainly recruited through the law office in Stuttgart run by Klaus Croissant. Before he fled to France, he ran a "lawyers' collective" and devoted most of his energy to looking after their interests. Susanne Albrecht was one of those who worked in his office. Two other women are known members of the same group and thought to be connected with the Ponto affair—Angelika Speitel, 25, who married one of the lawyers from Croissant's practice, and Silke Maier-Witt, the intelligence officer for the group. Just how these young women, most of them well brought up in decent families, became involved with terrorism remains a puzzle to West German authorities.

The truth is that they do not simply march up and apply, but gradually become involved after meeting people who share their anxieties about the state of the modern world, but who already have opted for violent solutions to those problems. They do not put themselves forward as candidates for membership; a terror group is like an exclusive club into which a friend invites you and once a member, you are expected to conform to the rules of that club.

One of the theories put forward by psychiatrists and criminologists to explain why so many German women are involved in urban guerilla activities is that it provides them with a form of liberation. Armand Mergen of Mainz University believes that these women need to emancipate themselves through violence. Because they are from good homes and have been well educated, they consider themselves superior to men and want to display that superiority in action. This may indeed be the true reason why women terrorists tend to be more brutal than their male colleagues.

A contrary theory is that women terrorists become sexually dependent on their male comrades. There is no doubt that sex is powerfully connected with political violence in the elitist groups we are examining. Certainly, so far as the European groups are concerned, there is ample evidence that many who take to the gun and the bomb start out by living in communes where partners are easily swapped and where experimental sex is part of everyday life. Many of the most active terrorists are marijuana smokers and some have taken to heavier drugs. Excitement, sensual pleasure and comfortable living outside normal routines, while still enjoying widespread approval for the high-minded ideology they preach, are all incitements to young people to involve themselves.

Another factor to be considered is that the postwar generation of German students seems obsessed by killing and death. How much such feelings are prompted by memories of the Hitler period and the horrors of the Nazi system, of which their parents were a part, is a question that needs much more detailed investigation than is possible in this book. Even so it is worth observing that there was something unnatural about the pleasure taken in German universities at news of the murders and kidnappings of 1977. After the kidnapping of Dr. Schleyer, wall writings at Heidelberg proclaimed, "It is impossible to hide our joy." The pleasure expressed in university pamphlets issued by some groups on the fringe of left-wing politics gave the impression that these groups had a hatred of the very concept of parliamentary democracy as well as its "bourgeois" representatives and institutions.

Kurt Reumann, a well-known German journalist analyzing such pamphlets in *Encounter* (October 1977), pointed out that after the murder of Siegfried Buback, the federal public prosecutor, the publications placed the moral guilt for his killing not on the terrorists, but "on that sociological catch-all, namely social conditions." So many of the groups were approving murder and asking

"Who will sentence to death Herr so-and-so?" that he felt compelled to ask: "Is the spirit of death abroad in the land?" It is certainly true that in the decade of West German terrorism, the feelings of compassion and humanity which stirred a whole generation into political action were soon corrupted into an avenging use of brutality and those gentle qualities were lost. Despite the divergence in personality and upbringing of the leaders of the Red Army Faction, they founded a movement that remains among the most feared and powerful in the world of international terrorism. Most of those founders are now dead, but the gang and its offshoots still flourish. Those early members who survived and the new recruits who have joined them seem to be not only more bloodthirsty, but more effective and more skilled with their weapons than those who launched the movement.

As the West German groups became more violent after the end of the Stuttgart trial in 1977, at which the original leaders were sentenced to long terms of imprisonment, a similar movement on the other side of the world began. The Japanese Red Army, which had been dormant for two years, carried out a most effective hijack in September 1977. By seizing a Japanese DC-8 airliner in Bombay and threatening to blow it up and kill the passengers of many nationalities, they forced the Tokyo government to pay a ransom of $6 million and to release six of their members imprisoned after earlier raids. It was a dramatic reactivation of the movement.

The Japanese Red Army shares many characteristics with the West German Red Army Faction. Its members, though more mystical, proclaim the same general philosophy, and the leader is also a woman, Fusako Shigenobu. The hijack to Bangladesh marked the thirty-second birthday of this fanatic who had been called the "Red Queen of Terror."

Fusako Shigenobu was born into the new Japanese society of the economic miracle after World War II and like her political sisters in Europe, she passed into the university ferment of the 1960s. Vietnam again was the cause, though the Japanese were also protesting the American occupation of Okinawa. The first act of her radical career occurred when she smuggled oak staves hidden in golf bags to demonstrators besieged in Tokyo University.

The Red Army, composed of a small force of students, intellectuals and other middle-class supporters, did not fare well in Japan. It was because of this failure on homeground that Shigenobu and her supporters turned towards the Popular Front for the Liberation of Palestine. Eventually a number of Red Army people went to the Middle East for guerilla training in the refugee camps. Their desire, they said, was to set up "international strongholds of the revolution" and Shigenobu became the friend of Leila Khaled, the Palestinian hijacker. It was in Israel at Lod airport that the Japanese carried out their most notorious action, slaughtering 26 people with grenades and machine-gun fire. Significantly, it was from the Middle East in 1977 that Fusako Shigenobu planned the Bombay hijacking which restored her Japanese Red Army as a fighting force, and it was Leila Khaled who collected the ransom money for the Japanese Red Army and the PFLP.

In a letter to the PFLP newspaper, *Al Hadaf*, Shigenobu spelled out the main theme of her terrorist philosophy after an earlier hijack:

These two operations were staged to consolidate the international revolutionary alliance against the imperialists of the world. We in the Red Army declare anew our preparedness to fight hand in hand with Palestinians and wage joint onslaughts at any time to defeat the Israeli enemy. We should not be bound by international laws or by resistance within the framework of these laws . . . because only revolutionary violence would enable us to defeat imperialists throughout the world . . .

Other leaders of the Red Army have followed the same themes, adding more detail. They plan acts of terror which they hope will spark the peoples' revolution, a revolution that would destroy capitalism and imperialism. Emperor Hirohito is one of their special targets. They believe he bears responsibility for the death of millions in World War II. But despite these grandiose aims, the Red

Army has spent most of its effort in trying to free its own members imprisoned because of their earlier actions. They are bound to the PFLP because they could not survive without the sanctuary and financial and logistic help provided by the Palestinians.

At his trial in Israel, Kozo Okamoto, the one survivor of the Lod raid, gave a frightening insight into the mentality of the Japanese terrorists. He was, he said, a soldier preparing for the Third World War—"We believe slaughtering of human bodies is inevitable. We know it will become more severe than battles between nations." Such bloodcurdling thoughts give some indication of the feelings of the Japanese Red Army and the fanaticism of the men and women in its ranks. Even though the group is not large in numbers, it has the capacity to create yet more bloodshed in the world.

The Red Brigades, which have terrorized Italy for several years, have strong affiliations with the other "red" revolutionary bands in the world, but the historic leaders of the movement are young people of extravagant personality. The life story of Renato Curcio, best known of the founders, handsome and bearded, is the stuff of which grand opera is made. Although the background from which he came was comparable with that of his West German comrades, there were extra touches that can only be described as Italian.

His father, a member of the Zampa family and brother of a well-known film producer, Luigi Zampa, had a respectable position in Roman society. Married to an elderly American heiress, Renato Zampa busily conducted other affairs, even within his own household. One of his mistresses was Yolande Curcio, a country girl placed in service with his family by the nuns. When she became pregnant, she was turned out of the house. Taking her child, whom she named Renato after his father, with her, she worked as a housekeeper in private houses and in hotels first in Italy, then in Switzerland and Britain. She now lives in a London apartment with her two poodles. She describes Renato as "a great idealist and revolutionary. Like all great men in history before him he has been put in jail for what he believes." According to her, Renato had a perfectly normal upbringing, and she can recall no traumatic events in his early life that might have impelled him to become a revolutionary.

After the death of Renato Zampa's wife, he offered to marry Yolande. She refused, though she did accept money, which provided her clever young son with an excellent education at good schools in Italy. Finally he went to Trento University in northern Italy, an institution that specializes in sociology and—as might be expected—is a hotbed of revolutionary activity.

Curcio is a 37-year-old of strict Roman Catholic upbringing, and we understand from conversation with Red Brigade members that it was his strong and unbalanced religious temperament combined with his new found enthusiasm for sociology that pushed him into violent politics. His first venture into this field was as a supporter of an extreme right-wing organization called New Order.

One of the star witnesses for the prosecution at the prolonged 1977 trial of Renato Curcio and his friends in Turin was Silvano Girotto, a 39-year-old Franciscan suspended from his religious duties. Known as the "Machine-gun Friar," he suddenly appeared in Turin dressed in jeans, anorak and gym shoes "to denounce these criminals." But this strange personality had himself played some role in the Red Brigades, which he joined in 1974 at the suggestion of a *caribinieri*, Captain Pietro Pignero, to spy on their activities. He was already known as the "Machine-gun Friar" because of his reputation as a guerilla fighter in Bolivia and in Chile. Whether or not this was justified is not known, for the friar is a fantasist who also claims that he once joined the French Foreign Legion. Nevertheless, he was accepted by the comrades of the Red Brigades, and familiar with their organization, was soon on friendly terms with Renato Curcio. Finally he denounced them to the *caribinieri,* making possible the arrest of Curcio. At the trial he declared, "I was convinced of the absurdity of their methods from the start." Before disappearing once he had testified in Turin, the friar denied that he had been paid by the police.

Renato Curcio's first steps into terrorism were taken in 1972, when he and his friends seized "enemies of the people" such as Etteri Amarilo, personnel manager at Fiat and then an executive at Siemens. They also seized a man called Bruno, described as a Fascist trade union leader. In each case after a mock trial before a "peoples' court," they beat up these men and released them. After some members of the gang had been arrested, they abducted a state prosecutor to try to secure their release.

In 1970 Curcio met and married a 25-year-old fellow student at Trento named Margarita Cagol. This thoughtful and gentle girl, the daughter of a rich Catholic and conservative local family was, until she took up sociology, mostly interested in music and dancing. There can be little doubt that it was the revolutionary atmosphere of Trento University that drew her into the terrorist field. In imitation of their colleagues in Berlin, the students there called it the free university, and many revolutionary leaders of the time such as Daniel (Danny the Red) Cohn-Bendit and Rudi Dutschke made appearances.

For her doctorate Margarita wrote a thesis on German workers' movements. Soon she was at work with her husband and his friends trying to persuade Italian workers to occupy their premises and begin the great revolution. However, they failed to convince the workers. Many of them were staunch Communist Party members and had no wish to involve themselves with and take orders from a bunch of sociology students.

In despair Renato and his friends decided—like many other such revolutionaries—that they had a mission to lead, even if the others stubbornly refused to follow. They heaped scorn upon the workers for their bourgeois attitudes and attacked the Communist Party for its divisive moves towards the softer brand of Eurocommunism. More and more, Curcio identified with an uncle called Armando who had died fighting the Germans with an Italian partisan unit. He always kept a picture of his uncle near him. The mythology of the partisans has an important emotive influence on the Red Brigades.

With support from southern groups known as Armed Proletarian Cells, Curcio and his wife began raiding in the Baader-Meinhof style. They collected ransoms, kidnapped and murdered those they considered their enemies. In 1974 Renato was taken by the police, but only a few months later Margarita led an armed raid on the prison at Castal Montferrato and rescued him.

That same summer of 1975 the Red Brigades kidnapped one of the Gancias, the Italian wine and aperitif family, and held him in a "people's prison"—a lonely farmhouse in Piedmont. There the security forces discovered them and besieged the farm for several days before making the final assault. As the *caribinieri* raced towards the farmhouse, Margarita hurled a charge of plastic explosive at them like a bomb. They opened up with automatics and killed her with two bullets in the chest. Renato was luckier. He managed to escape.

He survived as a terrorist leader for almost a year before he too was wounded and arrested. Threats and fresh terrorist acts continually postponed his trial and that of other squad leaders arrested with him. When the trial did finally open at Turin early in 1978, terrorists still at large shot dead one of the chiefs of the anti-terrorist group and then kidnapped Aldo Moro, one of Italy's most respected politicians.

Thus, only a few months after the autumn of terror launched by the West Germans and the Japanese, it was the new model Red Brigades who marched to the center of the world terrorist stage. Although the Moro kidnapping and the murder of high officials was ostensibly planned to secure the release of the old leaders from prison, events showed that the new men of the movement were tougher and better organized than the original Robin Hoods. For weeks on end they were able to throw the state into disarray. Here again there are close similarities with the Baader-Meinhof gang in West Germany where the same phenomenon was observed. In both cases the movements are still powerful and their links with the international terrorist fraternity appear to be strengthening. Compared to the West Germans, the Japanese and the Italians, American and British groups, who to some extent believe in the same causes, seem extremely mild. Nevertheless, there are those in the United States and Britain who set out on the same road, and similar groups may soon revive under a stricter leadership to bring the same methods of terror to bear in New York or Washington and London.

By their very names, organizations such as the "Third World Revolutionary Army" and the "American Revolutionary Army" give us some clue to the style of thought that brought them into being. A feature of these groups, often minuscule and of shifting membership, has been the grandiose nature of their titles.

Probably the most important of the U.S. subversive groups was the Weathermen, dedicated to provoking the authorities into repressive action that, they believed, would bring more support for terrorism. The name derived from a line in a Bob Dylan song: "You don't need a weatherman to know which way the wind blows." And for a while in 1969 and 1970, it began to look as though the wind might be blowing in their direction. Their aim of attracting attention was certainly fulfilled.

The Weathermen came into being as a result of squabbles at a conference in June 1969 of the Students for a Democratic Society (SDS), originally a liberal and near-pacifist New Left organization. Many supporters visited Cuba and Vietnam and, fired with enthusiasm for the revolutionary regimes in those countries, they began learning to make Molotov cocktails for the onslaught on American society. They declared that, unlike their counterparts in the Third World, they would make an antinational revolution, for otherwise they might fall into the trap of imperialist national chauvinism. The familiar old cliches poured from the mouths of these student revolutionaries. They tried in vain to merge with the Black Panthers. They made arson raids, and it is claimed that the Weathermen took part in some 500 incidents of bombing and raiding in 1969. They planted a bomb at the University of Wisconsin and demanded that the Reserve Officers' Training Corps there be disbanded and that Black Panther leaders under arrest be released.

In common with many world terrorist movements, the Weathermen were unable to put forward a coherent political program. Their original position paper made some attempt to describe the "correct path" for revolution in America. This paper was written by 11 young people, including Mark Rudd. The Weathermen were really the creation of Rudd, the leader of the 1968 Columbia University occupation, who declared himself a Marxist devoted to the destruction of a "corrupt imperialist pig society." His aim, like that of his European comrades, was to provoke repressive action and make it appear that brave resistance forces were fighting against the forces of repression. But most of their acts were more like student happenings than genuine guerilla operations. They were designed to shock the bourgeoisie and its morality by, for example, killing and eating an alley cat and expressing admiration for the murderous orgies of the Manson "family." On one occasion, however, they stole biological warfare material and threatened to infect city water supplies.

In America as in Europe, terrorist attacks with bombings, murders, kidnappings and hijackings were the illegitimate offspring of the mass-action movements that had originated with the protest demonstrations sparked by the war in Vietnam. Although state and federal authorities quickly developed techniques for coping with demonstrations, it took them longer to learn how to deal with terrorism. By the mid-1970s it was estimated that some 50 subversive groups were operational in the U.S., involving the participation of up to 15,000 people. It is doubtful that the Weathermen ever had more than 1,000 supporters, of whom very few were activists, and it all came to an end when their store of explosives in a Greenwich Village house blew up in March 1970. Several of the leaders were killed by this accident, and the movement, already going out of fashion, faded away. Mark Rudd, the surviving leader, went underground in 1970 and was not heard of again until he surrendered at the age of 30 to the New York City police seven years later.

For a while at the height of public agitation about the war in Vietnam, the Weathermen had looked dangerous, but this highly personalized band of urban guerillas was neither tough enough, nor devoted enough, to survive. The truth was that too many of its supporters were in it for kicks. They were "guns and grass" revolutionaries who enjoyed the excitement for a while, relished the lifestyle more than the politics and took pleasure that they could "epater la bourgeoisie." When they spoke of the people, it was obvious that they had never really been in touch with them and that they were simply working off their hang-ups.

Another offshoot of the Students for a Democratic Society was the Revolutionary Union, a Maoist group with more serious political appeal and a more mature following. One of the founders was Professor H. Franklin of Stanford University. With him were Robert Avakian, a student expelled from Berkeley in 1966, and Steve Hamilton. Financed from China by way of a Hong Kong communist-infiltrated union, the Revolutionary Union actually produced a manifesto, though it created less stir than the Weathermen. From the union developed yet another Maoist group called the Venceremos Organization, which had close contacts with Cuba. The organization sent a "brigade" to Cuba in the early 1970s.

An even more extreme group, the Symbionese Liberation Army (SLA), attracted much attention by its violent activities. It claimed to be a "loving" group, devoted to drawing together oppressed minorities in the "fascist" United States. It had a number of anarchist aims and was remarkable for the number of women it drew to the cause. Because they attracted so few militants, not more than 40, the SLA turned to dramatic action to attract attention and publicity.

The SLA is best known for its kidnapping of heiress Patricia Hearst, and her partial indoctrination. She was arrested together with two other SLA members trying to keep the organization alive after Donald De Freeze, the group's black leader, and five others had been killed in a raid by FBI agents and the Los Angeles police in Compton, one of that city's all black districts.

The end of the war in Vietnam deprived the small American terrorist movements of their mainspring. None of them was able to follow the lead of the international terrorist groups, though there is still a danger that race problems may provide new organizations with the necessary impetus for renewed action. Factions of Black Muslims have been involved in violent quarrels with other Black Muslim groups, and one of them, the Hanafis, attacked three buildings in Washington, D.C. and tried to hold 100 hostages. Their leader, Khalif Hamaas Abdul Khaalis, and 10 others were sentenced to long terms of imprisonment.

However, the main truly-terrorist threat in the United States came from politically motivated white groups. Revolutionary organizations comparable to those that plagued Europe grew from the New Left movement. The Weathermen group led by Mark Rudd advocated the creation of "a white movement to support the blacks in moving as fast as they have to and are able to." Their theory was that alienated high school students were the potential revolutionary class in America in alliance with Third World peoples. This was precisely the post-Marcusian philosophy spread by European university students and high school youths in the Paris revolt of 1968.

Apart from the Irish "territorial" bands already discussed, terrorist groups have made a poor showing in Great Britain. But for a time the Angry Brigade, similar in some respects to the Weathermen, did cause some alarm. From 1968 to 1971 the Angry Brigade planted 27 bombs and were involved in machine-gunning public buildings in Britain. An idea of their beliefs and the kind of people they attracted is evident in the words of simple faith spoken by Anna Mendelson, a young Essex University graduate. When defending herself at an Old Bailey trial on charges of possessing explosives and of conspiring with others to bomb in the cause of the Angry Brigade, she said: "If you convict us, we are not going to change. We will still be who we are, and what we believe. I know that the people in this dock with me are working together for a happier and more peaceful world. That is who we are. It is your decision."

This curious English group had many things in common with the Baader-Meinhof gang and with other international terrorist groups. Mendelson and a number of her friends were found guilty, and she was sentenced to 10 years imprisonment, though she was released in 1977 after serving only four years. Most members of the Angry Brigade were students and graduates from British universities who shared with their continental opposite numbers disappointment with the failure of the 1968 revolution in Paris. Both Anna Mendelson and John Barker, also sentenced to 10 years, were veterans of the days of elation at the Sorbonne, and they returned to London determined to further the causes behind whose banners they had marched.

The backgrounds of the people in the Angry Brigade were not unlike those we have considered in Europe. They too attacked the consumer society, which had so concerned the French students a few years before. Then, under the influence of a Spanish terrorist band called the "First of May Group," they began to use bombs to make their point, while living in communes and financing themselves by means of stolen checks and credit card frauds in the classic terrorist manner. When police moved in to arrest members of the group, they were beginning to imitate the Red Army Faction with raids on post offices and banks.

In passing sentence the presiding judge (Justice James), who had carefully kept the trial as apolitical as possible, told those found guilty: "I am sorry to see such educated people in your situation. Undoubtedly a warped understanding of sociology has brought you to the state in which you are."

Whether, as Mendelson predicted, those in prison have not changed is impossible to know. But since the trial there have been no further manifestations of the Angry Brigade, or any successor organization. So far as Great Britain is concerned, at the moment the terrorist field is a monopoly of the Provisional Irish Republican Army.

In the summer of 1978 there were modest signs of activity from right-wing terrorist groups in Britain. Letter bombs were sent to the communist newspaper *Morning Star* and to a left-wing bookshop. But these were minor incidents.

Two groups in particular attracted some attention, and both of them had a neo-Nazi flavor. Column 88, named in memory of Hitler whose name begins with the eighth letter in the alphabet, and the Eleventh Hour Brigade, an obscure and extremely small terrorist group, were both said to be plotting further action. Neither caused the public or the security forces any great concern.

However, terrorism still flourishes in other parts of the world. The same kind of people are still kidnapping, murdering, bombing and hijacking. The Palestinians again went into action to express their disapproval of President Anwar Sadat's historic pilgrimage to Jerusalem, and the Basque ETA group produced a more extreme faction just as the Spanish government moved towards satisfying some of their demands. And so it continues. As long as the young extremists of "left fascism" believe that violence is the only way to achieve their political aims, terrorism will continue on a greater or lesser level depending on the success of law enforcement agencies' efforts.

By looking at some of the leaders and their troops in the worldwide terrorist movements and by observing their personalities as well as their motivations, we have tried to reveal the complexity of the human factor in terrorism. Young people are drawn into violence for many reasons, but what happens to them then? How do the innocents learn the sophisticated techniques of their trade?

# 4

# Training: Indoctrination and Skills

Although terrorist groups rate political indoctrination of high importance in the training of their recruits, Carlos Marighella, the inspirer of all urban guerillas, was under no illusion about the importance of practical military knowledge. "No one can become a guerilla without undergoing a period of technical preparation," he declared in "Handbook of Urban Guerilla Warfare." "You can only become a good fighter by learning the art of fighting."

For the Latin American guru of terrorism, this involved everything from physical training to the learning of many kinds of jobs, especially those entailing manual skills. Writing in a fashion that would please a drill sergeant in any army, he preached physical training was the basis of the physical resistance that every good fighter needs. After such training, he wrote, the urban guerilla should learn to fight in different ways, some involving attack and others self-defense, just like a professional soldier.

Marighella urged his pupils to undertake what might be described as boy scout activities. They were to hike, camp, spend long periods in rough country and do mountain climbing, swimming, canoeing, fishing and hunting for food. In addition he considered it important to drive, pilot aircraft and handle motor and sailing boats. How many of the young ladies of Baader-Meinhof have these skills is unknown, but the military value of such training is undisputed.

The accomplished terrorist should know something of

the mechanics of radio, telephones and electronics; he should be able to make maps and plans, measure distance and locate his position on the ground by use of a compass. To survive in a society he is out to destroy, the terrorist should also acquire a knowledge of chemistry, as well as the ability to make rubber stamps and imitate other people's handwriting in order to forge documents convincingly. And of course, it is useful for the urban guerilla to learn basic first-aid skills in order to help wounded comrades. Marighella's section on technical training concluded:

The most important element in technical training, however, remains that of handling such weapons as submachine guns, revolvers, automatics, mortars, bazookas, FAL guns and other types of carbines—as well as knowledge of the various kinds of ammunition and explosives. Dynamite is one instance; it is vital to know how to use it, just as it is vital to know how to use incendiary bombs, smoke bombs, and so on. The guerilla must also learn to make and repair weapons, to make Molotov cocktails, bombs and mines, and how to destroy bridges, dislodge or destroy railway lines and sleepers.

The urban guerilla will complete his training in a specially organized technical center, but only after being tested in action, having actually fought the enemy.

This is a constant theme of terrorist training, that the recruit should prove himself in action before being given complete training, and there are many examples among the Germans, Palestinians and Latin Americans of this process. Indeed in some Latin American movements, the raw recruit is required, as an act of good faith, to kill a policeman or soldier before being fully accepted into the band.

The Montoneros in Argentina produced elaborate training manuals for their militants—15,000 of them according to claims by the leadership. The cover of the most ambitious work, which shows a strong hand clutching an automatic weapon, bears the title *Regulations for Organizing Political Military Activity*. Another, called the *Military Instruction Manual*, provides instructions to members on guerilla warfare as well as urban terrorism. The manuals also deal with more technical advice on the making of bombs and how to endure torture and interrogation.

In the matter of training guerillas for offensive action against German troops during World War II, a manual composed by the British Secret Operations Executive adopted a much brisker and more practical style than Marighella's instructions. In 32 pages it explained for beginners how to use explosives and small arms dropped to resistance groups in handy packs by the RAF. Hundreds of thousands of copies of this booklet, written in five languages as well as English and printed in a plain brown cover, were parachuted into occupied Europe. The text began:

The easiest way for small parties of offensively minded men to attack the enemy is by the use of explosives. Immense damage can be caused with a small quantity of supplies.

If the instructions given in this Booklet are followed carefully, even a person with no previous knowledge of explosives will be able to hit the enemy where it will do him most damage.

Put like that it all sounds very simple. But the modern terrorist movements operating on a worldwide scale go to some pains to instruct their young devotees in up-to-date methods of destroying society, and they do not by any means concentrate on military objectives.

The most effective instructors in the strictly martial arts of terrorism are without doubt the Arabs and Palestinians. Numerous training camps in the Middle East, set up to prepare young men and women for active service against Israel, at first turned out guerillas. The task of *fedayeen* soldiers was to fight a classic guerilla war against an occupying army. But after a while the same camps switched their attention to instructing hijackers and kidnappers to carry on the war by less conventional means. This was necessary because the commandos had failed to make any greater impact on Israel than the Arab armies had.

Late in 1971 the Popular Front for the Liberation of Palestine, through its many international links, began bringing in revolutionary-minded foreigners ready to help in PFLP campaigns. Among them was Kozo Okamoto, a 26-year-old student from Kyoto University who was already a member of the Japanese Red Army.

Early in 1972 he arrived in Beirut, Lebanon, by way of New York on a first-class ticket provided by his recruiters. In March PFLP instructors took him and three Japanese companions to the terrorist training camp at Baalbek, the famous ancient site in the mountains above Beirut. Okamoto reported that training began as it would have in any military establishment with a course of physical fitness to get the volunteers into shape. The Arab instructors quickly moved on to other subjects, starting with explosives drill and how to handle detonators and construct bombs. Then the small–arms experts took over, and the recruit practiced pistol handling and drill before progressing to the famous Kalashnikov rifle. Finally, they learned about grenades. All this was fairly standard basic infantry training and little more; but by mid-May, eight weeks later, the Japanese were considered ready for a special mission and drove to the terrorists' headquarters in Beirut for a briefing. Okamoto and his friends were then given special training for the job they were to do—an attack on Lod airport in Tel Aviv. At this point intelligence officers briefed them about airport procedures and the layout of the arrival building there.

A couple of days later the group flew to Rome, where they were armed and caught a French airliner to carry out the mindless massacre at the Israeli airport, in which 29 people—mostly Puerto Rican pilgrims—were killed when the terrorists opened up with Czech automatic rifles and hurled grenades at the passengers in the arrival lounge. Okamoto survived and under interrogation described his recruitment and training to Israeli security men.

It emerges from this example of a Japanese Red Army man who learned his deadly trade in Baalbek, one of several dozen Arab training camps in Lebanon at the time, that the training was neither long nor entirely thorough. It is typical of the kind of course offered in the Middle East.

The Japanese seem to have been apt pupils. Red Army

Faction members from West Germany taking a similar crash course made a less favorable impression on their instructors. They were as interested in smoking pot and making love as in learning how to kill effectively. The Germans behaved, according to one Arab, like a lot of tourists. Andreas Baader, the arrogant founding member of the gang, was called a coward because he refused to crawl beneath barbed wire while live bullets were fired over his head. Baader complained about this, saying that assault courses were not the right kind of training for urban guerillas.

In this he was not entirely wrong, though his reasoning probably had more to do with snobbery or laziness than military theory. A terrorist certainly needs discipline and has to be taught the virtue of obeying orders, but after that the need is more for a grounding in intelligence work than in strictly commando-type assault operations. Above all, he needs small-arms instruction, plenty of range practice and a thorough knowledge of explosives and detonators. It is clear from the study of many terrorist raids that training, whether given by the Arabs or by instructors from the operator's own movement, is not of a particularly high standard.

What the recruits lack in this respect they make up for in zeal and cruelty. And the truth is that far less formal training is needed by terrorists than that given in highly professional style to such units as the British Special Air Services or the West German anti-terrorist squad (GSG9), which rescued the passengers of the hijacked Lufthansa Boeing 737 at Mogadishu in Somalia. For terrorists do not need to be so precise, nor so careful to avoid unnecessary casualties as the forces of law and order operated by Western democracies.

One important subject terrorists pay attention to is the use of disguise. In successful groups international figures who have reappeared several times look quite different on each occasion. For example Carlos was not recognized at first when he led the raid on OPEC in Vienna. He was bearded, thinner in the face and the color of his dark hair had been altered. It is more than likely that plastic surgery had been used to remove his heavy jowls and to alter the shape of the plump face so well known to the French DST (Defence de la Securite du Territoire).

Western intelligence agencies believe that Prague has become the center for plastic surgery to change the appearance of known terrorists. Even without such expert attention, a terrorist can easily learn to change his appearance enough to fool security men, who have only out-of-date identity photos. A mustache, a bottle of dye, and a slight gain or loss of weight is usually sufficient.

Both the "territorial" terrorist groups acting in the Palestinian cause and the "transnational" groups, of which they later became one element, received a great deal of initial help from Arab countries. In the early days of the present wave of terrorism, Egypt and Syria were every bit as cooperative with the guerillas as Lebanon, Iraq and Syria. All these countries have helped to prepare groups for action. In addition, they provided instruction in intelligence work and helped to furnish arms and false documentation. Before the Yom Kippur War in 1973, the Egyptian Army ran six-month courses in special camps where the guerillas learned side by side with Egyptian troops. Basic instruction was provided in intelligence, frogmen operations and commando work. But there were also special training lessons with heavy weapons, Katushka rockets, recoilless guns and mortars. Most of the weaponry was provided by the Soviet Union. Such courses were intended for Palestinians serving as infantry with the Arab armies (there were some 8,000 Palestinian regular infantry), but a number of strictly-terrorist Arabs also benefited from such instruction.

The Yom Kippur War was the high point of general Arab support for the guerillas and terrorists. Since then, both Egypt and Syria have shown more interest in trying to solve the Israeli–Arab conflict by diplomatic means, with encouragement from the United States and, to a certain extent, from the Soviet Union. Their role as teachers of subversive warfare has been taken over by those who support the Rejection Front, that is Libya, Iraq, South Yemen and Algeria, who still believe that the Middle East problem can only be solved by force. Training colleges at Hit, Habbanya and Baghdad in Iraq hold as many as 2,500 Palestinian and other volunteers. But even there the Iraqi government has shown more caution lately and now keeps the *fedayeen* under fairly tight control. The lesson of Lebanon, where the aggressiveness and arrogance of the Palestinian groups provoked a ruinous civil war, has not been lost on neighboring Arab countries.

That is the problem with helping terrorists—a government can never be certain that they will not become over-ambitious and turn their weapons against the host state. Even the romantic and enthusiastic Colonel Qaddafi has recently shown more circumspection in his dealings with international terrorists, though he still offers them facilities, and a main PFLP training center and base is located at Nahar-El-Barad near Tripoli.

According to Major Omar Mehaishi, a former friend and one of Qaddafi's ministers who defected to Egypt, the colonel invited several members of Al Fatah and the PFLP to Libya a few years ago and put them in training camps under his personal supervision, together with apprentice Libyan terrorists. The largest of these camps was at Tocra, capable of training 5,000 men, and there were smaller establishments at Tarhuna, Misurate and Sirte. Among others trained were groups of the Libyan Special Intelligence Service: their first operation, an attempt to capture Omar Mehaishi, was a disastrous reflection on the quality of the training they had received. When Egyptian security picked up the seven raiders, each carried a regulation suitcase, all had bank rolls of $2,000 and they all wore identical standard Libyan army-issue underpants. The Egyptian secret service gleefully spread the story of the Libyans' lack of expertise and claimed that the Libyans had all confessed to having received special training with Russian-made bombs for use on Egyptian targets.

To use explosive devices of any but the simplest kind requires a good deal of training, and it is bomb work that really divides the pros from the amateurs. To explode an infernal machine effectively demands not only technical ability, but a cool head and a steady hand. It has often been proved by the Provisional IRA and, on at least one occasion, by the Red Army Faction, that lack of experience results in what the British Army calls "scoring an own goal."

When the Lebanese civil war was at its height, Wadi Hadad, former leader of the breakaway fanatics of the PFLP and without doubt the world's most experienced terrorist leader, set up a new training center in the People's Republic of South Yemen, formerly the British colony of Aden. Hadad was a doctor and an Orthodox Christian by upbringing, just like George Habash, leader of the mainstream PFLP. In earlier days the two men ran a clinic together in Jordan. But that was when they were concerned with healing rather than killing. Little is known about the personality of this skilled and ruthless man. At the time of his death, he was in his forties, a light-skinned Arab with a small mustache, of average height and a keen womanizer. With the approval of the South Yemen government, he took over a former British Army camp at Khayat, 15 miles from the port of Aden. Carlos joined him there to lecture and instruct as the organization's most-practiced field operator.

A good deal was learned about the methods of this camp when the Israelis seized a novice Dutch terrorist who arrived at Lod airport on a reconnaissance mission in September 1976. Lidwina Anna Jansen, an attractive female from Amsterdam, was a supporter of the leftist Red Aid organization in Holland who had drifted by way of radical student activities into terrorism. In Aden she attracted the attention of Wadi Hadad, who selected her for the reconnaissance mission after she attended his training course. She was to reconnoiter the Air France route from Paris to Tel Aviv and Bombay to lay groundwork for a hijacking.

She had first gone to Aden with a party of 15 like-minded Dutch young people and was taken to Khayat. The international nature of the training course was underscored by information she later gave to Israeli security interrogators. For apart from the Dutch group, she said she had met a party of 10 West Germans who arrived in camp in July 1976 and were greeted in person by

Wadi Hadad. They were put through their paces as cadet terrorists for six weeks by skilled instructors. The subjects were the familiar ones of weapons training, communications and tactics.

Jansen was useful to the PFLP, for, after a stay in Holland at the end of her course, she was able to fly into Israel, a near impossibility for any of the Arab trainees. But she did not play her role with any assurance and attracted the attention of the airport's sharp-eyed security guards. She was arrested and promptly confessed. Another Dutch youth from the same group was traveling with her, but he did not arouse suspicion and was able to slip through Tel Aviv before being arrested in New Delhi as a result of the information she gave the authorities.

While on her trip back home to Holland before the mission started, Jansen recognized in newspaper photographs two Arab fellow trainees from the terrorist school in Aden. They had been arrested in Istanbul after machine-gunning passengers waiting for an El Al flight. Four people were killed. The release of these two men was among the demands of the hijackers who forced a Lufthansa airliner to fly to Mogadishu in 1977, an act that demonstrated even more clearly the international ramifications of the Hadad training camp in Aden.

A mental hospital in Heidelberg may seem the unlikeliest of places to set up a terrorist training organization, but that is precisely what Dr. Wolfgang Huber and his wife Ursula did. In their Heidelberg Socialist Patients' Collective, they trained their mental patients to become terrorists to fight against modern society because, argued Huber, it was that society which had made his patients sick. The Working Circle (Explosives) in which the patients worked at their therapy, just as if they had been weaving baskets, taught them how to make bombs. They started by mixing small quantities of explosives and then taking their first bombs to the Odenwald Forest, exploding them by remote control and proudly taking pictures of their success.

It was members of the Socialist Patients' Collective—SPK—who occupied the West German embassy in Stockholm in April 1975 and coldbloodedly murdered two of the diplomats. When it became obvious that despite the killings the authorities were not going to give in to the terrorists' demands—the freeing of the Baader–Meinhof leaders—there was an explosion inside the embassy and Siegfried Hausner, who had trained in bomb making with the Working Circle, was mortally wounded. It is not known if he deliberately blew himself up along with the embassy or had "scored an own goal."

Another of Dr. Huber's protegees was Friedericke Krabbe, a student of psychology and sociology who, in the autumn of 1977, inherited the mantle of Ulricke Meinhof and Gudrun Ensslin as the woman leader of German terrorism. Her training had been complete, for the SPK had so-called working circles on dialectics, Marxism, sexuality, education and religion. On the more practical side the students were also taught radio transmission, photography, and judo and karate. They were shown how to jam police radios and required to take pictures of police buildings, offices and equipment. Ursula Huber even managed to demonstrate her skill by placing a bug in the senate chamber of the university to listen in to the senate's plans to close down her husband's clinic.

No such system of higher education in terrorism was available to the Provos in Ireland, though they did enjoy another advantage—some of their best recruits had already been trained during service in the British Army. One sergeant from the Parachute Regiment brought his skill with mortars to the PIRA. Renegade soldiers from the Irish Guards also have provided expertise for their compatriots. Some IRA members are encouraged by their leaders to join the British Army in order to get first-class military training. But in general the Provos lack lavish resources in either equipment or training. They must train in secret in Ireland, and therefore can only practice with their weapons and explosives in small groups on the lonely banks of the Shannon or on the coast of Northern Ireland near the Giant's Causeway, where they are under constant threat of detection by Irish or British security forces. Because of these restrictions, the Provisionals often display signs of undertraining. On numerous occasions captured Provos have admitted, "My gun jammed and I couldn't get it going again." That is no doubt partly because most of their weapons, old-model Stens and Thompson submachine guns, are no longer effective—the expensive Armalites are only entrusted to experts. But every good infantry soldier knows that jams are to be expected in field conditions, and the well-trained fighter takes immediate action to put things right.

Among the most effective training organizations for the new generation of transnational terrorists were those set up in Cuba after Fidel Castro came to power. After the Tricontinental Conference there in 1966 had proclaimed its faith in the struggle against imperialism, camps were set up under both Cuban and Russian intructors to formalize the training of young Latin Americans in guerilla warfare and terrorism. Castro himself knew the value of good training. Before launching his successful attack on Cuba, both he and Che Guevara had been coached by Alberto Bayo, an elderly Spanish colonel who learned his trade in the Spanish Civil War. With money supplied by Castro, Bayo bought a ranch at Santa Rosa near Mexico City and turned it into a guerilla school. For teaching underground warfare to these two successful pupils, the colonel received a down payment of $8,000.

Orlando Castro Hidalgo, a defector from Castro's DGI (Direccion General de Inteligencia) tells in his book, *Spy For Fidel,* how the training camps in Cuba were run: "One of the first functions of DGI was the running of special schools for the training of Latin Americans in guerilla warfare and subversive techniques. At one time, early in the sixties, as many as 1,500 men were being brought to Cuba for training . . ." Those who could not get there by air arrived clandestinely by Soviet freighter or fishing boat. On arrival in Havana they were grouped by nationality, and although a squad usually consisted of from 15 to 25 members, sometimes there were as few as three. For security reasons national groups were usually separated, and the different groups received specialized training. Venezuelans concentrated on guerilla operations and sabotage techniques, while Chileans, who in pre-Salvador Allende days came from a country with a strong Communist Party, were coached in using political methods to further their cause.

Guerilla warfare courses lasted from three to six months, but sometimes continued for up to a year. Promising recruits received additional instruction to become intelligence agents in their home countries.

A Venezuelan named Manuel Carrasquel later told a committee of the Organization of American States about the kind of training he had received. His group was taught tactics, weapon training, bomb making—especially how to blow up oil installations—map reading, cryptography, photography, falsification of documents and disguise.

When Carlos was at Camp Matanzas in Cuba, one of his professors was General Viktor Simenov of the KGB, who had been sent to Havana to help organize the Cuban secret service. Another instructor was Antonio Dages Bouvier, an Ecuadorian expert in guerilla tactics, who turned up again later in London and was involved in planning the hijacking that ended at Entebbe. Carlos' career indeed provides a thread through the maze of international terrorist training camps. Like other promising candidates from Latin America, he was singled out for further instruction in Moscow at the Patrice Lumumba University. Carlos became effective because he attended all the best terrorist schools—Havana, Moscow and finally the PFLP in the Middle East.

Lumumba University in Moscow, which gathers in students from all parts of the Third World, has many faces. It was set up by Nikita Khrushchev ostensibly to provide university education for the underprivileged, but it would be naive to suppose that it was not also used for propaganda purposes. According to one defector who taught there, 90 percent of the staff are connected with the KGB, and the Russian students, who provide a quarter of the 20,000-strong student body of the university, are carefully picked and then briefed for their task of spreading the communist word among the outsiders. Most of the foreign students complete their courses and then return home to become doctors, engineers and civil servants and take their place among the leaders of their countries. It is only then that the Russian students turn up as diplomats and journalists to renew friendships and often to put "old boy" pressure on their former class-mates to perform some service for the Soviet Union.

However, for the smaller percentage of foreign students who show enthusiasm and aptitude for clandestine activities on behalf of the cause, specialized courses are available. The elite of this group go on to be trained by Department V, the KGB's Assassination and Sabotage Squad, where they learn the dirty tricks of the business.

A training center for expatriate recruits was set up some years ago by a Colonel Kotov, who, after serving in Israel in the guise of a diplomat, moved to Lebanon where he had contact with Palestinian guerillas. When he returned to Moscow the KGB had already formulated its own terrorist courses. After rigorous weapons training international recruits were schooled in surveillance methods, how to follow someone without being detected and how to escape when they were being tailed. The final stage of the course was concerned with organizing and running a terrorist network. Students also received instruction in the use of disguise, fake identities and how to establish escape channels. The Russians later set up special courses in the Soviet Union and in East Germany for students to learn how to handle heavier and more modern weaponry. In particular they acquired the skills needed to operate SAM 7 hand-held missiles and to fire antitank weapons. Carlos passed through no less than four specialized training establishments run by the Soviet secret police near Moscow. After political indoctrination the specialities were sabotage, heavy weapons use and unarmed combat, including karate.

This raises the question of how far the Russians and the KGB are involved in transnational terrorism. Theoretically, the Soviets do not approve of terrorism, and officially condemn it as individualist and adventurist. Obviously, the Soviet Union has no wish to give too much support to terrorist extremists who deviate from the classic Communist Party line. Yet it is tempting for them to use such people as surrogates in the cold war against the capitalist powers, and in any case, by providing training and weapons for such terrorists they can at least keep a measure of control over them and prevent them from turning their activities towards the Soviet world. Another advantage of limited participation is that it enables the KGB to keep itself informed about subversive groups. Finally, the time may come when terrorism would be useful to the Kremlin as an extra weapon against their ideological enemies in Peking.

Whatever the reasons, it is certain that some help has been given to transnational groups by the Soviet Union. In 1975 two terrorists sent to prison in Holland for plotting to hijack a train and seize Soviet Jews as hostages testified that they had been trained at a village near Moscow.

It is through providing aid to Arab groups acting against Israeli interests that the Soviet Union has been drawn into supporting some terrorist activities. There have been numerous references to a Soviet training camp at Simferpol in the Crimea that can handle 400 trainees. There are also active training camps at Ostrova in Czechoslovakia and at Pankow in East Germany.

Such are the formal training facilities for those who seek to overthrow society by terrorist means. Instruction is provided for the most promising terrorist and for the group leaders. But there are many who go into action without courses, who simply learn by doing. We have already mentioned that Carlos Marighella, in his widely circulated training manual, wrote about bank robbery as a suitable entrance exam for apprentice guerillas. "Urban guerilla warfare," he said, "is a wonderful training school."

In Latin America many a terrorist has taken this traditional road into subversive activities. The truth is that only by taking part in a raid and by baptism of fire can a terrorist prove himself. The same is true of soldiers. However realistic their training, they need to go into action in order to find out if they have got the "stomach" for the job.

In several groups criminals have been welcomed into the movement for their technical skills, and sometimes for the doctrinal satisfaction the participation of genuine working-class outlaws gives to young middle-class or well-to-do terrorists beset by guilt. In any case, criminals can provide experienced help in how best to go about specialized forms of "fund raising."

The growing sophistication of terrorist training in Europe, now under constant pressure from highly specialized security forces, can be judged from an examination of a manual produced for the Red Brigades in Italy. Its owners had failed to comply with its last instruction, which was, "This book must not be left lying around" and police found it in a hastily abandoned terrorist hideout at 96 Via Gradoli, Rome. *Security Rules and Work Methods*—the title of this loose-leaf pamphlet—gives strict instructions on the comportment of terrorist groups. It advised them that to avoid drawing attention to themselves, they should appear to be respectable, proud of their homes and regularly employed, none of which are easy tasks for student killers. Apartments should be "proletarian, modest, clean, neat and completely furnished." From the outside everything should appear to be normal, with curtains, entrance light and nameplate in place. Window boxes are recommended to help provide an extra touch of respectability. The Red Brigades' instructor warned his charges not to make noise at night and to do everything possible to reassure the neighbors. Care must be taken before renting an apartment to ensure that the landlord did not live on the premises. Then the doors were to be fitted with burglar-proof locks. The pamphlet recommended great care in choosing a hideout to make certain that it was on a street where the police would find it difficult to keep watch from such traditional urban lookout places as bars, public buildings and warehouses. It warned that dirty cars attract attention and advised terrorists to spend time cleaning their cars rather than going to neighborhood cafes and bars where they might excite curiosity. In case all these precautions failed, the terrorists were ordered to retain as little compromising material as possible, keep their weapons and essential equipment in bags, and always be ready for a quick getaway.

It seems that in the case of the occupants of Via Gradoli, the strain of following the strict training recommendations and working at regular jobs had proved too much for the terrorists who participated in the kidnapping of Aldo Moro. Eventually they attracted attention during the great police search in Rome when a neighbor complained about a water leak in their apartment. The terrorists left behind a good deal of compromising evidence in the shape of false license plates, wigs and unused stationery stolen from police headquarters.

Even more important were the documents they left that revealed a good deal about the efficiency of their organization, proving that the Moro kidnapping had involved the complicated cooperation of nearly 60 people, including the 12 terrorists involved in the attack on the politician and his five-man escort, all of whom were killed. The group left behind bank notes linking them to ransoms collected from other kidnappings. Records found with the training manual showed that the group had spent $20,000 on firearms, again demonstrating that terrorist operations are costly.

An interesting example of "learn-as-you-go" terrorism is provided by Ulrike Meinhof. Until she took part in the Berlin operation to free Andreas Baader, she had no experience with violent crime. While she was on the run, she watched with interest as another member of the gang demonstrated how to start the engine of a stolen Mercedes by jumping the wires. They drove to a provincial town in the stolen car and broke into municipal offices, and there Ulrike learned how to open a locked door with a screwdriver. She entered the building and stole a quantity of passports, official stamps and one partially completed identification card. Instructions on where to send the stolen documents were contained in a coded message, but because Meinhof decoded the message improperly, they were sent to the wrong address and that mission failed.

The next task was to acquire weapons. Ulrike and her friends went to Frankfurt and, using stolen money, bought twenty-three 9 mm Firebird automatics from an Al Fatah man. They had to pay 450 deutsche marks per weapon, about three times the going rate at the time. The weapons were then issued to friends in an apartment belonging to a German journalist, and they went out to practice with them. A practice range was chosen in the woods near Frankfurt airport so that the noise of the jets would drown the noise of the shooting. It is in such ways that expertise in subversive warfare can be gained by the young terrorists, who are usually intelligent people, matching their skills against those of the authorities.

But in most cases the training of terrorists has become so formalized that regular courses are taught with final examinations of the most practical sort. Anyone wishing to join the Montoneros in Argentina, for example, must first undergo a two-month indoctrination course, during which the romantics and incompetents are weeded out. The course breaks down old loyalties and replaces them with a new set of values. Family loyalty is the first to be attacked, because it is the most basic of the old ties and the most difficult to eradicate.

At the end of the course, the aspirant takes a written examination that emphasizes the renunciation. A sample question is: what action would you take if your mother was in the hands of the enemy. Required answer: none. After the written examination there is a practical test in weaponry and explosives. Then comes the big moment. The final examination is simple: the candidate must shoot a soldier or a policeman. This explains why so many Argentinian policemen are gunned down as they leave their houses; they are easy marks for student terrorists passing final exams.

The reason for the act of killing is that it binds the would-be terrorist irrevocably to the organization. Up to that moment he or she could back out. But once the candidates have killed, they are committed. One woman, a nurse sickened by the killing, wanted to get out. The Montoneros sent a killer squad to her home. When they burst in, her mother pleaded, "Shoot me, not her." The killers shot them both. Similar executions have been carried out by Baader-Meinhof and by the PFLP on members who wanted to return to a normal life. There is no way out except by death.

# 5

# Money: The Budget of Death

Money is the fuel of terrorism. The belief that the use of terror is the poor man's method of waging war is no longer valid. The Palestinian, Latin American and West German groups that seek to destroy the bourgeois way of life enjoy lifestyles equal to those of the richest sections of the affluent society.

One or two impoverished groups remain, notably the South Moluccans, who pursue their hopeless campaign in Holland with meager resources. Their cause is such an impossible and unpopular one that no major power and no well-established terrorist group can see any great advantage in supporting them, and so far, they have not learned to hold up banks or kidnap for ransom. Elsewhere, the picture of the ragged revolutionary living off the land, stealing his weapons and supplies from "the forces of repression," is as outmoded as red-coated soldiers. Modern terrorists must be rich and the transnational groups must be very rich indeed—first-class airline tickets are expensive.

Ever more complicated arms have to be paid for, so do safe houses, radio sets, cars and hotel rooms. The terrorists themselves have to be paid and need expense money to fit into the societies in which they operate. If, for example, an observation team of three were to keep watch over a businessman in order to stage a kidnapping, they would have to dress in a fashion that would not excite comment in smart restaurants. As an Irish policeman put it when talking about a well-dressed Provo who had just been sent to prison: "Only the stone-throwers wear jeans. Most of the hard men are smartly dressed—they can afford to be with all the money they have coming in from bank raids." Harry Duggan, the leader of London's Balcombe Street gang of the IRA, was described as "looking like a junior hotel manager."

Michel Moukharbel, Carlos' adjutant in Paris, was also the assassin's bookkeeper and kept detailed records of the money that he and Carlos spent on their various enterprises. Because of these details—hotel bills, train fares, car rental accounts—the authorities were able not only to trace Carlos' movements but to construct a picture of the financial infrastructure of terror. This infrastructure closely follows the normal financial pattern of big business, even down to pension schemes for the disabled and the widows and families of those killed on "company business."

When Colonel Qaddafi set up his own multinational terrorist organization, he established a fund to provide this kind of social insurance. One of his men, who surrendered after hijacking a plane to Kuwait, told interrogators that the Libyan leader had promised his team before they set out that he would pay compensation of $500,000 to the families of any of them killed on the mission. Hans-Joachim Klein, who was wounded during the OPEC operation, had his pain eased by an insurance payment of $200,000 from Qaddafi. The Libyan fanatic has become to terrorism what Lloyds of London is to shipping. Their worlds, in fact, actually overlap, because Lloyds pays out on the aircraft hijacked by the people whose lives Qaddafi insures.

And so the expenses mount. Cars cannot always be stolen—the theft might attract too much attention—and so they have to be rented. Radio and electronic equipment must be bought, and if the group is mixing its own explosives, the ingredients have to be purchased. The well-placed "sleepers" whose services are only called upon at crucial moments have to be funded. Officials have to be bribed, and still more money is spent in the mundane business of running offices. Paper and typewriters must be bought, and telephone bills need to be paid. People, even the most dedicated of terrorists, have to eat and drink and be clothed. The air fares for a five-person hijack team could easily amount to $6,000 in addition to the money spent on the reconnaissance team. When totalled up the funds needed to finance one hit team are comparable to the annual expenses of a small company.

Where does the money come from? The answer to that question depends on the type of organization involved and on the countries likely to support it. The IRA, for example, has always relied on funds collected by sympathizers in Ireland and especially upon money donated by sentimental Irish Americans, who are easy touches for claims that the money is needed to relieve the hardship brought by the so-called brutality of the British Army. Some of the donors of course actively support the bombers and the murderers, but most turn a blind eye to the inevitable destination of their money. Even the people who run the Northern Ireland Aid Committee in New York City seem genuinely to believe that the money they collect will be used for humanitarian purposes. But the British Army has traced too many Armalites captured in Belfast back to gunshops in New York for this belief to hold water.

However, after a campaign by the British government and the government of the Irish Republic to explain the true nature of Provisional IRA activities to Irish Americans, there was evidence that by 1977 this emotional money was drying up. The raffles, dances and monthly commitments raised $600,000 in 1972, but five years later this sum had fallen to $150,000. The Provos were forced to return to the traditional form of terrorist fund raising—the robbing of banks. They enjoyed no small success. It was estimated that the Provos stole £2 million ($4 million) in 215 attacks on banks in one year and in December 1977 Jack Lynch, the Prime Minister of the Irish Republic, was forced to impose stringent measures to deal with the increase in armed bank raids.

In one of the classic paradoxes of terrorism, the richest terrorists are the Palestinians, who come from the poverty of the refugee camps. They have never needed to rob banks—except of course during the Lebanese civil war, when they were able to walk into deserted banks and load the entire contents of vaults onto trucks. This paradox stems from the fact that their movement attracted support from the Arab world at precisely the moment when the oil states of the Middle East were beginning to enjoy their immense, newly acquired wealth. Because even conservative and antirevolutionary Arabs could not resist the emotional appeals to help free Palestine of the Israelis and to recover the holy places of Islam lost to the Jews, money poured into the coffers of the Palestinian organizations. This flow of money also entailed recognition by the Arab states that none of them was strong enough to tackle Israel openly on the field of battle and that the only way to hurt the Israelis was by means of terrorism. But that was before the Arabs realized that control of the supply of oil gave them a weapon far more powerful than even the nuclear bomb.

What gives this situation a touch of Alice in Wonderland is that the oil states know that they are next on the terrorists' list after the Israelis. Yet, by the warped logic of Arab politics, they are forced to provide the money to keep the terrorists active. They make an attempt at rationalization by giving their donations not directly to the terrorists, but to the Palestine Liberation Organization. However, since the terrorist groups are an integral part of the PLO, the money inevitably filters through to them and from them it is passed on to the transnational gangs, thus uniting oil money with German nihilists, Japanese revolutionaries, Latin American romantics and Turkish nationalists. The Palestinians are indeed the plutocrats of terror.

It was estimated in 1975 that Al Fatah, the largest of the groups that make up the PLO, had an income of almost $200 million; according to the Israelis, the Popular Front for the Liberation of Palestine, the most extreme of the Arab organizations, had a similar sum at its disposal. In July 1977 *Time* magazine reported that when Yasser Arafat flew to Saudi Arabia to ask King Khalid to persuade the Syrians not to attack the Palestinians in Lebanon, the Saudi government refused. But as a kind of consolation prize, Crown Prince Fahd wrote Arafat a check for $5 million. This gift was in addition to the annual $25 million subsidy from Saudi Arabia to the PLO.

Saudi Arabia is just one source of revenue. Kuwait and the Arab Emirates also provide substantial contributions as a kind of *danegeld* to ensure that guerillas are not tempted to become too active in their territories. In brief, the whole Arab world backs the Palestinian movements with money. One of the most generous backers is Colonel Qaddafi, who spares no financial effort to keep the Palestinians in action. With a production rate of 1,737,000 barrels of oil a day, Libya amassed a balance of payments surplus in 1975 of $1.7 billion. It is estimated that Qaddafi paid some $40 million from his ample reserves to Black September, while similar sums went to other organizations and substantial amounts were spent on providing arms and equipment for the terrorist movement. He justly deserves the name "paymaster of terror."

In addition to his regular contributions to Palestinian liberation groups, Qaddafi also offered large bonuses for successful operations against Israel. To express his appreciation to Black September for their action at the Munich Olympic Games, he gave them a cash reward of $10 million. After the seizure of the OPEC oil ministers in Vienna, Carlos received a gift of some $2 million. In addition, ransom money for the lives of the Saudi and Iranian ministers kidnapped on that occasion brought some $25 million into the Palestinian coffers. Terrorism in these circumstances can be a profitable business.

It was estimated that in 1976 organizations under the PLO umbrella received around $90 million from the Arab states. In addition the Palestinians who live and work in the Persian Gulf oil states pay a five percent tax on their incomes "to sustain the cause." Colonel Qaddafi is harsher. He imposes an eight percent tax on Palestinians employed in his country. The Palestinians also receive large sums as gifts from rich individuals anxious to prove their enthusiasm for the cause—and there is no shortage of Arab millionaires.

With such a huge income the Palestine Liberation Organization has come to resemble a multinational business corporation, with an amalgam of terrorism and diplomacy as its end product. Hardly any of its resources are used to improve conditions in the refugee camps of the Middle East, where Arabs live in disgustingly squalid conditions. There is reason in this seeming inconsistency, for the camps provide the endless flow of recruits for terrorist duties. An improvement in conditions there, which is certainly possible, would erode the causes of bitterness that keep good and decent Arabs always ready to fight and destroy Israel. Even the poor in the camps are themselves forced to contribute their mite.

Most of the money is spent on military training and on terrorist operations. But a good deal also goes to finance the huge bureaucracy that now controls the movements. They have modern offices with executives, public relations people, secretaries in pretty dresses and the whole paraphernalia of a modern business corporation—although the young men in the offices spoil the cut of their pants with pistols stuck in their waistbands. In addition to its headquarters in Beirut, the PLO also runs its own diplomatic service with offices that have near-diplomatic status in no less than 100 countries and maintains an observer delegation at the United Nations. The heads of these missions in the more important countries of Western Europe and the United States are paid up to $1,500 a month. Such sums are in stark contrast to the pay of a guerilla who gets only $70 plus family allowances each month.

Over the last couple of years, the Palestinians have nevertheless had some financial embarrassments, for the civil war in which they were engaged in Lebanon, their power base, cost them a great deal. One calculation puts the cost at $100 million, because the organization had to purchase heavy weapons and had to provide for thousands of their troops who were injured and maimed in the fighting, as well as making allowances for their dependents.

During the Beirut fighting one major business establishment remained untouched, for it was strongly protected throughout by regular Palestinian troops. No harm came to the Arab Bank Ltd., a strong financial institution based in Amman, Jordan and presided over by a

Jerusalem-born Arab. In the Middle East this bank, which has assets of over $4 billion, is often called the "PLO Bank," for it is generally believed that the Arab Bank handles the investments made by the organization in European and American stock exchanges. The PLO is estimated to have an investment portfolio of some $100 million. In Beirut it owns hotels and has bought land on the West Bank of the Jordan—in Israeli-held territory. Such investments give a measure of independence from the financial pressures of Arab governments.

In recent years the Palestinian organizations have increased their revenue by commercial ventures such as poultry farms, nightclubs, and factories and workshops producing handicrafts, clothes and furniture. But not all their business enterprises are so respectable. Palestinian leaders have let it be known that they have made big money from the illegal sale of drugs in Israel. But they are less talkative about their share in the international marijuana traffic through Lebanon. In the summer of 1977 the trial and conviction in London of a British drug smuggler revealed a profitable trade in marijuana designed to bring large sums of money to the Palestinian organizations. The marijuana, grown in northern Lebanon, was taken in trucks through Turkey and Bulgaria to Yugoslavia, where the hidden cargoes were split up and smuggled across Europe to Britain in secret compartments built into private cars. The supply from Lebanon dried up during the worst period of the civil war, but the Palestinians became active again as soon as the fighting died down. Had the network not been uncovered by international narcotics squads, it is believed that the next consignment would have netted about $1 million. This traffic was a two-way business. The transports that delivered the marijuana through Turkey were to have returned loaded with weapons made in Eastern Europe, paid for with the drug profits. If the traffic had continued there is no doubt that pot smokers in fashionable London would unwittingly have been helping to provide terrorist weapons for Palestinians—and through them, possibly the IRA as well.

Terrorist funds, like all kinds of big money, attract corruption and criminals. Several PLO officials with aspirations above their terrorist station were thrown into prison for gambling away a $500,000 chunk of the organization's money in Cairo's casinos. And even the more modest funds of the Provisional IRA have proved too great a temptation for sticky-fingered comrades. One Provo who acquired £100,000 ($200,000) for the cause by a particularly successful bank raid transferred it to his own account in the United States. No doubt he will subscribe generously to the Northern Irish Aid Fund—if he lives to enjoy his loot.

Even terrorists who proclaim the purity of their motives are susceptible to the rustle of bank notes. Carlos, the celebrated anti-bourgeois, is no slouch when it comes to enjoying the good life in the best restaurants on his expense account, and he has made a fortune from his post as chief overseas assassin for the Palestinians. It is one of the ironies of the modern world that the West, with its dependence on Arab oil, provides some of the wealth that is passed on to people dedicated to destroying the fabric of Western society.

In other parts of the world, terrorists have to work harder to make their money. A good example of self-financing is provided by the ERP, the Ejercito Revolucionario del Pueblo or People's Revolutionary Army of Argentina who, although formed as the armed wing of a Trotskyist revolutionary party, might well be described as the capitalists of terror. Formed in 1970, it concentrated its military cells on fund raising by "expropriation" or, less politely, bank robbery and kidnapping for ransom. Estimated to be 5,000 strong by 1974, ERP ranks were increased by Tupamaros escaping from Uruguay and Mirista radicals who fled from the military coup in Chile that toppled the Marxist Salvador Allende government.

Their initial capital came from a bank raid in Cordoba that brought in a mere $300,000, but the ERP rapidly increased this by kidnapping a business executive whose ransom netted $1 million. Not unnaturally, this success pointed the way to a profitable line of business, and they switched their activities almost entirely to kidnapping the executives of major companies, especially of the multinationals who had set up business in Argentina and had filled many of their senior posts with their own countrymen. The kidnappings, therefore, fulfilled three functions. They brought in a great deal of money; they enabled the ERP to maintain a correct radical approach; and they pleased xenophobic Argentinians by attacking foreign concerns and foreign officials.

As a result of this branch of terrorist enterprise, the ERP rapidly built up a central fund of some $30 million. They did not, however, always have things their own way. The authorities were opposed to ransom deals and tried to foil them wherever possible. In 1972 after the completion of negotiations for the $1-million-dollar ransom of Oberdan Sallustro, a Fiat executive, the police discovered and attacked the hideout where he was being held. Four of the terrorists were captured. But Sallustro paid a greater price than the ransom money. He was murdered when the police stormed the "people's prison."

The following year, after a partially-successful attempt to seize a Ford Motor Company executive in Buenos Aires during which the victim was wounded, it was reported that the company had handed over $1 million for "protection" against any new attempt. It is not uncommon for big firms to pay up in this way in order to avoid trouble—in the same way that some airlines make regular payments to ensure that their aircraft are not hijacked. This was one of the ERP's Robin Hood actions. In accordance with their instructions the ransom was paid in the form of medical supplies and other help to the poor.

In the early 1970s the amount of money demanded by ERP continually escalated—$2 million for Charles Lockwood, a British executive of Acrow Steel, $3 million for John R. Thompson, the American president of Firestone Tires Argentinian subsidiary—until eventually it reached the then record of $14.2 million for Victor Samuelson, an Exxon executive. After Samuelson had been held for almost five months, the company agreed to the terrorists' terms, but the revolutionaries then kept the victim for another 49 days to give them time to "launder" the money.

In June 1975 the Montoneros, the other main Argentinian terrorist group, who follow a leftist-Peronist philosophy, announced that they had pulled off the most lucrative kidnapping to date: $60 million in cash and $1.2 million in food and clothing distributed to the poor in exchange for the lives of Jorge and Juan Born, sons of Jorge Born, chairman of the Bunge y Born commercial empire. Jorge Born was held for nine months while the negotiations were conducted, but his brother Juan was so affected by his imprisonment in a "people's prison" that the Montoneros feared for his mental health and his life; rather than jeopardize the deal, they made a realistic business decision and released him before the ransom was paid. There was no indication given about the method in which the ransom was paid, but in Argentina it is believed that the money was delivered in several instalments brought into the country by couriers from abroad.

The government ordered an inquiry into the group's accounts after the ransom had been paid in order to ascertain whether tax or exchange control laws had been violated. Either because there had been no violations or because Bunge y Born represented too powerful a slice of the Argentinian economy for the government—then beset with economic problems—to take on, nothing substantial has emerged from this inquiry at the time of writing.

The authorities have, however, pursued another investigation with the utmost diligence. In August 1976, an executive jet with two pilots and a lone passenger crashed in the mountains south of Mexico City. The plane had been hired in the name of David Graiver, the 35-year-old scion of the Graiver family of Polish Jews who had settled in Argentina in the 1930s and had become powerful bankers in the large but unpopular Jewish community in Buenos Aires. Graiver was a financial whiz-kid, a flamboyant wheeler-dealer who juggled enormous sums of money. It seemed that he had run out of luck. Although all three bodies were dreadfully mutilated, his was unhesitatingly identified by his brother Isidoro. He was cremated and his wife Lidia carried his ashes back to Argentina in a brass urn.

When Graiver crashed, so did his empire. Banks in America, Belgium and Argentina investigated his dealings. When the figures were computed, it appeared that some $50 million of other people's money was unaccounted for. It had all the hallmarks of a massive international fraud.

Then eight months later the affair took on a new dimension when *La Nueva Provincia,* a right-wing newspaper connected with General Iberico Saint-Jean, a hardline rightist who had been head of the secret police, accused Graiver of being the investment banker of the Montoneros. The newspaper alleged that Graiver had channeled at least $17 million of the Montoneros' money through his Banco Commerical de la Plata into investments in Argentina and abroad. This was at a time when the Montoneros' profits from their kidnappings were far in excess of their immediate needs, and so they did what any major business concern would do—invested their excess capital. The Argentinian government now estimates that the Montoneros were getting $130,000 a month from their investments, and according to his enemies—and he had many—David Graiver was providing the revolutionaries with the same "hot money" services he had already arranged for top men in the Peronist regime.

The newspaper investigation of Graiver provided detailed information about the business cover of the terrorists. Every month two well-dressed men, known as Dr. Paz and Dr. Penaloza, took the high-speed elevator to the twenty-ninth floor of the Graiver bank in the center of Buenos Aires. Because it was equipped with so many security devices, this office was known as "the bunker." Once there, they would collect their monthly interest in cash, stuff it into their briefcases, have a cup of coffee and leave a half hour later to put the money at the disposal of the local leaders of the terrorist campaigns being fought in the towns and the countryside.

The junta led by General Jorge Videla was by now conducting a repressive but successful campaign against the terrorists, and followed up the newspaper accusation by claiming it could prove that Graiver was willingly handling Montoneros funds and, in fact, had become so enmeshed that his banking empire depended on the inflow of terrorist money. General Videla announced: "This so-called Graiver group worked for the subversives. They received millions of dollars in deposits to be invested here and abroad for the benefit of subversion, and they knew where the money had come from." Evidence against Graiver began to accumulate and the police had a windfall when they raided a Montoneros safe house and found documents linking him with the organization's finances.

The government then took action against the Graiver family and its associates, arresting some 300 people. A dramatic twist was given to the investigation when Juan Graiver, father of David, was questioned by the police and then released. The next day four young police officers in sports clothes went to see the elder Graiver again, and he asked, "Who are you, Montoneros, or what?" The police said they were guerillas. "Take it easy," Juan Graiver is reported to have said. "I'm a decent sort who pays his debts. We are going to give you your money back." Naturally enough he was extremely worried because after the collapse of the Graiver financial empire, the Montoneros, sharing the anxieties of ordinary investors, were demanding to know what had happened to their money. They were asking the sort of questions that did not allow Graiver to sleep well at night.

In December 1977 a court martial, composed of military officers sitting in secret, sentenced David Graiver's father, Juan, his widow, Lidia, and his brother, Isidoro, to 15 years' imprisonment, the maximum, for collaborating with terrorist groups. Five other relatives and associates were sentenced to lighter terms. The military communique announcing the sentences did not give any details of the trial but military sources said that the substance of the charge of investing stolen funds abroad had been obtained by questioning Jorge Rubenstein, a financial adviser to the Graiver banking establishments. Rubenstein will never again be able to answer questions; he died "while in the custody of the security forces."

There are many questions still to be answered, however. What happened to all the money? How much was the case against the Graivers part of the current wave of anti-Semitism in Argentina? And the most tantalizing of all, is David Graiver still alive? In April 1978 Robert Morgenthau, the Manhattan District Attorney, declared "There is a basis to believe he is still alive." Other sources quoted in the *Wall Street Journal* said it seemed likely that Graiver was behind the Iron Curtain. The South American financier and five of his banking staff had been charged by a grand jury in New York City with conspiracy, misappropriation of funds and falsification of bank records in an international financial scheme involving six countries. The district attorney announced that his detectives were searching for Graiver and that they would seek the help of Interpol. This news began fresh speculation in Argentina, where it is generally believed that Graiver became involved with the terrorists after the seizure of his brother Isidoro by the Montoneros early in the 1970s. After Isidoro was freed, it was generally believed that the family had paid a ransom, but later there was speculation that David Graiver made a deal to manage the Montoneros' money in return for his family being left alone. What does seem certain is that the Montoneros lost a sizable chunk of their ill-gotten and unwisely invested money. It proved, in fact, that capitalism does not always pay, even for terrorists.

The Baader-Meinhof group and its successors in West Germany have, of course, set out to prove this point from the opposite direction. From the beginning of their existence, they geared their organization to theft following the precepts of Carlos Marighella, the Brazilian terrorist who taught that bank robbery was the just way of financing revolution. The fact that he was killed while practicing what he preached did not deter the Germans. They mounted six bank robberies within two months in 1972 and walked away with $185,000.

Ulrike Meinhof set out her justification for robbing banks in her pamphlet *Urban Guerillas and Class Conflict*. She wrote:

No one claims that bank robbery of itself changes anything . . . for the revolutionary organization it means first of all a solution of financial problems. It is logistically correct, since otherwise the financial problem could not be solved at all. It is tactically correct because it is a proletarian action. It is strategically correct because it serves the financing of the guerilla.

But the West German terrorists also had financial help, as did the Japanese Red Army, from Arab funds made available to them in return for services rendered, such as attacks on Israeli offices and factories producing for the Israelis. The Red Army Faction did not need to acquire on its own the large sums that some terrorist movements required, for a great deal of its support was provided by well-to-do German sympathizers. There was never any shortage of comfortable apartments in which the terrorists could hide, and cars and equipment were easy to acquire in an affluent Western country. Even though Andreas Baader liked his comforts and Ulrike Meinhof complained when she had to live in an unheated building, money was never a problem for these middle-class terrorists. Meinhof had money of her own, and many of the young female terrorists were able to get funds from their prosperous parents.

Klaus Rohl, husband of Ulrike, revealed in his biography that both of them had been secret members of the Communist Party from 1956 until 1961. He further stated that his magazine *Konkret* had been subsidized by Soviet funds. On clandestine visits to Eastern Europe, he and Ulrike had collected upwards of one million marks by way of Prague.

Whenever the Baader-Meinhof crowd did run short of money, they simply organized more bank raids. Even in 1977 that same process continued. So common was it for West German banks to be held up at gunpoint that they became known as "terrorist treasuries." Robbers were making off with up to $5 million a year, most of which went into terrorist fighting funds.

The early bank raids did not always produce as much as the Baader-Meinhof gang would have liked. In one case Baader managed to steal only 8,000 deutsche marks, a few thousand dollars, having failed to notice a carton of notes worth more than 10 times as much. His comrades mocked Baader for his failure, saying: "You could earn that much doing dirty work for *Konkret* magazine." Other members of the gang went in for small scale fraud. One of the terrorists declared that he had lost his travelers' checks and claimed the insurance on them in the Middle East. After he had collected the money, he flew back to Europe and cashed the original travelers' checks. A cheap little trick but then, all things are permissible as long as they serve the cause.

Perhaps the most revealing words on the financial philosophy of terrorism were those of Horst Mahler, who, on entering a bank, declared: "This is a stick-up! Hands up and keep quiet and nothing will happen to you. After all, it's not your money."

Bank robbery has been a principal means of financing underground terrorist activities in the U.S., supplemented by occasional ransoms and contributions in dollars and kind by wealthy sympathizers. In a "Mayday communique" in 1977, the George Jackson Brigade claimed credit for a series of six successful Oregon bank robberies. They were undertaken in the aftermath of an unsuccessful bank holdup on January 23, 1976, which resulted in a shoot-out with police in Tukwila, Washington. The Brigade barely made a profit for all their efforts, netting an average of a little over $4,000 per robbery. A 1970 Boston bank robbery that resulted in the death of a policeman was revealed to be part of a series of terrorist operations in 1976, when Susan Saxe was tried and found guilty after two of her accomplices turned state's evidence. Saxe was also convicted of a Philadelphia bank robbery as well as the theft of arms from the Newburyport, Massachusetts National Guard Armory.

The most publicized terrorist bank stickup in the U.S. was, of course, the one in which Patty Hearst participated just eight weeks after she was kidnapped by the Symbionese Liberation Army in 1974. After considerable courtroom theatrics, she was sentenced to seven years in prison for her role in the holdup.

All in all, however, American terrorists have neither required nor obtained the large sums of money needed by their West German, Italian and Middle Eastern counterparts to underwrite expensive hijacking operations and the costly apparatus of true multinational terrorism.

While bank raids and small-time chicanery have kept terrorists in many countries afloat, the really big profits come from hijackings and kidnaps. As a result of the kidnapping of the politician Peter Lorenz in West Berlin, five imprisoned terrorists were released and flown to South Yemen with 20,000 deutche marks apiece as pocket money. While this did not equal the coup of Wadi Hadad, the old master—who in 1972 forced Lufthansa to pay $5 million into his PFLP fund, at a time when it was cut off from the main stream of Arab money, in return for the release of a hijacked jumbo—it did help.

Hadad, incidentally, smarted for years over this hijacking because the South Yemenis charged him a $1-million-dollar "landing fee." His hit team also failed to discover that one of the passengers was Joseph P. Kennedy III, the son of the late Robert F. Kennedy and obviously worth more in ransom money than all the other passengers put together.

In Italy the Red Brigades took a leaf out of the Mafia's book when they began operating their terrorist network as a money-making organization. When anti-terrorist investigators made a breakthrough in the mid-1970s and succeeded in arresting the original Red Brigades' leadership and breaking their networks, they discovered detailed accounts. By that time ransom money and protection payments had amassed in such quantities that the Red Brigades had an annual budget of one billion lira. The terrorists' finance managers had prudently invested large sums. It was estimated that 300 million lira had been invested in real estate, and the income from this was used to purchase weapons, cars and equipment. Some of the property bought by Red Brigades was used to provide safe houses and "people's prisons," but usually their real estate was used simply to provide a solid reliable income. Like the Palestinians the accountants of the Red Brigades put aside large sums to pay their terrorist operators, and they also operated a social security system to look after the dependents of those killed or imprisoned in the course of their terrorist activities. Despite the healthy income enjoyed by the Red Brigades, they still had money worries. While in prison awaiting trial, Renata Curcio complained about the high and increasing cost of keeping underground units operational.

The Japanese Red Army has always had the reputation of being as much a mercenary force as an ideological one. Because the Japanese police cracked down on them after their first small operations at home, this group was forced to flee and re-form abroad with no visible means of support. They went to work for the Palestinians in return for subsidies to keep their movement alive, but also turned to hijacking to maintain a semblance of independence. However, they were not particularly successful, and so the Red Army's woman leader, Fusako Shigenobu, planned a series of kidnappings of Japanese businessmen in Europe to restore the financial situation. The entire Red Army treasury—$10,000—was sent by courier from the Middle East to Paris to finance the operations. But the courier was arrested at Orly airport and on examination, the money proved to be a poor forgery.

The Red Army had to turn again to the PFLP to bail them out. It was not until the summer of 1977 that the Red Army made a startling comeback by seizing a Japan Air Lines plane just after it had taken off from Bombay and forcing it to fly to Bangladesh and then to Algiers. The Japanese government abjectly surrendered to their demands and agreed to release a mixed bag of six imprisoned terrorists and criminals. They thus provided the Red Army with a renewed fighting force. And, by handing over a ransom of $6 million in used $100 bills, they provided the capital to reestablish the Red Army as a powerful force in international terrorism, part of the new group that was being set up in late 1977 by Wadi Hadad and Carlos in Baghdad until halted by Hadad's death.

We said at the beginning of this chapter that money is the fuel of terrorism—without it nothing runs. But at the same time it is probably the easiest of essentials for terrorists to obtain. For once they have abandoned normal morality and convinced themselves that anything is justified in pursuit of their cause, then bank robbery, kidnapping and hijacking become not only permissible, but actual acts of virtue. When this philosophy is joined with the sophisticated investment of its rewards and is backed by the flow of Arab petrodollars to organizations judged to be of assistance to the Palestinian cause, there are fortunes to be made. But these are not fortunes to be frittered away by playboys or to be invested wisely for the benefit of mankind. They are fortunes to be used in destroying the democratic civilization that has evolved in the Western world, the fruit of 3,000 years of struggle. Remember that Stalin started his revolutionary life as a bank robber.

# 6

# The Weapons
# of Terror — Guns

The weapons of terror have become industrialized since
the Old Man of the Mountains sent his Assassins armed
with their long knives to persuade his enemies of the
justness of his cause, and Jael, one of the first of the
"freedom fighters," carried out the political assassination
of Sisera by hammering a tent peg through his skull. But
the three essential requirements of such weapons remain
the same: availability, simplicity and efficiency. Other
requirements have been added over the years. It is now
necessary for terrorists to be able to kill a number of people from a distance, so firepower has become important.
This entails the use of automatic weapons, but not those
with too rapid a rate of fire, for the limited amount of ammunition that can normally be carried on a mission of
terror precludes its waste. The guns and ammunition
must have stopping power, for it is dangerous to allow a
victim the capability of firing back; one lucky bullet
could wreck the whole operation. To conduct urban terrorism, weapons need to be concealed, so miniaturization
is also essential. When these characteristics are added to
easy access to guns and the bullets to load them and the
simplicity that precludes weapons jamming at a vital
moment, the perfect weapon of terror emerges.

The following weapons possess these requirements to a
greater or lesser degree; some are more efficient than others, but they all carry the same guarantee of usage.
These are the chosen weapons of terrorism.

## Kalashnikov or AK 47 (Plate I)

This Russian assault rifle is the true weapon of revolution. The brilliant invention of a Siberian peasant boy who became a solider and designed weapons while he was convalescing from a wound received in the tank battle for Bryansk in World War II, hundreds of thousands of various versions of this rifle have been made in Communist–bloc countries and supplied to the Soviet Union's clients and revolutionary movements around the world. It is the standard weapon of the Iron Curtain countries, several Arab armies, the Palestinian movements, Cuba and numerous armies in black Africa. Its success stems largely from its reliability. It functioned in Vietnam under conditions that jammed the American M 16. It can be smothered in mud and sand and will still work perfectly. Solid and dependable, it is the weapon for ill-educated peasant armies, used by Black September at Munich, Palestinian raiding parties across the Israeli border, and by ZANU (Zimbabwe African National Union) guerillas in Rhodesia. There have been reports that the IRA also has a small number. Two hundred and fifty of them were seized when the IRA arms ship *Claudia* was captured in 1973.

*Assessment:* This excellent weapon is reliable and, despite its short barrel, not noticeably less accurate than Western rifles. It has good stopping power. Captured Kalashnikovs were preferred by U.S. troops in Vietnam and by Israeli soldiers to their own weapons.

## VZ 58 V Assault Rifle (Plate 2)

This Czech-designed and -made weapon was used by the three Japanese Red Army terrorists when they carried out the massacre at Lod airport in 1972. They used buttless VZ 58s and grenades, which they had hidden in their luggage. Following this exploit a unit of the Japanese Red Army gave itself the name VZ 58. It is sold commercially by Omnipol, the Czech arms manufacturer.

**Assessment:** This effective weapon at first sight resembles the AK 47, but it differs quite dramatically in design and manufacture. It is not as foolproof as the AK 47 in that it can be assembled and fired without the locking piece, thus causing an explosion in the breech. It can fire the same rounds as the AK 47, but the magazines are not interchangeable.

### Skorpion VZ 61 (Plate 3)

This tiny, Czech-made machine pistol is one of the most popular weapons of terrorism. It was used by the Red Brigades to kill Aldo Moro, and ballistics showed that it was the same gun used previously to kill Francesco Coco, the chief prosecutor of Genoa. It has also been supplied to a number of African countries and forms an important part of the arsenal of urban guerillas in southern Africa. The Skorpion has been used particularly by assassination gangs in Johannesburg. It was found in the cache of weapons left behind by Carlos in one of his Paris hideouts and was used in the attempted assassination of Princess Ashraf of Iran in Juan les Pins on the French Riviera in September 1977. It is a standard weapon of the Czech security forces. The cartridge is unique for weapons made in Communist-bloc countries because it is of American design.

**Assessment:** This has all the necessary qualities for a weapon of terrorism. It is light and so small it can be easily concealed. The Skorpion has an effective rate of fire and is deadly at close range. It can also be fitted with a highly efficient silencer. The silencer reduces the effective range to about 100 yards, but since terrorist operations are rarely carried out at a range of more than 10 yards, this is of no consequence. The silencer, apart from deadening the sound of shooting, spreads the shot around, giving the weapon something of a shotgun characteristic and making a hit more probable. It is no longer being made, and existing stocks are being sold off by Omnipol.

## Heckler and Koch MP 5 (Plate 4)

This submachine gun was developed from the G 3 rifle which is a standard weapon of West Germany and 34 other countries. Made at the Heckler and Koch factory outside Stuttgart from designs under development by the German Army towards the end of World War II, the G 3 is also produced in Britain and France. The MP 5 submachine gun version has become almost as widely used by terrorists. It is particularly favored by the Baader-Meinhof gang's successors and was used in the kidnapping of Hans-Martin Schleyer in Cologne in September 1977. The MP 5 has been issued to the various police forces of West Germany and has also been bought by the security forces of several other nations. Those used in the Schleyer kidnapping, in which three bodyguards and a driver were killed, were among a batch stolen in Switzerland. A drawing of the MP 5 set against the background of a five-pointed star forms the insignia of the Red Army Faction, which carried out the kidnapping.

*Assessment:* This conforms to the highest standards of West German automatic weapons production. It is probably the most efficient terrorist weapon now in production. It fulfills all the requirements and is particularly suitable for German terrorists because it can be stolen from police armories, and the ammunition is available in quantity.

## Armalite AR-18 (Plate 5)

This American-designed rifle is the favorite weapon of the IRA terrorists who hide in ruined buildings or take apartments with a commanding view and then pump a burst of small, high-velocity rounds into an army vehicle or patrol. Originally produced as the successor to the AR-16, the standard American infantry weapon in Vietnam, it was not adopted by the U.S. Army because so many AR-16s had been produced. It has, however, been produced commercially in Japan, California and, under license, by the Sterling Armament Co. in England. One version, the AR-180, which has only a single-shot capacity, is sold as a sporting rifle in both New York and London. The IRA has acquired some of these weapons from Japan, but most of them come from the gunshops of New York, where they are bought legitimately and then smuggled in small batches on board ships sailing to Ireland. Some of these AR-180s have been modified by IRA gunsmiths to fire bursts, but most remain single-shot rifles and are only issued to expert shots who are able to get off three or four aimed rounds very quickly. It is the weapon that has killed more British soldiers than any other in Northern Ireland.

**Assessment:** This weapon's accuracy and the penetrating power of its small bullet make it deadly. The bullet can penetrate body armor, medium steel plate and steel helmets at 500 yards and inflict a devastating wound. The shock of even a minor wound inflicted by these high-velocity rounds can kill. It is, however, too large a weapon to be used in a normal terrorist operation. It must be broken down and smuggled into and out of a firing position by "gun carriers."

## Thompson Submachine Gun (Plate 6)

This weapon, which achieved such notoriety as the gangsters' Chicago Piano, was originally designed by General John Thompson as a means of breaking the stalemate on the Western Front in World War I by giving Allied troops portable firepower for their attacks on the well-defended German trenches. His prototype, produced in 1917, was called the Trench Broom, but it had not been accepted by the authorities at the time the war ended. Then, despite its gangster phase, it languished until the start of World War II, when it was mass-produced and used in quantity by the Allies. By then, however, it had become the favorite weapon of the old-style Irish Republican Army gunmen in the trench-coat and Tommy-Gun era. The IRA has retained its affection for the gun and, although it has been replaced by more modern weapons, there are still a number of well-oiled Thompson's hidden in rabbit holes and barns throughout Ireland—and some of them are occasionally taken out and used. It is estimated that nearly 1.5 million various models of these guns were made. The Thompson was also used in London by the Angry Brigade, to date Britain's only native terrorist movement of the Baader-Meinhof type. (It collapsed in 1972 when most of its members were arrested and sent to prison for long terms the following year.)

*Assessment:* A first-class World War II field weapon that proved extremely effective for house clearing, it is too big and cumbersome to appeal to modern terrorists. It would seem that only the romanticism of the IRA and their availability keeps the Thompson in use in Ireland. The old-fashioned drum magazines, which held either 50 or 100 rounds, are still available, but these gangster models tended to jam under field conditions and were replaced by straight boxes in the military version.

### Sten Submachine Gun (Plate 7)

Mass-produced for the British Army and the European resistance movements during World War II, over two million Sten guns were produced and its offshoot, the Sterling, is still in service with the British Army. Since a great number of these weapons were spread around the world—thousands were parachuted into occupied Europe—many drifted into the hands of terrorist organizations. They are, however, too large for most urban terrorist work and have largely been replaced by smaller, more efficient automatic weapons in the European and Middle Eastern terrorist movements. The IRA, however, still retains its affection for the Sten. One of them was found among the arsenal of the Balcombe Street gang of Provos in London and, like the Tommy Gun, it is brought out of its caches during times of trouble in Ireland. It too was used in London by the now-defunct Angry Brigade. Models of the Sten range from the mass-produced, crude

Mark II, to the rather elegant, wood-stocked and silenced Mark VI. The Mark II is the most common version used by terrorists.

*Assessment:* This excellent mass-produced weapon provides automatic fire at close range, but because it was mass-produced, the Sten has several dangerous quirks. It tends to jam so that it will not fire or, even more disconcerting, jams on full automatic. This was principally because the lips of the stamped metal magazine could easily be damaged. The fault was largely rectified in later models. Another dangerous quirk was that a sharp blow on the butt could jar the bolt out of its safety catch and cause the gun to fire. A number of British soldiers jumping from the backs of trucks and hitting their Sten butts on the road shot the men behind them. Nevertheless, it is an efficient weapon when used as the IRA's Balcombe Street gang did, to spray a crowded restaurant in London from a passing car.

### M 1 Carbine (Plate 8)

This World War II weapon, like the Tommy Gun and the Sten gun, has virtually disappeared from the armories of terrorism except those of the IRA. Two of them were among the weapons captured from the Balcombe Street raiders, who were the most successful of the Provisional IRA's Active Service Units operating in England. It was developed by the Winchester arms company in a very short time; the design was accepted in October 1941 only one year after the U.S. Ordnance Department had issued a specification for a light rifle. Production began almost immediately and the huge total—3,527,827—of various models of this carbine were made by nine companies.

*Assessment:* Because it is light and handy, this carbine was particularly suited to jungle warfare, and for that reason is also suitable for street fighting. Reliable and safe with no vices, it is a useful weapon for training recruits and is used for that purpose by the IRA.

**Beretta Model 12 Submachine Gun** (Plate 9)

This compact, accurate weapon is the latest of the Beretta series of submachine guns and is issued to commando units of the Italian Army. It has also been sold to countries in Africa, South America and the Middle East. Two of these were among the equipment used by the Carlos gang to mount the raid on OPEC headquarters in Vienna. Carlos carried one of them and the other was used by Hans-Joachim Klein, who was seriously wounded when a bullet from an OPEC guard hit the magazine of his Beretta, fragmented, and riddled his stomach.

*Assessment:* This weapon ranks with the Czech Skorpion as one of the most efficient automatic weapons. It is simple, elegant, has two safety systems, and with a 40-round magazine, gives terrorists a heavy concentration of firepower in an urban guerilla situation. With its metal stock unfolded it can also be used effectively at longer ranges.

**Astra .357 Magnum** (Plate 10)

This is the Big Bertha of assassination weapons. Made in Spain, it is on sale commercially in the U.S. and Britain. The size of its bullet and its tremendous power makes death almost inevitable if the gun is used at close range. The Balcombe Street gang used it to kill Ross McWhirter, publisher of *The Guiness Book of World Records*, in 1975—because he had offered a reward of £50,000 ($100,000) for the capture of the Provisional IRA's Active Service Unit that was terrorizing London. This particular gun was found in the Balcombe Street arsenal and was matched by ballistics experts. A similar gun was used to murder London businessman Alan Quartermaine while he was being driven home in 1974. Ballistics tests show that the gun that killed Quartermaine was used to cover the retreat of an IRA squad after a bomb attack on the Naval and Military Club in London in December 1974.

*Assessment:* This brutally efficient weapon's only drawback is its size. It is the most powerful handgun in the terrorist armory.

## M 52 Pistol (Plate 11)

This is another well-made, reliable weapon designed and manufactured by the Czechs, who seem determined to remain independent of Soviet armories. It has been phased out of front-line service in Czechoslovakia and passed on to various "liberation groups." Carlos had a number of these weapons in his various caches in London and Paris. He used one of them to kill Michel Moukharbel, the friend he thought had betrayed him, and two French police inspectors. Carlos seriously wounded Commissaire Jean Herranz in a shooting in the Rue Toullier when he was being arrested in a girl friend's apartment.

*Assessment:* For the close ranges at which terrorists are taught to use pistols, any reliable weapon is just as effective as another when it comes to killing. Where the M 52 differs, however, is in its extremely powerful cartridge, which gives it a muzzle velocity of more than twice that of a standard military service revolver. One of the shots that killed Moukharbel as he was lying on the floor passed through his body, the floorboards, the ceiling of the apartment below, a molded plastic table and then buried itself so deeply in another set of floorboards that it was impossible to dig out. It is an assassin's weapon.

## Browning High Power Pistol (Plate 12)

This is probably the best known of all the automatic pistols. Designed in 1925 by the gun genius John Moses Browning, it was used in various versions throughout World War II by the Allies and was also made in Belgium for the special use of the Nazi SS. Many thousands have been produced, and it has drifted into general use throughout the world. It was a gun of this type that Carlos fired at British department store executive and Zionist Teddy Sieff in December 1973. Sieff was lucky that Carlos did not use the Czech M 52, the other pistol in his armory, for although the Browning is high-powered, Sieff's strong front teeth absorbed the impact of the bullet, which came to rest a fraction of an inch away from his jugular vein. If Carlos had used the M 52, its even higher-powered cartridge would probably have taken the Zionist leader's head off. Ballistic tests showed that the Browning found in Carlos's London cache was the gun used in the Sieff operation. Gudrun Ensslin of Baader-Meinhof was carrying one of these guns when she was arrested in a boutique in Hamburg.

**Assessment:** This reliable, effective weapon for close-range work and the ammunition for it are readily available. One of its advantages is the large capacity of its magazine, which holds 13 rounds.

### Makarov Pistol (Plate 13)

This is the Soviet equivalent of the Browning pistol and is in general service with the Russian-supplied armies of Eastern Europe and Soviet–client nations. It is also made by China. Like the Browning, many thousands have been made, and it is now in general use throughout the world. The Makarov has come into terrorist hands particularly through the Palestinian terrorist organizations, which have been supplied from the Soviet arsenals. The most spectacular operation in which it has been used was the Carlos-led assault on OPEC headquarters in Vienna on December 21, 1975. Each of the six-member kidnapping team carried a Makarov as a personal weapon, with a mixed bag of submachine guns, grenades and explosives. Gabrielle Krocher-Tiedemann, a member of the German Baader-Meinhoff gang who took part in this operation, carried two. With them she murdered two men, an Austrian policeman and the bodyguard of the Iraqi oil minister. Carlos used his Makarov to kill a senior member of the Libyan delegation who grappled with Carlos and almost succeeded in wresting the terrorist's submachine gun from him. Carlos, at the time of writing, is still alive. Gabrielle was arrested gun in hand by Swiss police on the French frontier in 1977.

**Assessment:** This is a solid reliable piece of machinery. Simple to use, it proved its worth as a close-range weapon of terrorism in Vienna.

### Tokarev (TT-33) (Plate 14)

This Soviet pistol has now been replaced by the Makarov in the Eastern European countries, but it is still effective and is used by many Asian-communist countries with numerous filtering through to Arab terrorist groups. One variant, the 9 mm Parabellum Tokagypt, has a curious history. It was made in Hungary and supplied in large quantities to President Nasser when he was seeking the arms refused him by Secretary of State John Foster Dulles. The Egyptians were, however, not impressed by it and deliveries were halted. But it was a powerful weapon, accurate at long range, and since there was no comparable 9 mm Parabellum being made in the United States, American arms dealers contracted to buy the surplus stocks. The guns were then stamped with the name Firebird. But once again the sale was canceled when the U.S. government rescinded the import licenses. The Firebirds were then put on the commercial market in Europe, and a large consignment found its way to the Arabs. It was these pistols with which Ulrike Meinhof and Andreas Baader were taught to shoot at an Arab training camp in Jordan and which eventually became the standard weapon in the Baader-Meinhof armory. A number of Firebirds were bought by gang member Rolf Pohle from West German gunshops. He used forged papers and licenses but was eventually caught when an arms dealer in Ulm became suspicious of his papers. Meinhof herself bought 23 Firebirds from Fatah for 450 deutsche marks each, paying nearly four times the open retail price for customers licensed to own a handgun.

*Assessment:* This is an old-fashioned pistol in the traditional style, but despite its military obsolescence it is still an effective weapon of terrorism—as the Baader-Meinhof gang has proved.

## Walther P 38 (Plate 15)

This pistol is so popular with the Italian Red Brigades that they have become known as the P Thirty-eighters. In 1975 they started a clandestine journal entitled *Mai piu Senza Fusile (Never Without a Gun)*, and the P 38 was that gun. It has been used in kidnappings and particularly in the crippling shootings where Red Brigade members ambush and shoot victims—journalists, lawyers, policemen, etc.—in the legs.

*Assessment:* This is a modern weapon, in service with the West German armed forces and available in a commercial version. It is simple to operate and works effectively under most conditions. It is a good all-purpose weapon.

## Smith and Wesson Revolver (Plate 16)

Nearly one million of these revolvers were produced from 1940 to 1945 and they became a standard weapon of the American and British armed forces. The revolver was also issued to police forces in the United States, England and Ireland. A large number of Smith and Wessons have come into the possession of the IRA, who have used them in many assassinations. Two of them were found among the armory of the Balcombe Street gang. One of the gang, Edward Butler, who was later sent to prison for life, always carried a .38 Smith and Wesson. "I would not go shopping without it. I carried it everywhere." It is a favorite weapon of the Kneecappers, for with its low muzzle velocity it cripples without destroying.

*Assessment:* Cynical weapons instructors in the British Army were fond of saying that the best way to bring down an enemy with one of these revolvers was to throw it at him. Certainly it takes an expert shot to hit a person at anything over 10 yards. Nevertheless, at short range this is a reliable and effective weapon, and there have been many funerals in Ireland to prove it.

### RGD–5 Anti-Personnel Hand Grenade (Plate 17)

This modern Russian grenade was used by the FLOSY (Front for the Liberation of South Yemen) terrorists in Aden in their attacks on the British Army, and the sight of one of these smooth-skinned, apple-green bombs rolling towards a patrol along an alley was always fearsome. It was used by the Vietcong and also by Carlos and his gang during the raid on the OPEC headquarters in Vienna. Hans-Joachim Klein threw one of them at the policemen on guard at OPEC shortly before he was wounded in the stomach by a ricochet off the butt of his submachine gun. Those used in Aden were made in China and supplied to FLOSY by Peking.

*Assessment:* This light grenade can be thrown for some 35 to 40 yards and, with its killing radius of 18 to 22 yards, is an effective weapon. Its egg-shaped steel body has a serrated liner that bursts into a pattern of killing fragments—deadly in a confined space.

### SAM 7 Strela (Arrow) (Plate 18)

The SAM 7, translated, is the seventh model of surface-to-air missiles produced by the Soviet Union. It is also known by the NATO code name of Grail but achieved its fame as SAM 7, along with SAM 2 and SAM 6, in shooting down Israeli aircraft during the Yom Kippur War in October 1973. Its use by terrorists was first revealed earlier that year when Italian police raided a top-floor apartment at Ostia just three miles along the main flight path from Rome's airport and found two SAM 7s hidden in a closet.

*Assessment:* This hand-held antiaircraft weapon is similar to Western missiles such as the American Redeye and the British Blowpipe and like them was developed for battlefield use by individual soldiers to protect units against low-level strafing. Its infrared guidance control automatically homes in on the heat given off by an attacking aircraft's engine. It can be confused by electronic countermeasures and evasive action by high-speed fighters, but would be deadly against big jetliners approaching slowly along a flight path. Its drawback is that its high-explosive warhead is not particularly powerful and a large, well-built aircraft could, if not hit in a vital area, survive its explosion. Its advantage as a terrorist antiaircraft weapon is that it can be carried around in the backseat of a car and fired whenever a target comes within range. All airport security officials must now take note of the possibility of its use. At London's Heathrow regular army exercises are held on the assumption that terrorists armed with SAM 7s are mounting an attack.

### M 26 Grenade (Plate 19)

This is a standard U.S. Army weapon, known as a fragmentation grenade because its coiled inner liner is notched to fragment when the grenade explodes and thereby cause the largest number of casualties. This has given rise to its own language; U.S. troops in Vietnam who thought that their officers were becoming too zealous in their search for a fight with the Vietcong were apt to throw an M 26 in the officer's vicinity. This became known as "fragging." The M 26 became notorious as a terrorist weapon after a large number were stolen by the Baader-Meinhof gang in 1971 from the U.S. Army base at Miesau in West Germany. They were then distributed to various terrorist organizations throughout Europe. The Japanese Red Army used these grenades in their occupation of the French Embassy in the Hague in September 1974; Carlos used them when he killed two and wounded 34 customers in his attack on Le Drugstore in Paris, which was designed to coincide with the Japanese occupation of the embassy; and his gang carried them during the OPEC raid in December 1975. The identification of this stolen batch of grenades by their serial numbers enabled the security forces of Europe to connect the links between terrorist groups as the grenades were passed on from one to another.

*Assessment:* The notched inner lining of this grenade, coiled under tension, makes it a deadly antipersonnel weapon, ideal for terrorist use in crowded places, where the maximum number of casualties can be inflicted and the maximum amount of terror caused. It has secure safety devices and its 16-ounce weight gives it the right balance for throwing.

### RPG–7 Portable Rocket Launcher (Plate 20)

This Russian weapon is the artillery of terrorism. It was used extensively by the Vietcong and was feared by U.S. soldiers both in its role as an antipersonnel fragmentation weapon and as an antitank rocket that could blow the turret off a modern tank. The rocket launcher has been supplied to the Rhodesian rebel organizations and to the various Palestinian groups. In strictly terrorist actions it was used on two occasions by Carlos' gang in Paris when they attempted to destroy Israeli passenger jets on the runway at Orly. This is possibly the weapon that a mixed German and Palestinian "commando" operation attempted to use against an El Al plane at Nairobi airport in 1976, another raid that was foiled by an Israeli secret service tip-off. They have also been used against British Army posts in Northern Ireland by the Provisional IRA, who obtained a small batch from Colonel Qaddafi. A much larger consignment was seized when the arms ship *Claudia* was captured off the Irish coast on the last stage of its run from Libya.

*Assessment:* This is not a particularly accurate weapon, especially at long range and in high winds. Nevertheless, it can do a fearsome amount of damage. It is simple to make—Al Fatah has its own RPG factory—and easy to fire, but care must be taken to make sure no one is standing behind the weapon when it is fired, since the burning gases from the rocket motor can do almost as much damage as the grenade itself. It gives an individual the ability to deliver an explosive charge the equivalent of a medium gunshell and then pick up the launcher and walk away with another half a dozen projectiles slung in a bandolier across the shoulders. In urban guerilla actions it gives the terrorist an artillery capacity denied the security forces in the early stages of a confrontation.

## M 60 General Purpose Machine Gun (Plate 21)

A great fuss was made early in 1978 when the IRA paraded one of its newly acquired M 60s, standard equipment in the U.S. Army. From three to six of these machine guns were believed to have been smuggled into Northern Ireland from the Middle East via Cyprus and Antwerp concealed aboard a tanker. They were displayed during a parade marking the sixth anniversary of Bloody Sunday (when the British Army opened fire during a riot in Londonderry and killed 13). One M 60 had already been used in January in an ambush of three Royal Ulster constables in Londonderry. The feeling was that this blatant attack was done to demonstrate that the Provisional IRA was not yet finished—a view that had been increasingly expressed by the government. Certainly the appearance of the M 60 gave credence to the Provos claim that they were receiving shipments of sophisticated weapons and were by no means at the end of their rope. By the middle of 1978 two of these weapons had been captured by security forces, one in the Irish Republic and one in Northern Ireland.

*Assessment:* This is an excellent infantry weapon, but it has serious drawbacks as a weapon of terror. Most terrorist weapons are used in ambush and in urban surroundings. The M 60 has too fast a rate of fire, is too heavy and too long to be a successful weapon of urban warfare. It could be used by the IRA in open country firefights, but even there it has its drawbacks, for in order to change a hot barrel the second man on the gun is issued a "mitten asbestos MI 942," which he uses to pull the barrel out while the first man presses down on the stock with his right hand and lifts the fore-end with his left. Such complicated operation is not suited to the tactics and circumstances of terror operations. It is essential in this type of warfare that a weapon be light, simple and not require more than one person to handle it. One could say that anything an M 60 can do in this role, an Armalite can do better. It is in fact a weapon of propaganda rather than of terror.

The Japanese security forces, cleaning up after the final student attempts to block the opening of the new Tokyo airport, discovered several examples of a new weapon of terror, a sophisticated cattle prod, a two-pronged electrical staff about three-feet long connected to a current-producing beltpack. This weapon can deliver a charge of some 500 volts and is capable of knocking a person out and, in some cases, of killing. This could be an effective weapon in the type of mass street battles in which the Japanese specialize.

An even more extraordinary weapon was used to kill the Bulgarian defector Georgi Markov in London in September 1978. Markov, who had broadcast details of Bulgarian leaders' sexual habits, fell ill and died after complaining of being jabbed in the thigh while waiting for a bus on Waterloo Bridge. At first it was thought that he had been killed by a poisoned umbrella, but an autopsy showed that he had been shot by a surgical "gun" normally used to inject radioactive pellets into cancer victims. In Markov's case the gun was used to fire a tiny, poison-packed pellet into the back of his leg. A similar pellet was extracted from the back of another Bulgarian defector-broadcaster, Vladimir Kostov, who was attacked in Paris but recovered. The authorities know the identity of the man who carried out the attacks and know that he was ordered to do so by the Bulgarian secret service.

Stefan Bankov, a Bulgarian exile living in the U.S., revealed in September 1978 that he had been temporarily paralyzed by a liquid spilled on his shoulder by unidentified foreigners on a plane in 1974. Other similar attacks resulting in at least two fatalities involving Croatian exiles living in the U.S. were reported in late 1978. Privately, U.S. officials conceded that assertions by the Croatian-American community that the attacks were the work of the Yugoslav secret police were well founded, if unproven.

# 7

# The Weapons of Terror—Bombs

The modern terrorist's bomb still fulfills the same function as the crude device of The Professor: it is used to kill, or threaten to kill, and thereby destroy the economic and social life of a country; to instill fear; in fact, to terrorize. But the bombs, their mechanisms and their explosives have become far more efficient. They are easier to make and safer to handle, can be made much smaller, and can be triggered by a variety of ingenious methods, thus enabling them to be used in circumstances that were out of reach of nineteenth-century terrorists. Terrorists of that period could derail a train, but they did not have at their mercy jumbo jets carrying 400 people at 600 miles per hour 35,000 feet above the ground. The derailing of a train could kill a number of people, but when an airliner is blown out of the sky, everybody dies. So not only are today's bombs more efficient, they are capable, because of the development of mass air travel, of causing far greater loss of human life and material and of instilling the maximum amount of fear. It is this potential that makes the aerial hijacker's slab of plastic explosive such a powerful weapon.

In this chapter we propose to show how the modern bombers go about their business. If the information is not as detailed as some of our readers might wish, it is because we have set out to report how things are done and not to provide a textbook on how to make bombs. Every schoolboy knows how to mix gunpowder and pack it into a cardboard tube to make a firecracker, quite a number know how to make explosives out of fertilizer, and most people who have served in the army know how to handle plastic, gun cotton, fuses and grenades. There is a great deal of expert knowledge freely available. We do not wish to make it any easier for people to construct bombs but intend to demonstrate how the bombers use their explosive expertise to attack society.

One of the difficult tasks of law enforcement agencies is to cut the terrorists' supply of explosives. When the terrorists are supported by countries with diplomatic representation, this becomes almost impossible, because those countries that actively encourage terrorism have no compunction about using their diplomatic cloak to smuggle weapons and explosives to surrogate warriors. Libya has been particularly guilty in this respect. Colonel Qaddafi has often used his diplomatic missions abroad to supply Soviet-made arms and explosives to "anti-imperialist" terror groups in many different countries. His embassy in Rome has been very busy in this field on various occasions.

The advantage of such a supply route is that once the supporting country has decided to send arms, the terrorists do not need to go through any risky process to obtain them. The lines of communication are secured by diplomatic usage. The explosives supplied are of a military type, usually plastic, which is stable and can be molded to any required shape. A circle of it can be used to cut down a tree, or it can be wrapped in a destructive embrace around the exhaust pipe of a car.

Palestinian terrorist groups are also heavily involved in the supply of arms and explosives to groups that support their cause. Their favorite explosive is again military plastic. The stability of this explosive makes it easy to smuggle—sometimes molded into innocent shapes like children's putty—by boat, car, even the knapsacks of traveling students. This last method was the one used by the Scottish anarchist Stuart Christie. He was arrested in Madrid in August 1967 carrying five packets of plastic (French in origin, not Arab), seven detonators and chemicals for making explosives. They were to be used by Spanish anarchists in an attempt to blow up Generalissimo Francisco Franco at a soccer match. A military type of plastic, RDX, was used in a bomb planted on the London Post Office Tower's observation platform in October 1971. Responsibility for this bombing was claimed by the Kilburn Battalion of the IRA, and experts who examined the remnants of the bomb and its timing device saw no reason to dispute this claim. It was a typical IRA-type, delayed-action bomb.

The second main source of supply is the theft of commercial explosives from mines and quarries. It is a simple matter to raid the magazines of such isolated places and often—with the connivance of sympathizers on the workforce—these missions have provided much of the explosives used by American terrorists, the IRA and the South American movements. California's New World Liberation Front mailed or planted a total of at least nine bombs with explosives its members stole from a Fenton, California quarry in a single raid in February 1975. The British Angry Brigade used French commercial explosives in their bombs. These explosives, Nitrotex, Nitromite and Gomme L, were handed over to women couriers by French sympathizers and smuggled into Britain on the ferries that cross the English Channel. At that time there was no means of tracing the explosive ingredients of a bomb except to its manufacturers. But since then, security forces have met with some success, especially in Britain and Ireland, in making the source of commercial explosives identifiable by the insertion into each batch of either a combination of colored threads or certain chemical compounds that can be identified after an explosion and so traced to the point where it was switched from legal to illegal use. This device helps to make things more difficult for terrorists.

The third main source of supply is that most peaceful of pursuits, gardening. It is here that we come into an area where it is best not to publish too many details, but it is commonly known that the IRA makes a large proportion of its bomb explosives from a mixture of certain types of chemical fertilizer and diesel fuel. The bomb that killed a physics researcher at the University of Wisconsin in 1970 was a simple mixture of nitrogen fertilizer and fuel oil bought on the open market by Karleton Armstrong, the man who later pleaded guilty to making and detonating the bomb. In an agricultural society such as Wisconsin's or Ireland's it is impossible to control the sale of large quantities of both fertilizer and diesel fuel for tractors. And this type of mixture will always be available to the bombers although the manufacturers are being urged to cut the explosive ingredients to as low a proportion as possible. The disadvantage of this type of explosive is that it is quite difficult to detonate and needs a priming charge of gun cotton or a couple of sticks of gelignite. The advantage is that it can be obtained and transported in bulk and is therefore ideal for the 100-pound and 200-pound car bombs that have caused such damage in Northern Ireland.

Another way of obtaining explosives is by raiding military bases. But any terrorist who does this must be prepared for a pitched battle if things go wrong with his plans. It is a tactic pursued more in South America than anywhere else. An even more desperate method, usually only attempted by guerilla movements in the initial stages of their development, is to remove the filling from unexploded shells and bombs. This is a most hazardous method and those who practice it are more likely to meet a sudden end than their enemies.

Having obtained the explosive the terrorists must build it into an "infernal device" and provide the fuse to set it off. Fuses come under four main headings: flame, chemical, electric and mechanical.

Flame fuses are probably the least used because their comparatively fast burning time allows the bomber little time to get clear of the explosion and because the burning fuse provides visible evidence that something nasty is going on. Military or commercial fuses of various types provide a fixed burning rate per foot, so that the time between ignition and explosion can be judged by cutting the fuse to a certain length. It is fitted into a detonator, normally a metal tube about two inches long filled with a sensitive explosive, usually fulminate of mercury. The detonator is fitted into a priming charge of explosive buried in the main body of the explosive. When the flame reaches the detonator it explodes, setting off the priming charge, which in turn sets off the main charge. Such detonators can also be exploded by firing a cap similar to that used in the base of a bullet cartridge, or by passing an electric current from a battery through a fuse wire or a wire filament such as that used in a light bulb.

Chemical fuses are basically similar to the fuse used by Ossipov, The Professor in Conrad's *The Secret Agent*, but modern methods call for a vial of acid to be crushed inside something that provides a time lag. The most popular is a rubber contraceptive. The acid gradually burns through the rubber before it comes in contact with the chemical and produces the spark that sets off the explosive. Metal containers can also be used. A rough guess can be made about the time that the acid will take to do its work, but this is an inexact form of time fuse because it is almost impossible to judge precisely the strength of the acid, the strength of the container and therefore the length of time the process will take. And if the contraceptive is faulty, the result could be even more embarrassing and far more dangerous than if it were used for its proper purpose. In their initial bombs the Angry Brigade used a combined chemical-mechanical fuse in which sulfuric acid dropped slowly on to a retaining tape. This burned through and released a striker.

Electric devices are the most common form of time fuse. They involve the use of clocks and watches wired so that when the hands reach a certain position on the clockface, they touch terminals connected to a battery, which then, with the circuit completed, sends a charge of electricity through the detonator and explodes the bomb. Baader-Meinhof used clockwork egg timers to provide the spark for some of their bombs, and in Belfast the IRA bought up a supply of the clockwork buzzers that signal when time is up on a parking meter. Although both these devices have limitations because of the lack of flexibility in their timing sequence, they work efficiently enough as long as a delay of no more than an hour is needed.

Another method, familiar to moviegoers, is that of wires strung from an explosive charge and connected to a plunger, which when depressed produces a current and sets off the bomb. This type is commonly used to set off heavy charges placed under roads, in culverts and hedges or in buildings. A plunger is not always necessary. The charge can be exploded by completing the circuit on a battery. However, this system requires wires to be trailed through a building or across fields and they can be detected by security patrols. Also, since the bombers must be within visual distance of the bomb to detonate it at the correct time, they are susceptible to detection and capture.

A more remote, and therefore safer, form of electric fuse is the radio fuse. By using the same system as that used for controlling model planes and boats, the bomber can send a signal that will explode his bomb instantaneously. Depending on the strength of the signal, the operator could be miles away, receiving the order to fire by telephone or by some form of visual signal.

Another form of electric signal was used by the Israelis when they killed Mahmoud Hamshari, the PLO representative in Paris, after the Munich massacre in 1972. They staked out his apartment, noting the time when his French wife, Marie-Claude, took their daughter, Amina, to nursery school. One Israeli, posing as an Italian journalist, made contact with Hamshari on the pretext of interviewing him. While they were meeting at a cafe, another member of the execution squad took an impression of the lock on the door of the apartment. The "Italian" arranged another meeting with Hamshari. This time, using a key made from the impression, the second Israeli walked into the apartment and fitted an electronically controlled bomb into the base of Hamshari's telephone. The next day the phone rang just after Mrs. Hamshari and Amina had left. Hamshari answered it. A voice at the other end said: "This is the Italian journalist who has a rendezvous with you today. That's really you, Mr. Hamshari?" The Palestinian replied, "Yes, this is Mahmoud Hamshari." As soon as he said that, the telephone blew up in his face. He lived long enough to tell the police what had happened, and they were able to piece together the electronic device that had killed him. The trigger mechanism was based on the same sort of mechanism as that fitted to scrambler telephones.

Mechanical fuses, at their simplest, are activated by pulling a safety pin that releases a spring, which in turn causes a firing pin to strike a detonator as in a hand grenade or closes an electrical circuit or, by friction, produces a spark. These fuses can be set off by opening a door, lifting the lid of a box of chocolates or opening a car trunk, actions that involve the movement of some component.

Pressure fuses are another simple form of mechanical detonation. A bomb may be set under a car seat, a floorboard or a mattress so that the pressure of the victim's body will release a plunger and so explode the bomb. A more sophisticated pressure bomb is that used in aircraft. These bombs work on the barometric principle and are so delicate that the change in pressure exerted on the bomb as the aircraft rises through the atmosphere sets it off.

The decision on what type of fuse to use is dictated by several factors: what fuses are available, the level of expertise of the bombmaker and the type of bomb desired. There is no point in making time bombs if there are no delayed-action fuses available. Similarly, it is futile to make a bomb to throw into a crowded restaurant if it cannot be fitted with an instantaneous fuse. It is the combination of the explosive, the case, the fuse and the timing that makes the perfect bomb.

At its simplest, the modern bomb is still crude. The IRA often uses several sticks of gelignite or dynamite bound together and set off by a short length of combustible fuse. These bombs are often wrapped with six-inch nails or coach bolts, which create a lethal burst of shrapnel when the bombs explode. Other simple bombs are constructed of lengths of pipe filled with pieces of metal junk, which, with a certain grim humor, the IRA calls "shipyard confetti." The Baader-Meinhof gang used army water bottles as outer cases for their initial bombs, and they too made pipe bombs, 7½-inch sections of steel pipe 6½ inches in diameter. As Jillian Becker describes them in *Hitler's Children,* her excellent account of the gang, "each of these had a bottom plate welded on to it and a top plate with a narrower pipe sticking out into which a screwing thread was cut." Pipe-terminating nuts were then screwed into the narrower pipe and "the detonators were fitted into these nuts and connected on a circuit to a 50-volt dry-cell battery via an egg timer giving a maximum delay of 60 minutes." Baader-Meinhof also used a larger version, converting gas cylinders into bombs.

The problem for terrorists is that these crude devices are so simple to make that every raw recruit thinks he is a professional, and before they learn the errors of their ways it is too late: they have "scored an own goal" and blown themselves to pieces.

The use of commercial explosives that have started to degrade, to "sweat," is one cause of accidents, and, astonishingly enough, so is the practice of smoking while making bombs. One theory claims a carelessly handled cigarette was the reason the Weathermen blew themselves out of existence when they were making bombs in their Greenwich Village headquarters in 1970. Three of them died and although a regrouped Weather Underground has carried out some bombings since then, they no longer pose a serious threat.

But the greatest cause of "own goals" is clumsiness when setting the electrical systems on time bombs. It is very easy to bring the terminals into contact with each other. For this reason IRA experts instituted a safety device so that the young people they sent to plant bombs could not blow themselves up. This device was a simple pin that had to be withdrawn before the clock started to tick. But many of the youngsters were in so much of a hurry to get away or were so frightened of the bomb itself that they neglected to take out the pin. The expert instructors then attached tags to the pins ordering the bombers to return the pins in order to prove that they had set the bomb properly. This had unfortunate results for at least one of the experts when a young bomber still forgot to take out the pin: the army found the youth's unexploded bombs with the pin very conveniently directing them to the expert's address.

In their campaign to wreck the economy of Northern Ireland, the IRA have learned that fire is their best friend. With explosives, and especially detonators, becoming more difficult to obtain, they have turned away from big, destructive bombs to easily concealed small ones, which they surround with cans of gasoline. One of their favorite devices is an incendiary bomb made out of a tape recorder cassette. Such machines are comparatively easy to smuggle past the British Army and the police and to conceal in piles of flammable merchandise in shops, timed to go off after the store has closed. One special incendiary bomb was defused by the army after the IRA had tried to plant it at Fortwilliam Golf Club. It consisted of a golf bag filled with five pounds of commercial explosive, a timing unit, an incendiary mixture, three gasoline containers and one pound of firelighters. Another of the IRA's tricks is to make use of the safety mesh that encloses most business premises in Northern Ireland. They build a hook into the bomb and then hang the bomb from the safety mesh.

The car bomb, filled with explosives and made dangerous to handle by booby traps, is very much an IRA weapon. A car stuffed with 200 pounds of explosives can cause absolute devastation in town centers. Sometimes the IRA bombers have their little jokes. In 1977 they hijacked a whole fleet of bakery vans. They filled several with explosives which, when they went off, showered Belfast with loaves of bread, but they left the others, locked but harmless, on street corners. Each one had to be dealt with— usually by the army blowing off their doors with a controlled explosion—and the resulting cost and disruption was considerable. The army in Belfast has developed a number of techniques for dealing with such incidents. They have Sniffers, dogs trained to smell out explosives and chemical devices. They also developed the Goliath, which looks like a large toy tank. This remote control invention is used to inspect a suspect vehicle and, if necessary, blow open doors or destroy what could be a bomb by firing a shotgun at it.

The other common form of car bomb is the concealed device inside a car designed to kill the driver. There are a number of types, the simplest being the Mafia type, which is a bundle of explosives wired to the starting system so that when the ignition is switched on, car and driver are destroyed. This was used so often that most people in danger prudently inspected their engines before turning their ignition keys. This precaution was circumvented by attaching plastic to exhaust pipes that exploded when the pipes grew hot enough, or, as in the case of Mohammed Boudia, who was PFLP's chief operative in Europe, putting a pressure bomb under his car seat. He was killed by an Israeli hit team, but his death had the unforeseen result of bringing Carlos back to the terrorist scene, for Carlos, "sleeping" in London, was called upon to replace Boudia.

Professor Gordon Hamilton-Fairley, a cancer specialist, was killed in October 1975 when he bent down to examine a suspicious package under his neighbor's car in a London street. The package was designed to kill the professor's neighbor, Conservative Minister of Parliament Hugh Fraser, an outspoken opponent of the IRA, when Fraser drove off.

Another way of killing a person in a car is the Big Bang, designed to destroy a vehicle as it passes a certain spot. The British Army has become only too familiar with mines buried in the roadsides of Northern Ireland. This is an account of one such mine as reported in *Visor*, the British Army newspaper in Ulster:

A two-day clearance operation, involving an overnight stakeout of a suspected explosive device within fifteen hundred meters of the border resulted in the successful neutralization of a one hundred and fifty pound terrorist landmine.

The device, dug into a roadside verge, consisted of homemade explosive packed into three beer kegs. Each keg, apart from containing fifty to eighty pounds of explosive, had a five to ten pound booster charge attached and all three kegs were linked to explode simultaneously. The mine was to have been electrically detonated and a command wire was discovered, partially buried along a hedgerow, which led to the firing point concealed in a nearby derelict building.

The authors of this book, on one of their visits to Northern Ireland, landed by helicopter close to the southern Armagh border soon after a similar device, made out of a milk churn, had been destroyed by the army. It had made an impressive hole in the roadbank and the road and shattered windows over a wide area.

Often the army is not lucky enough to discover these ambushes before they are sprung, and the resulting explosions have been known to somersault 10-ton Saracen armored personnel carriers.

The IRA have a special liking for culvert bombs, packing explosives into the drains that run under many Irish roads. The army has become very suspicious of these culverts and always checks them before driving across. The Israelis used to do exactly the same in the early 1970s when Palestinians would cross the border and lay culvert mines. But the Israelis had a special device—a girder sticking out of the front of an armored car with a steel-plated seat welded to the girder's end. The crew members of the armored car would then take turns to perch on the seat and study the road surface for mines and wires. It was truly a "hot seat."

It was a matter of shame and stupidity that similar caution was not used to guard Christopher Ewart-Biggs, the British ambassador to Dublin, who was assassinated by a culvert bomb 180 yards from his official residence in July 1976. There were only two ways for the ambassador to travel before he reached main roads. There is no doubt that a routine inspection before he left the house would have found the mine, which consisted of at least 100 pounds of explosives and was detonated by wire from a wooded hill some 300 yards from the road.

Another man killed by a version of the culvert bomb was the prime minister of Spain, Admiral Luis Carrero Blanco, in December 1973. He made the mistake of traveling by the same route every day. His killers took a basement room on that route and dug a tunnel 20 feet under the road. They planted three charges of nearly 40 pounds each under the street, timed to explode at intervals of one-tenth of a second to match the speed of his car. Red sighting marks were painted on a wall facing the terrorists' house so that they would know when to detonate. One of the assassins sat in a window with a walkie-talkie watching the marks. When he gave the command another assassin pressed the plunger and Carrero Blanco was blown, literally, over a church.

A less certain way of killing a man, but one that when widely practiced causes much alarm, is the letter or parcel bomb. Richard Clutterbuck, in *Living With Terror,* tells how to recognize a letter bomb:

It is likely to be at least a quarter, and more probably, half an inch thick—so it will feel like a paper-back book or perhaps a folded report or pamphlet, rather than a simple letter. It will, however, probably feel heavier than if it contained the same thickness of paper. The explosive may "sweat" causing greasy marks and there may be a smell of marzipan. The package will also bend in a different way, either giving a suspicious feeling of rigidity or an equally suspicious feeling of lack of elasticity—in other words, it may have the "dead" feeling of putty or clay, rather than the springy feeling of a pamphlet or a sheaf of papers.

Such a device, containing only three or four ounces of explosives, can kill if it is opened close to the body. Dr. Ami Shachori, the Israeli agricultural attache in London, was killed by one in September 1972. It was a thick buff-covered envelope measuring six inches by three. It exploded as he opened it. Most of the blast funneled downwards towards his desk so that he escaped the initial explosion, but by the worst possible piece of luck, he was killed by a splinter from his shattered desk.

That bomb, and most of the others that were sent at that time to Israelis and Zionist sympathizers around the world, was set off by a mousetrap-style mechanism. A spring attached to a detonator is folded back when it is put into the envelope and is held in position by the pressure of the closed envelope. When the envelope is opened, the pressure is released and the spring strikes the detonator head. Another method of fusing a letter bomb is to use an incendiary adhesive that sparks when the envelope is opened. Parcel bombs are more efficient because they contain more explosives and give less evidence of their contents. A batch of gaily wrapped Christmas parcels looking like boxes of chocolates was sent to Israelis in 1972; the parcels were found to contain eight ounces of explosives—more than enough to kill.

The Israelis are themselves experts in the use of letter and parcel bombs. Bassam Abu Sherif, spokesman for PFLP, is hideously scarred—the result of opening a similar box of chocolates—and a number of other Palestinian officials have been killed and wounded by letter bombs.

A most bizarre form of letter bomb came to light in October 1972 when a Dutch Jew received a letter posted in Karlsruhe, West Germany. He was suspicious and passed the letter to the police, who found it was not a letter bomb but a poison gas bomb. It contained 40 grams of cyanide in powder form. In chemical reaction with the oxygen in the air, it would have produced cyanide gas.

Another terrifying development in bomb making was perfected by the International Spanish Communist Party, a Maoist group, who in January 1976 taped a bomb to the chest of Dr. Joaquin Viola Sauret, a former mayor of Barcelona. The bomb was booby-trapped so that it could be safely removed only when instructions were sent by the terrorists. These instructions were not to be given until certain demands had been met. But the bomb went off prematurely, killing Dr. Sauret and his wife and injuring one of the terrorists. It was similar to one that had killed Jose Harques, a rich Catalan industrialist in May 1977. He refused to believe that it would explode, tore it off his chest and died.

Perhaps the most cynical form of terrorist device is the barometric bomb. This appalling weapon is designed to destroy an aircraft in flight and therefore everybody on board: innocent men, women and children, even sympathizers with the terrorists' cause, all die. In August 1972 two Palestinians in Rome, Adnam Ali Hashan and Ahmed Zaid, picked up two young English women on vacation. The women fell for the handsome Palestinians who suggested that they should all go to Israel. The women agreed, and the Palestinians bought them tickets to fly to Lod airport and gave them a tape recorder. At the last moment the two men, who were posing as Iranians, said they had to fly to Tehran to collect money. They all arranged to meet in Jerusalem. The women, fortunately, did not carry the tape recorder onto the plane as hand luggage, but had it put in the baggage compartment with their other luggage. The tape recorder was filled with explosives and its barometric firing device was set to explode when the plane reached a certain height. It exploded precisely as it was designed to do, but the force of the explosion was contained by the armored compartment, built into all El Al planes following tests with explosions in mid-air over the desert. The damaged plane landed safely, and when the two girls told their story, Hasham and Zaid were arrested in Italy. But like all captured terrorists they were an embarrassment and a potential liability to the authorities and were soon given "provisional liberty" on the curious grounds that the explosive charge they used "was not adequate to destroy the airliner." They disappeared from Italy as soon as the prison gates opened.

Radio-fired bombs are the latest to come from the bombers' bag of tricks, and at first sight they seem to have the advantage over all other bombs of being absolutely under the control of the bomber. There is no need for the bomber to light a fuse or to start a mechanism that will fire at a fixed time—unless it is stopped manually—or even to trust to the uncertain effect of acid on a contraceptive. The terrorist can decide when the explosion is going to take place, make adjustments for unforeseen circumstances, and advance or retard the timing of the explosion. And all this can be done from a point of safety with almost nothing to connect the bomber with the bomb. The terrorist might even be out with his child, playing with a radio-controlled model airplane. A certain signal is sent and the bomb blows up. There is a drawback, however, for if the security forces are sufficiently adept at signals intelligence, they, in turn, could send signals to blow up the terrorists with their own bomb.

And that brings us to booby traps. Almost anything can be booby-trapped. A pipe can be boopy-trapped so that when it is lit, it blows the smoker's head off. A dead soldier can have his backside stuffed with explosives, that will blow up those sent to carry in the soldier. Likely souvenirs, weapons and field glasses, can be booby-trapped so that they explode when picked up. A favorite ploy in Belfast is for a caller to report suspicious activity in an abandoned house. The army, who cannot ignore such reports, must investigate, and booby traps could be anywhere, a trip wire across the door, a mine under a loose floorboard. It is as easy as the schoolchild prank of balancing a bucket of water on top of a door. With a wild imagination and sufficient expertise, anything can be booby-trapped. And dealing with the traps involves a tedious, dangerous battle of wits between the bomber and the bomb disposal squads. Occasionally the two sides get to know each other's work very well, even to appreciate the finer points of a good technical piece of work carried out by the opposition.

This war within a war becomes personal when antihandling devices are included in a bomb's mechanism. They include fuses that are sensitive to x-rays and are designed to explode when suspicious parcels are x-rayed. Another antihandling device is a photoelectric cell that explodes the bomb when it is exposed to light, either by the opening of a suitcase bomb or when a torch is shone on a bomb hidden in a dark place. Then there are "trembler" devices, which are activated after a bomb has been carried to the place where it is to explode. When the bomb has been set, any movement will cause a steel ball to roll or a pendulum to swing, either action completing an electrical circuit and thereby exploding the bomb. And there are fuses connected to secondary fuses that explode when the first fuse is made harmless and withdrawn. The simplest looking bomb of a type that the bomb disposal expert has defused many times can be adjusted to contain one of these devices. It was in this fashion that London's Balcombe Street gang killed a bomb disposal expert, Captain Roger Goad, in August 1975. Fortunately there are not many bombers with the expertise to fit these booby traps, but truly, the bomb disposal experts earn their pay.

One type of bomb remains to be discussed, the ultimate: the nuclear bomb. In essence the terrorists' task in constructing a nuclear weapon is the same as that in making a conventional bomb. First he has to acquire the material and then he has to build the bomb.

Of the two tasks the acquisition of the material is the harder. For with the information contained in a good university library, any reasonably bright student of physics can do the theoretical work. And that is precisely what a

20-year-old student at Massachusetts Institute of Technology did in just five weeks in 1975 using published technical works. He did it in answer to a challenge by a television program; the producer of the program said in stunned disbelief: "We found it was frightfully easy to design such a bomb. Basically it is simply a matter of bringing two shaped pieces of plutonium together with sufficient force for them to 'go critical.'" According to evidence given in 1977 at a public inquiry in Britain into building a nuclear fuel reprocessing plant at Windscale, only 8 kilograms of plutonium are required to produce a bomb big enough to wipe out a city center. Scientist Kit Pedler, creator of British television's *Doomwatch* series, explained in an article in the London *Daily Express* of May 8, 1977 that "if a solution of plutonium nitrate was dried, packed as crystals into two stainless steel mixing bowls and surrounded by ordinary blocks of TNT, a nuclear explosion would probably occur if the critical mass of the nitrate when imploded had been calculated properly."

The British Royal Commission on Environmental Pollution, headed by Sir Brian Flowers, put the technical side of building a "nuke" into perspective in a report in September 1976 when it said, "The equipment required would not be significantly more elaborate than that already used by criminal groups engaged in the illicit manufacture of heroin." In fact the technical know-how is well within the capabilities of one of the IRA's bomb experts, a point made by the French magazine *L'Express* (January 27–February 2, 1975), which presented a scenario of a group of terrorists stealing containers of potassium nitrate from a factory. "It is not necessary," the magazine said, "to be a Nobel prize winner to extract plutonium from this solution." And then, in a series of children's how to do it book illustrations, the magazine showed how a bomb could be made.

How easy is it then to fulfill the other task, to acquire the explosive material? In 1972 Professor Theodore Taylor undertook a study for the Ford Foundation of the security at six U.S. nuclear installations. He found that plutonium was being carried across the country in ordinary trucks with only two persons on board, without an escort and without radio contact. Since Taylor made his report, security has been considerably tightened, at least in the United States. But, Taylor insists, it is still not strong enough to stop a determined band of terrorists. In 1975 the FBI revealed that in the previous year it had conducted serious investigations of seven letters threatening to explode nuclear bombs in Boston, Des Moines, San Francisco and Lincoln, Nebraska.

In 1976 a report by the British Royal Commission on Environmental Pollution stated that terrorists could make a crude but effective nuclear weapon using stolen plutonium and argued that the British government had not appreciated the full implications of this possibility. It also reported that members of the commission who visited nuclear installations in Britain got the impression that not enough attention was given to some aspects of security. We understand that their criticisms centered on the lack of security on shipments of radioactive material. British security arrangements have now been strengthened and the Ministry of Defense is playing a large part in guarding shipments. The greatest danger, according to Sir Brian Flowers, Rector of Imperial College, London, comes from an "inside job," the persistent theft of small quantities of nuclear material by someone working in the reprocessing and fabrication plants. According to the FBI, there are two known instances when government employees smuggled out of guarded U.S. facilities enough special nuclear materials to manufacture atomic bombs.

Ralph Lapp, the nuclear scientist, estimates that a worker taking out 20 pellets of atomic fuel a day for 160 days would accumulate enough plutonium to make a bomb equivalent in power to the one that destroyed Nagasaki.

The blackmail potential of such a weapon is enormous. A leaflet called *Towards a People's Bomb,* which was published in London in 1972 by a London group called Undercurrents, told its readers how to extract plutonium and even published a diagram of a crude bomb. It might have worked, but the implications of its threat were that if it was detonated in the luggage check in Charing Cross station, it would destroy, among other things, "Buckingham Palace, the Houses of Parliament, Scotland Yard and the Elephant and Castle—not to mention vaporizing a fair chunk of the River Thames." What government could resist the demands of a terrorist group if proof was given that a nuclear weapon had been placed in just such a spot? The whole world could be held to ransom.

There are other ways in which nations can be held to ransom or even dealt crippling blows by terrorists and individual madmen. Water supplies could be poisoned, the theft of nerve gases—one minuscule drop of which can kill a person—could create panic, and as we saw at the beginning of 1978, agricultural terrorism could be employed to wreck a nation's economy. The discovery of a few Jaffa oranges injected with mercury had a serious effect on Israel's citrus fruit sales. An organization which called itself the Arab Revolutionary Army claimed that it was "poisoning thousands of export-selected oranges before plucking" and "poisoning thousands of oranges during export preparation." "Our aim," it said, "is not indiscriminately to kill your population, but to sabotage the Israeli economy." In fact, the oranges were not poisoned in Israel, but a few were jabbed with hypodermic syringes filled with the contents of broken thermometers by Palestinian sympathizers in a number of northern European countries.

The people who jabbed the oranges with mercury-filled syringes were able to induce fear. And that is what terrorism is all about. That fear would be multiplied a million times if all the dangers of a nuclear explosion—explosive destruction, fire, radioactive poisoning, the genetic effect on future generations—were used in the cause of terrorism. The Big Nuke is the ultimate weapon of terror.

# 8

# Tactics and Strategy: And How Democracy Fights Back

Although the Euro-Arab terrorist offensive of 1977 proved again that a good deal of the urban terrorist's time is devoted to fund raising, it also demonstrated that the tactics are geared to ensure that the transnational groups should become self-perpetuating. Tactically, the terror club needed to secure the release of West Germans, Japanese and Arabs who had been captured in earlier raids. The Japanese Red Army in particular was short of trained operators and the hijacking of one airliner was all that they needed to put them back in business after a two-year respite in their activities. And it was with the cooperation of one powerful Arab group, and with support from the Germans, that they were able to carry it out successfully.

A gang of five experienced terrorists took over a Japanese Air Lines DC-8 carrying 156 passengers soon after it had taken off from Bombay. They obtained from the Tokyo government the release of six imprisoned terrorists and were paid a ransom of $6 million for the lives of their hostages. It was a classic, successful terrorist operation.

Just to complete the familiar picture, the Japanese and their released comrades made their way to one of the traditional havens for hijackers—Algiers. From there the 11 men and women terrorists were able to make their way back to their base in the Middle East, ready for further action—and with the money to finance it. Part of their wealth was paid into the funds of their backers, the PFLP.

While that operation was taking place, the Red Army Faction in West Germany, which had already killed a prominent banker and the public prosecutor responsible for the trial of the Baader-Meinhof leaders, kidnapped Hans-Martin Schleyer, an industrialist and leader of the employers' federation. The kidnappers then entered into weeks of negotiations, bargaining his life against the release of their own leaders incarcerated in the fortress prison at Stammheim.

Chancellor Helmut Schmidt's government refused to give in and played the long, hard bargaining game, demanding proof that the terrorists did indeed hold their prisoner alive, while encouraging the terrorists by asking a number of Third World countries whether they would agree to the prisoners being delivered to their countries.

Then a dramatic development took place that demonstrated how the international terrorists have improved their coordination and become more sophisticated in their tactics. They increased their pressure on the West German government by mounting a new hijacking from an entirely different quarter. Four Palestinians, two men and two women of Wadi Hadad's PFLP-Special Operations, operating from Baghdad, seized a Lufthansa Boeing 747 homeward bound from Majorca packed with German tourists and a party of six beauty queens. Demanding the release of the same Baader-Meinhof leaders as the kidnappers of Schleyer, together with two Palestinians held in Turkey (the same pair that the young Dutch woman Lidwina Jansen recognized at the Aden training school), they forced the aircraft to fly around the Middle East until finally it landed at Mogadishu in Somalia. There, while the bargaining continued, the West German government ordered a counter-raid, Entebbe style.

This was conducted with great skill and dash by 28 men of the GSG9, the 180-member anti-terrorist force that had been created and trained for just such an operation. This time it was the terrorists who died. But what was even more important in the long term was the fact that a British Army major and noncommissioned officers (NCO's) from the British Special Air Services Regiment also went to Mogadishu, taking with them cardboard-bodied grenades that stun and blind their victims for some six seconds but do no permanent damage. These grenades were developed by the SAS specifically for dealing with hijackers. Here at last was a fine example of cooperation between Western powers in fighting the common enemy. For the SAS men, goggled to protect themselves from the grenades' effect, put the hijackers out of action long enough for the German commandos to have at them and shoot them without harming the passengers. For once the terrorists were literally blinded by science.

It was a famous victory that heartened the anti-terrorist forces, who had had little success since Entebbe. Yet it was only one battle won, and much remained to be done. Although the forces of terror had been beaten, they were still able to strike back by murdering the unfortunate Dr. Schleyer, whose body was dumped in an abandoned car in Alsace. The hunted kidnappers took refuge in the Middle East. The fact that the imprisoned Baader-Meinhof leaders, Andreas Baader, Gudrun Ensslin and Jan-Carl Raspe, were able to commit suicide in their maximum security prison after learning that the attempt to free them had failed, produced an immediate countereffect. Those sympathetic to the radical cause demonstrated, and some West German establishments in other European countries were bombed because the radicals believed that Baader and his comrades had been murdered in prison. Others who were not at all sympathetic to terrorism found it difficult to eradicate the suspicion that even if the authorities had not murdered their prisoners, they had remembered the axiom—"Thou shalt not kill but needst not strive officiously to keep alive." As we have seen in earlier chapters describing the rise of the terrorist movements, it is an event of this kind that can influence the young and eventually provide more recruits for the infantry of terror.

While the long drama of the 1977 autumn offensive played itself out, it seemed that political life in Germany was at a standstill, paralyzed by governmental concentration on this one problem. Chancellor Helmut Schmidt was unable to receive James Callaghan, the British prime minister, and he had to postpone his own official visit to Poland. It began to look as though the maxim of Ulrike Meinhof—"A few dozen fighters, who go into action without endless talk, can fundamentally change the political scene"—had been proved correct. Popular clamor for the death penalty and ever more security measures stimulated by the wave of terror played into the hands of the Red Army Faction and their international friends. For shooting in the streets and police revenge is what terrorism feeds upon.

The perverted, yet naive, intention of Baader-Meinhof was to bring about "fascisification" of West Germany, in order to provoke "a revolutionary reaction from the masses." In the face of this, the West German government at first stood fast and remained reasonable, and finally it was bold and exasperated enough to refuse the terrorists' demands and then to strike back and use legitimate force against violence. In this West Germany finally received strong public support from its partners in the European community, Britain and France. Before the nations of Europe finally joined themselves into a Common Market, there was a plan to achieve unity through the creation of a European Army. But this plan came to nothing. So it is one of the ironies of history that the terrorists, by their revolutionary activity, have helped to persuade European leaders to unite their armies in the nucleus of a Common Market anti-terrorist force. If the process continues this may eventually result in a strengthening of Western European unity in an alliance against the very forces that seek to destroy its way of life.

A further heartening sign that the industrial democracies were strengthening their combined resolve to contain international terrorism was provided by the summit conference of leaders of the U.S., Britain, West Germany, France, Italy, Canada and Japan in July 1978. Meeting in Bonn they unanimously agreed to take stern measures against countries that refused to extradite or prosecute terrorists and hijackers, or refused to return hostages and aircraft. The matter was raised by Takeo

Fukuda, prime minister of Japan, and the powers agreed to punish such offending nations by suspending their air traffic connections with the seven nations. Suggestions that an economic boycott might be organized were rejected on the grounds that it would be unworkable.

This plan is the strongest collective effort against terrorism to date. It seems likely that countries such as Libya, Algeria and South Yemen may be discouraged from offering safe havens to terrorists by this threat to refuse landing rights in all signatory nations to their national air carriers. The statesmen of the West certainly hope that their stand against air piracy will discourage terrorists and hostage-takers in general.

Faced with a common international enemy, the nations of the West consulted and secured general approval for a counteraction. The tragedy is that it had taken no less than five years for these sophisticated societies to combine against a multinational terrorist force, not strong in numbers—there are probably less than 1,000 activist men and women—but which by its tactics had spread death and fear throughout the world.

The truth is that when the hijackers, assassins and kidnappers first began to strike their tactics took the West by surprise. Their acts were unexpected in liberal countries where freedom of expression exists, in democracies whose one over-riding advantage is that governments can be changed by the simple process of voting, without men having to go out in the streets and kill in order to bring down an unpopular administration. It might be conceded that in Latin American tyrannies guerilla tactics could be justified as the only way to overthrow brutal regimes; it might be expected that the Palestinians, and even the Irish, might take up arms in the cause of national aspiration. But why should innocent men and women be slaughtered by gunmen in peaceful democracies? The first response was that the terrorists must have some reasonable demands and that therefore their aims should be studied and attempts made to deal with their grievances. It is in the nature of Western societies to listen to argument and to try to discover what has gone wrong. Added to that, in West Germany and in Japan there remained feelings of guilt about earlier regimes whose brutalities had plunged the world into war.

If the young, and especially the university intellectuals, were alienated enough to take up arms in the cause of changing and improving society they should be heard and perhaps heeded. That was the attitude, and during the time it took for us to realize that the terrorism was in fact a destructive aberration of reformist thought, rather than a worthy expression of disquiet, governments chose to give in to their tactical demands and to hope thereby to satisfy them.

By the time the true nature of terrorism was understood and the West was prepared to recognize the terrorists' strategic demands for the fraud they were, the tactics had hardened into a formal pattern, and their surprise value had been lost.

There is no mystery about the tactics. They shocked only by their unexpectedness and novelty, and by the fact that television coverage of violent events brought them into every home. The main terrorist activities consist of:

1. murder by gunning down people in the streets;
2. assassination of political leaders and other well-known people;
3. bombing of public places or the homes of private individuals;
4. kidnapping of prominent people for ransom or the release of prisoners;
5. hijacking aircraft and using the safety of the crew and passengers as a bargaining counter to secure the same aims;
6. armed bank robbery and raids to get money, weapons, documents, etc.

If there is no mystery about the methods, it is equally true that there is no magic formula or secret weapon that will easily counter them. It is obvious that in each case straightforward security measures involving more efficient police work, security checks and personal precautions need to be taken for protection against terror. But even more important is better intelligence work and

Plate 1
**Kalashnikov or AK 47**

| | |
|---|---|
| **Weight** | 9.5 lb (unloaded) |
| | 11.31 lb (loaded with full magazine) |
| | Later models, unloaded, weigh just over 6.5 lb |
| **Length** | 34.2 in |
| | 27.5 in, with butt folded |
| **Magazine** | Curved metal box holding 30 rounds |
| **Cartridge** | 7.62 mm. Steel core gives penetrating power to short bullet |
| **Muzzle velocity** | 2330 ft/sec |
| **Rate of fire** | 100 rounds a minute automatic |
| | 40 rounds a minute single shot |
| **Maximum effective range** | 330 yd |

| | |
|---|---|
| **Weight** | 6.9 lb (unloaded) |
| | 8.4 lb (loaded with full magazine) |
| **Length** | 33.2 in. |
| | 25 in, with butt folded |
| **Magazine** | Curved metal box holding 30 rounds |
| **Cartridge** | 7.62 mm |
| **Muzzle velocity** | 2330 ft/sec |
| **Rate of fire** | 90 rounds a minute automatic |
| | 40 rounds a minute single shot |
| **Maximum effective range** | 440 yd |

Plate 2
## VZ 58 V Assault Rifle

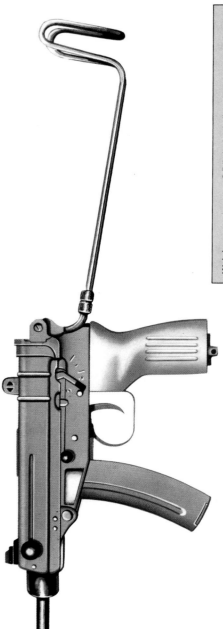

Plate 3
**Skorpion VZ 61**

| | |
|---|---|
| **Weight** | 3.5 lb (unloaded)<br>4.4 lb (loaded with full 20-round magazine) |
| **Length** | 20.2 in<br>10.6 in, with steel frame butt folded over top of barrel |
| **Magazine** | Slightly curved metal box holding 10 or 20 rounds |
| **Cartridge** | .32 (7.65 mm) automatic pistol cartridge |
| **Muzzle velocity** | 1040 ft/sec |
| **Rate of fire** | 840 rounds a minute automatic<br>40 rounds a minute single shot |
| **Maximum effective range** | 219 yd with butt<br>55 yd with butt folded |

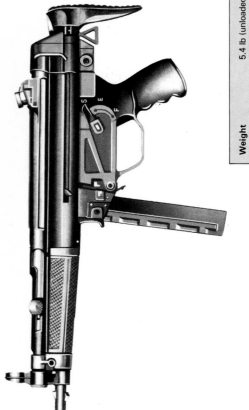

| | |
|---|---|
| **Weight** | 5.4 lb (unloaded)<br>6.48 lb (loaded with full 30-round magazine) |
| **Length** | 26.77 in<br>19.29 in, with telescopic butt retracted |
| **Magazine** | Straight metal box holding<br>10, 15 or 30 rounds |
| **Cartridge** | 9 mm Parabellum |
| **Muzzle velocity** | 1312 ft/sec |
| **Rate of fire** | 100 rounds a minute automatic<br>40 rounds a minute single shot |
| **Maximum effective<br>range** | 220 yd |

Plate 4
## Heckler and Koch MP 5

| | |
|---|---|
| **Weight** | 7 lb (unloaded) |
| | 7.75 lb (loaded with full magazine) |
| **Length** | 36.38 in |
| **Magazine** | Straight metal box holding 20 rounds |
| **Cartridge** | 5.56 mm (.223) |
| **Muzzle velocity** | 3250 ft/sec |
| **Rate of fire** | 80 rounds a minute automatic |
| | 40 rounds a minute single shot |
| **Maximum effective range** | 500 yd |

Plate 5
**Armalite AR-18**

Plate 6
**Thompson Sub-machine-gun**

| | |
|---|---|
| **Weight** | 10.5 lb (unloaded) |
| | 12.1 lb (loaded with full 30-round magazine) |
| **Length** | 32 in |
| **Magazine** | Straight metal box holding 20 or 30 rounds |
| **Cartridge** | .45 automatic pistol cartridge |
| **Muzzle velocity** | 920 ft/sec |
| **Rate of fire** | 120 rounds a minute automatic |
| | 40 rounds a minute single shot |
| **Maximum effective range** | 220 yd |

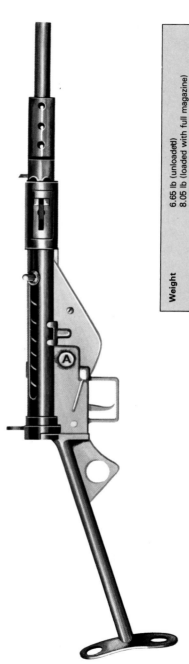

| Weight | 6.65 lb (unloaded) |
| | 8.05 lb (loaded with full magazine) |
| Length | 30 in |
| Magazine | Straight metal box holding 32 rounds feeding horizontally into left of gun |
| Cartridge | 9 mm Parabellum |
| Muzzle velocity | 1200 ft/sec |
| Rate of fire | 128 rounds a minute automatic |
| | 40 rounds a minute single shot |
| Maximum effective range | 200 yd |

Plate 7
**Sten Sub-machine-gun**

Plate 8
**M1 Carbine**

| | |
|---|---|
| **Weight** | 5.19 lb (unloaded) |
| | 5.80 lb (loaded with full magazine) |
| **Length** | 35.58 in |
| **Magazine** | Straight metal box holding 15 rounds |
| **Cartridge** | .30 short rifle |
| **Muzzle velocity** | 1970 ft/sec |
| **Rate of fire** | 40 rounds a minute single shot |
| **Maximum effective range** | 330 yd |

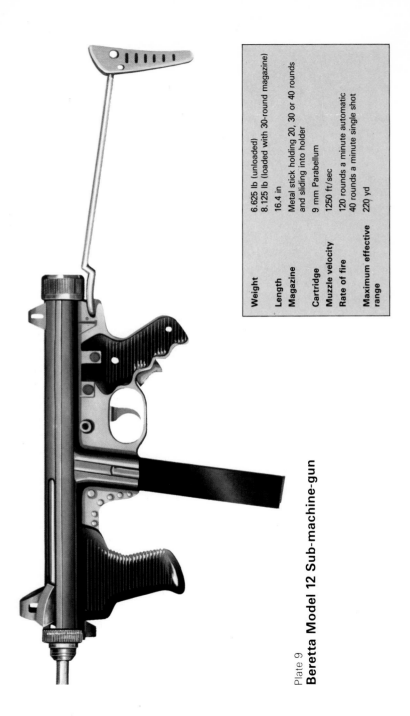

| Weight | 6.625 lb (unloaded) |
| | 8.125 lb (loaded with 30-round magazine) |
| Length | 16.4 in |
| Magazine | Metal stick holding 20, 30 or 40 rounds |
| | and sliding into holder |
| Cartridge | 9 mm Parabellum |
| Muzzle velocity | 1250 ft/sec |
| Rate of fire | 120 rounds a minute automatic |
| | 40 rounds a minute single shot |
| Maximum effective range | 220 yd |

Plate 9
**Beretta Model 12 Sub-machine-gun**

Plate 10
## Astra .357 Magnum

| | |
|---|---|
| **Weight** | 2 lb with 6-in barrel (unloaded) |
| **Length** | 11.25 in with 6-in barrel (other barrel lengths are 3, 4 and 8.5 in) |
| **Magazine** | Six-chambered cylinder |
| **Cartridge** | .357 of various types |
| **Muzzle velocity** | 1410–1550 ft/sec depending on cartridge used |
| **Maximum effective range** | 55 yd depending on barrel length |

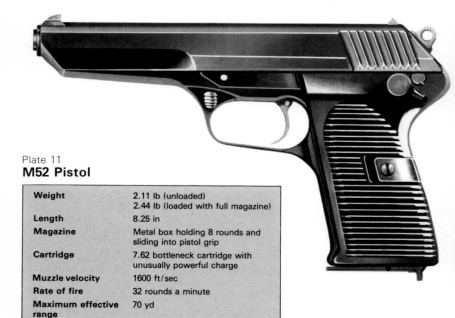

Plate 11
## M52 Pistol

| | |
|---|---|
| **Weight** | 2.11 lb (unloaded) 2.44 lb (loaded with full magazine) |
| **Length** | 8.25 in |
| **Magazine** | Metal box holding 8 rounds and sliding into pistol grip |
| **Cartridge** | 7.62 bottleneck cartridge with unusually powerful charge |
| **Muzzle velocity** | 1600 ft/sec |
| **Rate of fire** | 32 rounds a minute |
| **Maximum effective range** | 70 yd |

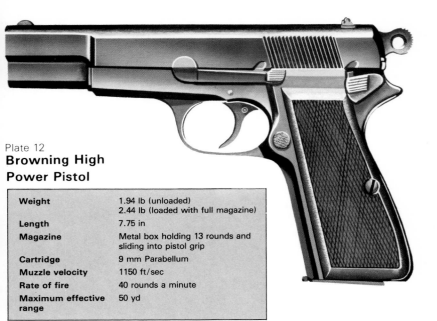

Plate 12
**Browning High Power Pistol**

| | |
|---|---|
| **Weight** | 1.94 lb (unloaded)<br>2.44 lb (loaded with full magazine) |
| **Length** | 7.75 in |
| **Magazine** | Metal box holding 13 rounds and sliding into pistol grip |
| **Cartridge** | 9 mm Parabellum |
| **Muzzle velocity** | 1150 ft/sec |
| **Rate of fire** | 40 rounds a minute |
| **Maximum effective range** | 50 yd |

Plate 13
**Makarov Pistol**

| | |
|---|---|
| **Weight** | 1.46 lb (unloaded) |
| **Length** | 6.3 in |
| **Magazine** | Metal box holding 8 rounds and sliding into pistol grip |
| **Cartridge** | 9 mm |
| **Muzzle velocity** | 1023 ft/sec |
| **Rate of fire** | 35 rounds a minute |
| **Maximum effective range** | 54 yd |

## Plate 14
## Tokarev (TT-33)

| | |
|---|---|
| **Weight** | 1.88 lb (unloaded) |
| **Length** | 7.7 in |
| **Magazine** | Metal box holding 8 rounds and sliding into pistol grip |
| **Cartridge** | 7.62 mm Tokarev<br>9 mm Tokagypt |
| **Muzzle velocity** | 1378 ft/sec |
| **Rate of fire** | 32 rounds a minute |
| **Maximum effective range** | 55 yd |

## Plate 15
## Walther P38

| | |
|---|---|
| **Weight** | 1.7 lb (unloaded)<br>2.125 lb (loaded with full magazine) |
| **Length** | 8.6 in |
| **Magazine** | Metal box holding 8 rounds and sliding into pistol grip |
| **Cartridge** | 9 mm Parabellum |
| **Muzzle velocity** | 1135 ft/sec |
| **Rate of fire** | 32 rounds a minute |
| **Maximum effective range** | 54 yd |

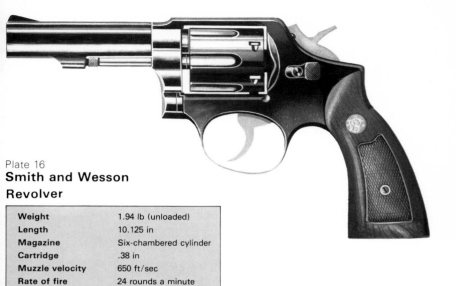

Plate 16
**Smith and Wesson
Revolver**

| | |
|---|---|
| **Weight** | 1.94 lb (unloaded) |
| **Length** | 10.125 in |
| **Magazine** | Six-chambered cylinder |
| **Cartridge** | .38 in |
| **Muzzle velocity** | 650 ft/sec |
| **Rate of fire** | 24 rounds a minute |
| **Maximum effective range** | 44 yd |

Plate 17
**RGD-5 Anti-personnel
Hand Grenade**

| | |
|---|---|
| **Weight** | 0.69 lb |
| **Length** | 4.5 in |
| **Diameter** | 2.25 in |
| **Colour** | Apple green with RGD-5 (in Cyrillic) written on body |
| **Explosive** | 110 grams of TNT |
| **Fuse** | Percussion with delay of 3.2 to 4.2 seconds |

Plate 18
## SAM 7 Strela (Arrow)

| | |
|---|---|
| **Weight of launcher** | 20.3 lb |
| **Weight of missile** | 20.25 lb |
| **Length of launcher** | 53 in |
| **Length of missile** | 51.2 in |
| **Rocket motor** | Three-stage solid propellant |
| **Maximum range** | 3792 yd |
| **Maximum height** | 6560 ft |
| **Guidance system** | Infra-red |

Plate 19
## M26 Grenade

| | |
|---|---|
| **Weight** | 1 lb |
| **Length** | 3.9 in |
| **Diameter** | 2.25 in |
| **Colour** | Standard US Army olive with yellow lettering |
| **Explosive** | 155 grams of TNT-based Composition B |
| **Fuse** | Electrical impact |

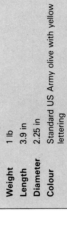

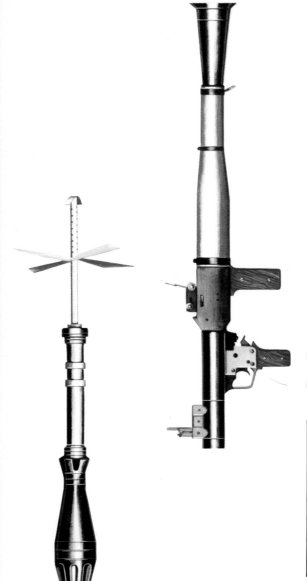

Plate 20
**RPG-7 Portable Rocket-launcher**

| | |
|---|---|
| **Weight of launcher** | 15.4 lb |
| **Weight of grenade** | 4.95 lb |
| **Length of launcher** | 39 in |
| **Calibre of launcher** | 1.5 in |
| **Calibre of projectile** | 3.3 in |
| **Range, static target** | 555 yd |
| **Range, moving target** | 330 yd |
| **Penetration of armour** | 12.6 in |

| | |
|---|---|
| **Weight** | 23.09 lb (unloaded) |
| **Length** | 43.5 in |
| **Feed** | Disintegrating link belt |
| **Cartridge** | 7.62 mm |
| **Muzzle velocity** | 2800 ft/sec |
| **Rate of fire** | 550 rounds a minute cyclic |
| | 200 rounds a minute automatic |
| **Maximum effective range** | 2000 yd with tripod |
| | 1000 yd with bipod |

Plate 21
**M60 General Purpose Machine-gun**

a greater effort to discover who the terrorists are and how they operate. The routines of security need to be improved, while freedom of movement and action for individuals is preserved. There is the rub. For the most effective defense against terrorism is undoubtedly to set up a police state such as that which exists in the Soviet Union, where anybody can be declared an enemy of the state and incarcerated without any process of law. And any dissident can, and often is, sent to a mental home for "treatment." Such dire precautions of course involve the setting up of a gigantic apparatus of state security.

Such procedures are unthinkable in the West, and what has to be contrived is a system of increased security that does not impose too many restrictions on freedom. That said, it must be obvious that some freedom must be sacrificed in order to protect citizens from death and intimidation by terror and the very fabric of the state from disintegration. For example, it may be tiresome and even humiliating to be body-searched and have security people examine one's most personal possessions in a suitcase, but it is greatly preferable to being blown up in mid-air, or threatened with revolvers by demented terrorists to whom you must cringe for permission to go to the toilet in a hijacked aircraft. The real battle of wits, which calls for skill and nerve, takes place when terrorist acts involve the kidnaping of individuals or the holding hostage of groups of people. In such events a body of violent case law has built up over the last 10 years, and to a large extent the moves on both sides have become as ritualistic as a folk dance.

Let us take the early aircraft mass hijackings carried out by Arab terrorists. Two or three pirates boarded an aircraft with concealed arms and grenades; one moved forward to threaten the crew while the others held the passengers at bay. Then the leader announced over the plane's radio that he was captain of the martyr squad now in command of the aircraft. His tactic was to fly it to an airfield in a safe country, or one sympathetic to his cause, and there to utter increasingly terrible threats until the government of the place from which the aircraft came agreed to his demands.

In the case of the mass hijacking to Dawson's Field in Jordan in September 1970, when outside governments were unused to such high drama, it was not long before they gave in. Even the British government with its long tradition of respect for the rules of law, speedily released Leila Khaled, the Palestinian terrorist, who had unsuccessfully tried to seize an El Al flight that landed at London airport. Although she ought to have been held, charged and tried, the government was only too pleased to be rid of her in exchange for the safety of passengers on a BOAC flight held at the desert airport.

Large sums of money were paid out, airliners and new crews were provided, solemn communiques were read out and convicted killers were released from prison. Then, as one raid followed another, the attitudes of governments began to stiffen. The Israelis, accustomed to living with violence, showed the way. They placed armed guards on El Al flights, armored the vital parts, locked the door to the cockpit and refused to be blackmailed. That at once reduced the number of attacks on their flights. But it was not until after the sensational hijacking of the Air France flight from Athens to Entebbe with more than 300 passengers on board that a new game developed. The story of the Israeli commando raid upon the terrorists who had separated the Jewish passengers from the rest and were holding them hostage at Entebbe is well known, and its successful aftereffects gave new courage to governments throughout the world.

As the international terrorists increased the number of their raids, Western governments began to make the necessary preparations for firmer action. Slowly the means of communication between different police forces were improved—though the flow of information between countries is still not fast enough and there remains a tendency, demonstrated again by the French in the Abu Daoud affair early in 1977, simply to shuffle off responsibility by getting rid of a wanted terrorist through immediate expulsion. Even so there are hopeful signs.

Although the United States was slow to respond to the international terrorist threat, President Jimmy Carter gave orders in March 1978 for the establishment and training of a specialized force 200 strong. This was a delayed response to the clear demonstration of the efficacy of the German GSG9 and the British SAS. The new force, to be called Blue Light—which recalls the flash and bang grenades used at Mogadishu—will have special weapons and equipment. The specially selected recruits at once began training under the command of Colonel Charles Beckwith, a 49-year-old Green Beret with wide experience in clandestine operations in Vietnam. Some of his recruits on the course at Fort Bragg, North Carolina, were veterans of the 1970 raid into North Vietnam on the Son Tay prison camp.

It was the lesson of the Mogadishu raid that belatedly convinced the President that new steps were urgently needed to remedy the nation's lack of means to cope with such incidents. Until then only small groups of U.S. troops had received sporadic training in anti-terrorist operations. The new unit will take several months to complete its course, and the Pentagon estimates that not for two or three years will it reach the proficiency of West German and British units. Meanwhile an emergency force of 60 Blue Light troops will plug the gap.

Because the British Army has gained long experience in subversive warfare during the colonial wars—it has been engaged worldwide since the end of World War II—a specialized military unit was already in existence to cope with the new techniques of terror. The Special Air Service, with 1,000 carefully selected officers and men highly trained for delicate operations, was ideally suited for use in so-called Phase II operations—when a situation has developed with which the police are no longer able to cope. At this point they must call in superior firepower and essential military skills.

The 22nd SAS Regiment provides just such an elite anti-terrorist unit, which is held on a three-minute standby. It can also call on army bomb disposal teams and conventional infantry and even armored vehicles if necessary. The process is officially known as MACP— Military Aid to the Civil Power.

Since World War II the SAS has fought in Malaya, Kenya, Oman and is in action day after day in Northern Ireland. Its units have served in small groups, the equivalent of terrorist cells, in many parts of the world both in uniform and plain clothes. Recruitment tests for this volunteer unit are very strict and only 19 of every 100 are accepted for SAS service. Selection procedures include personality tests planned for the selection of those who have above-average intelligence, are assertive and self-sufficient without being too extroverted or introverted.

The SAS has added a new speciality by training on mock aircraft and developing new methods of storming an aircraft taken over by hijackers. In consultation with the weapons research department of the British Ministry of Defense, they experimented with a whole new range of "dirty tricks" weapons, including the nonlethal flash and bang grenade used at Mogadishu. They guard London airport in moments of crisis and are ready to hunt terrorists anywhere in the world. A team went to Rome to advise on tactics after the kidnap of Aldo Moro.

In London there already existed a bomb squad accustomed to dealing with Provisional IRA outrages. It was expanded and its methods improved as it was transformed in 1976 into an anti-terrorist squad, which was kept busy by Provo activity, and was therefore sensitive to the possibility of international terrorism as well.

After the massacre of the Israeli athletes in Munich in 1972 and the disastrous police counterattack, the West German government set up its own specialized paramilitary unit known as GSG9 (Border Protection Group 9) under the command of a tough professional officer named Ulrich Wegener. The recruits are all intelligent, exceptionally fit and highly trained in everything from swimming to karate and knife fighting. In fact, their training more than lives up to the rigorous super-boy scout instruction to which Marighella thought his terrorists ought to be subjected. Their small-arms instruction covers everything from a Smith and Wesson .38, machine pistols and machine guns to the Mauser 66 sniper rifle. Ulrich Wegener has a large budget and uses it to purchase the very latest anti-terrorist weapons. After five years of careful preparation, their first big operation at Mogadishu lasted seven minutes and was totally successful.

The West German force had received advice and training from Israel's General Intelligence and Reconnaissance Unit 269. This group descends from an anti-terrorist unit developed by General Arik Sharon, who led Israeli forces into Egypt in the Yom Kippur War. Among its battle honors are Entebbe, and the freeing of 90 hostages aboard a Sabena aircraft that had been seized by Palestinians and forced to land at Lod airport in 1972.

The French have a 40-member special squad composed of men of the Gendarmerie National (which is the oldest regiment in the French Army), known as Gigene. This unit has already proved its value in action abroad when it rescued the children of French servicemen hijacked on their school bus by terrorists operating in Djibouti in 1976. In addition there are special anti-terrorist brigades of police, set up after the Munich massacre. Some of these men were on standby duty in Holland during the capture of the French Embassy in the Hague by Japanese terrorists. For assault operations the Italians rely on the 50-man Squad R Anti-commando, which was called to Rome airport when the hijacked Lufthansa DC-9 from Majorca landed there in November 1977. But huge forces of police and troops were called in for the anti-terrorist sweeps and searches after the Moro kidnapping.

In Holland a special squad of marines assaulted the train captured by South Moluccans. They too received help and advice from a detachment of the Special Air Service from Britain, although they turned down the offer of the "stun grenades," preferring to use their own method of throwing the terrorists off balance—low-level flights by fighters whose pilots suddenly cut in their afterburners.

Not until such forces as these were in existence and the political climate had been created for them to intervene in a crisis did governments feel able to take a tougher stand in the negotiation phase, that precedes any assault on terrorists who have seized hostages.

After Mogadishu West Germany began a counteroffensive, dispatching three-man *Zielfahndung* (target squads) to snatch terrorists in foreign countries. This, of course, could only be done with the cooperation of authorities in the countries concerned. A notable success was scored through this new form of international cooperation when one such squad grabbed 28-year-old Angelika Loder, 27-year-old Gudrun Sturmer, and 28-year-old Gabriele Rollnik, at Bourgas, a resort on the Bulgarian Black Sea. These terrorists were all involved in the raid on the Moabit prison in Berlin that released Till Meyer, a member of the June 2nd Movement on trial for numerous offenses. He too was arrested in Bulgaria and flown back to West Germany. This was the first recorded case of cooperation being given by a Communist East European state in the war against terrorism.

The obvious success of the Israeli assault at Entebbe and the West German one at Mogadishu created a rather smug feeling that so long as Western states took a strong line against terrorists—provided they had at their disposal a specially trained commando force—all would be well. This is a dangerous supposition, for as many things can go wrong in a counterterror raid as in any form of warfare. Thorough training of the assault troops is important, but even the best trained troops in the world are not always victorious unless they are lucky. The good guys do not always win, and in some future operation it is only too likely that some action on a foreign airfield will end in carnage among innocent passengers as well as the troops involved.

As if to point up this message, there is the example of the Egyptian commandos at Larnaca airport, Cyprus. They were good troops from the Egyptian Army, an army that succeeded only a few years ago in making a crossing of the Suez canal against the opposition of the Israeli Army, also one of the best in the world—yet their antiterrorist raid ended in farce and disaster. In February 1978 two Palestinian gunmen made their way into the Hilton Hotel, Nicosia, and shot and killed Yusuf Sebai, an Egyptian editor and a personal friend of President Anwar Sadat. They then took hostages and eventually forced the Cypriots to provide them with an Air Cyprus plane. Finding every airport in the Middle East closed to them, they eventually returned 21 hours later to Larnaca.

Furious at the murder of his friend and having received intelligence reports that Palestinian terrorists were moving into Cyprus to rescue their brethren, President Sadat determined to take bold action, Mogadishu style. He dispatched a force of commandos, which had already liberated one hijacked aircraft in Egypt, across the Mediterranean to Cyprus.

General Nabil Shukri personally commanded the 72-man force aboard an Egyptian Air Force Hercules with orders to get the two terrorists and free the airliner they were holding. Insufficient diplomatic preparation had been made for this raid, however. Although President Sadat and President Spiros Kyprianou of Cyprus later gave quarrelsomely different accounts of the affair, it seems clear that the Egyptians did not have clear authorization for their mission. The result was that when the Egyptian commandos assaulted the plane, they were attacked by forces of the Cypriot National Guard, lost 15 dead, and were unable to get into the aircraft. The terrorists, frightened by the battle going on around the plane, eventually surrendered to the Cypriots, were tried and found guilty of murder.

But the confused battle of Larnaca demonstrates how easily things can go wrong if anti-terrorist assault forces are not highly trained and are not given proper backup from their own government. It may serve as a warning to any government planning such action.

While in Western countries the police and the military developed their assault techniques, which are much more delicate than those of the terrorist, who does not care whether or not innocent people are killed, other methods were put forward. Academics analyzed terrorists' actions and habits. Psychiatrists started to probe the terrorist mind, and to suggest ways in which trained negotiators might exploit their weaknesses in the bargaining phase of a terror action.

The first instinct in dealing with those who hold hostages, and are besieged, is to attack them. But that may simply result in the death of those held prisoner. There is no place for cowboys in a terrorist scenario.

One of the pioneers of the victory-through-talk technique of dealing with such situations is Dr. Harvey Schlossberg, former director of psychological services for the New York City Police Department. It was he who devised the methods of talking out the hostage-holders and who along with Captain Frank Bolz, a career detective and commanding officer of the New York Hostage Negotiating Team, established the widely used negotiating technique. We quoted Bolz in our first chapter as saying: "We aim to bore them to death." Their method of operation is two-edged. They set out to calm the hostage-taker while at the same time increasing the pressure upon him, until he can be convinced that the only way out for him is to free the people he holds. In practice it has been proved that the best person to conduct the negotiations is a police officer or some similarly recognizable representative of authority with a psychiatrist giving advice but remaining in the background. Members of the Federal Bureau of Investigation and representatives of over 1,500 police agencies have been trained by the Bolz-Schlossberg team, and the FBI is now training additional negotiators from police departments throughout the country in these techniques.

What has been demonstrated by the use of such methods is that the advantage does not always lie with the terrorist. A display of firmness, which breaks down the willpower of the terrorist, can compel him to surrender his hostages without bloodshed. In 1975 the Irish security authorities tried out this technique in the 18-day siege of the Provos Eddie Gallagher and Marian Coyle, who had kidnapped the Dutch businessman, Dr. Tiede Herrema, and were demanding the release of several comrades—especially Gallagher's mistress, Rose Dugdale—in return for his life.

Troops and police surrounded the house in County Kildare where Herrema was being held and made use of modern surveillance gadgets, cameras and listening devices in order to discover every move and word of the kidnappers. Psychiatrists then advised the negotiator to choose times when the terrorists were relaxed but in low spirits to press them to surrender. At moments of tension they were soothed with offers of food and comforts. The authorities were particularly fortunate in this case in that the calm and strong personality of Dr. Herrema himself made it possible for him to bring his own strength to bear in the developing relationship with his captors. Eventually it was Eddie Gallagher and Marian Coyle, renowned for their wildness even among the Provos, who broke and surrendered. None of this would have been possible had not the Irish government made it clear that they would not capitulate under any circumstances and that they refused to make any deals or concessions. Such tactics demand a strong will and a realistic appreciation of what can happen.

During the Herrema incident the Irish authorities called upon the resources of the Scotland Yard Technical Support Branch to take advantage of the latest surveillance and monitoring technology and for help with communications. This branch in Britain works closely with the anti-terrorist squad that we have already discussed. Both units played a notable part in employing the "wait-them-out" technique against the IRA in the siege of Balcombe Street in London in December 1975. Four of the Provo's Active Service Unit, which had murdered publisher Ross McWhirter and had terrorized London's West End with bomb attacks, were chased into an apartment in Balcombe Street where they held the occupants prisoners in their own home. The commissioner of police made it clear from the start that he would make no concessions and surrounded the apartment with men of the Metropolitan Police Special Patrol Group. This SPG squad consists of uniformed men trained to use Smith and Wesson .38 revolvers and can be given more powerful support by members of D11, marksmen of the specialist firearms squad. The SAS were alerted in this case and prepared a number of attack plans, but once again the terrorists, faced with the inevitability of death or prison, surrendered and released their hostages unharmed.

It must not be forgotten that the first step in such operations is to discover the place where the terrorists are holding their victims. Until they can be pinned down and surrounded, no action can be taken at all. The kidnap in Rome early in 1978 of Aldo Moro showed the power of the

Red Brigades and the impotence of security and police forces, who for weeks on end were unable to track down the terrorist hideout where Moro was being held. The talk-out technique depends entirely on good detective work, and it cannot be stressed too strongly how important it is for the police either to infiltrate terrorist movements or to get informers from their members. Without detection nothing can be done. Hijackers, always in search of publicity, perform part of the security task themselves by announcing where they are, but kidnapping, where the lair remains secret, is a stronger form of terrorist war.

In order to succeed it is essential that the talk-out specialists know that a well-armed force of police is in position to take action if it becomes necessary. Even in Britain where police and public alike have long opposed the idea of an armed police force, it is now recognized that in present-day conditions the forces of law and order must have specialist weapons available. It is better from every point of view to employ policemen trained with the right weapons than to use soldiers. The police are trained in a different fashion and a soldier is in the nature of things disposed to be more aggressive than his civilian colleague in uniform. There are perhaps some advantages here in the European system of policing, where it is customary to have a third force of gendarmes who are neither simply police nor entirely soldiers.

This means that, along with the psychological method of dealing with terrorists, attention must be paid to providing the forces of order with the best possible weapons for the job. Revolvers and pistols have the advantage of being light and easy to conceal in delicate situations, but they are not always accurate. One of the newer weapons now recommended for such work is the L39AI sniper's rifle with the Rank image-intensifier night sight, particularly when it is remembered that most police actions requiring weapons take place at night. But the disadvantage of such a weapon is its penetrating power. Like many modern weapons it is too powerful to be used by any but the most accurate and most-disciplined of marksmen, for its bullets can penetrate concrete and ricochet over 100 yards and are therefore highly dangerous in built-up areas. British police units now tend to favor the Parker-Hale .222, a high-velocity rifle without the fault of overpenetration.

A new American submachine gun, the 180, is now coming into use fitted with a laser sight. The advantage of this weapon is that the laser beam itself terrifies the terrorist as it seeks him out, and can of itself bring about a peaceful surrender, for there can be few things more frightening than to see a red spot centered on your heart and to know that if the person behind the beam pulls the trigger, you're dead. The laser sight also makes the weapon easier to aim so that less training in marksmanship is needed.

In the Balcombe Street siege a police officer conducted the negotiations with a psychiatrist advising him. But when South Moluccan terrorists captured a train holding many hostages in Holland in the summer of 1977, it was the psychiatrist himself who negotiated with the terrorists. The siege ended only when Dutch Marines stormed the coaches after the terrorists had been alarmed by Starfighter jets buzzing the train. Although the psychiatrist in question, Dr. Dick Mulder, is a specialist in the talk-out technique, and has the authority of a colonel in the reserve, having dealt with previous sieges by Palestinians, the Japanese Red Army and other South Moluccans in Holland, criticisms were afterwards voiced of the way the negotiations were conducted. Anti-terrorist experts and other psychiatrists claimed that Mulder had not been sufficiently authoritative and had failed to put enough pressure on the Moluccans.

He later explained his technique in detail. He believes that the first step is to build up a psychological picture of the terrorists, a difficult thing to do during phase one, which is the most dangerous period when the terrorists are acting wildly, making extravagant threats and often shooting. After making it clear that there is no quick solution and that he and the government are ready to wait, he even favors allowing the terrorists to speak to the press and television on the grounds that this satisfies their inflated egos.

At this time Dr. Mulder also prepares for phase two by arranging to have one direct telephone line to the terrorists for his own use. He begins to assert his own will by cutting off all other communication, then controlling what the terrorists shall eat and at what time. He claims that he eventually can tell them when to sleep by bidding them goodnight. In this way it is possible for the psychiatrist-controller to know what the terrorists are doing throughout the day.

In the view of the Dutch expert this leads ineluctably to phase three, which starts when the terrorists begin to feel that they are losing their campaign. Their natural reaction is to want to go back to the shooting and adrenalin-pumping time of phase one. At this point threats are made all over again and great care must be exercised by the controller.

The situation was particularly delicate in this particular case because the Moluccans in the train were holding 56 hostages, while another group held 105 children in a school not far away. Both groups demanded the release of imprisoned comrades and recognition of a non-existent independent state of South Molucca, which it was not in the power of the Dutch government to grant. Significantly, the Moluccans were to some extent prepared for Dr. Mulder's technique, for he had already employed it against their friends in an earlier siege. This is the first known case of terrorists having undergone psychological training as a result of earlier experience. At first they neither made contact with the outside world, nor asked for contact to be made with them; until there was some means of talking, it was impossible for the negotiator to begin his work.

The terrorist leader was called Max and he told Mulder that he did not want any psychological talk. So the Dutch colonel had to find another basis for conversation, chatting and suggesting things that could be done, like starting to clean the train. Max again did not respond but began to talk mystically about the sadistic side of Moluccans and declared that he was willing to stick out the siege for a year if necessary. It was at this point that the psychiatrist began to worry about the state of mind of the hostages and to wonder whether or not they had the inner resources to survive for a long period. There were also doubts about the ability of Max to sustain his leadership in increasingly difficult circumstances.

As discipline on the train broke down after 20 days, Mulder had to admit that the talking-out technique was unlikely to succeed and he advised the government that the time had come for military action. Here again the psychiatrist thought fit to suggest the tactics to be adopted. The attack should be made at dawn when the terrorists were least alert. Mulder was able to tell the military commander that most of the Moluccans slept in the front coach. The psychiatrist also hit upon the idea of getting air force Starfighters to dive low over the train with afterburners blasting in order to throw the terrorists off balance. Finally the marines attacked, killing Max and five other Moluccans. Unfortunately two hostages were also killed, largely because they stood up despite having been told to lie down when the assault started. When Mulder was interviewed at length on BBC television, he said that he could now speak freely about the tactics he had employed because the terrorists were by now perfectly familiar with them and he therefore would have to devise a fresh approach for the next situation.

As in true warfare it is sometimes the defense and sometimes the attack that has the advantage. It would be foolish to forget that terrorists are intelligent and crafty people perfectly capable of learning operational lessons from experience. There is evidence that Provos in Ireland have been trained to resist the modern interrogation techniques of the British Army. Their men are taught, for example, to avoid looking into the eyes of the questioner and how to evade his trickeries. At Mogadishu the new grenades caught the raiders by surprise, and the new lightweight bulletproof vests worn by the GSG9 group made them less vulnerable. Although these facts are unlikely to find their way into terror training manuals for some time, there can be little doubt but that in some Middle East camp terrorist instructors are trying to buy the right kind of goggles and bulletproof vests for their teams next time.

Events in Rome early in 1978 showed that members of the Red Brigades had learned tactical lessons about the psychological warfare aspects of their campaign. The Red Army Faction and other groups had always insisted, once their victim was incarcerated in a "people's prison," on the broadcast of communiques laying down the political aims of their group. The Red Brigades employed different tactics. Instead of boring the public with their policy statements, they announced that Aldo Moro was himself on trial before their "people's court." Moreover they issued a series of letters written by Moro that sowed doubt and confusion among fellow members of his Christian Democratic party, whom he accused of betraying him and whom he berated for failing to accept the Red Brigades' demands that might save his life. The accusatory and self-pitying tone of his letters created a political effect to the advantage of the terrorists.

There were plenty of Italians who took the letters at face value, as though they had been written by a statesman in normal circumstances. But terrorist watchers and psychiatrists who have specialized in this field know that after a man has been held even for a few days by threatening terrorists, it is likely that only those with the strongest will are capable of writing letters anything like the ones they would normally compose. It is not torture, not even simply the fear of death that causes aberrations of the mind. Just the circumstances of loss of freedom and loss of hope can transform a person's way of thinking. The exploitation of such circumstances is a dangerous new development in terror techniques. It is ironic that if such methods were used in liberal societies against captured terrorists, there would be cries of "torture," and strong protests and demonstrations.

Although anti-terrorist squads have greater resources for inventing and improving their equipment, the terrorists also take advantage of published material to improve their tactics and weapons. It is suspected, for example, that they have been buying a Swiss army handbook detailing easy sabotage methods originally issued to army NCOs but later put on semi-public sale. Entitled *Handbook on Guerilla Warfare*, it was written for the guidance of Swiss soldiers should their country ever be occupied by enemy forces. In autumn 1977 the Swiss were asked to take steps to prevent it from falling into the wrong hands.

The security forces of Western nations must remain constantly on the alert not only to counter terrorist raids but to stay ahead of the game. Whenever a particularly dramatic terrorist raid takes place, the public at large begins suggesting what should be done. The public, unlike both terrorists and anti-terrorists, always have formulas based on wishful thinking and a belief in magic weapons. During the autumn offensive of 1977, the old suggestion was again put forward that gas should be pumped into hijacked airliners to put the pirates, and indeed the passengers, to sleep. How simple that sounds.

Such hopes were effectively dashed by Professor D. R. Lawrence of the pharmacology and therapeutics department of the University College Hospital Medical School in a letter to *The Times* of London in late 1977. "When I consider the technology and skill required of my specialist colleagues in anesthesia, caring for one unconscious person at a time, I tremble for the likely loss of life if a planeload were simultaneously anesthetized. Utopia might possibly develop such a gas, but Utopia would presumably have no need of it . . . ."

The second panacea of public opinion is the death sentence for terrorists. For would not that deprive the terrorists of further targets since they are always demanding the release of imprisoned colleagues? This too is a false argument. Death penalties would do no such thing, for it would be a negation of democracy for terrorists to be shot on the spot after battlefield-type courts martial and such action would provide the terrorists with the support they so desperately need; if the sentences were not carried out immediately, the lengthy processes of appeal before sentencing could reasonably be carried out and would provide ample time for the terrorists' comrades to launch raids in order to secure their release.

And so the war goes on, just like any other war, with both sides seeking advantages, changing their tactics and strategy, introducing new weapons and methods. There is no easy road to victory.

# 9

# The Who's Who of Terror

Terrorist organizations emerge for a variety of reasons; they flourish like laboratory cultures basking in the warmth of radical chic and international publicity, but each needs its own special cause to bring it to life. For some, like the Palestinians and the South Moluccans, it is nationalistic—they use terror as one of their weapons in trying to establish their national right to an area of territory. For others, like the Baader-Meinhof gang and the Japanese Red Army, the cause is world revolution. Some, like the Spanish and Italian groups, have internal political reasons for turning to terror, and there are others still, such as the Moslem insurgents in the Philippines and the Warriors of Christ the King in Spain, who owe their existence to religion as much as to politics.

In each case the origin seems simple. The combination of a grievance and a vision can make a person throw a bomb. But after the first clear burst of enthusiasm, rationalization tends to blur the motives. Some of the Palestinian groups, for example, have developed a commitment to world revolution almost as total as their devotion to the recovery of their homeland. The failure of the West German and Japanese groups to offer a viable alternative society to the one they want to destroy points to anarchy. And the cynical support of the Soviet Union for almost any group that could embarrass the West, whatever that group's political alignment, blurs the picture even more.

Nowhere could there be more confusion than in the welter of reasons the Provisional IRA gives for its campaign of terror. National, political, social and religious causes mixed together with a generous dollop of historical mysticism provide the Provos with their rationalization. The Provos are, of course, unique. But they do demonstrate the great range of justification that exists for blowing up movie theaters, hijacking airliners and assassinating "bourgeois pigs." And even the Provos are bound by two basic laws of the terrorist experiment:

1. The use of violence is obligatory in order to induce fear and chaos.

2. It must be aimed at the people and the institutions of the established order.

This may seem to be a statement of the obvious. But these laws are the foundation of terrorism, for they provide the cement that surrounds each terrorist brick and binds together into a unity of purpose even those who are violently opposed to one another.

This unity is often disguised. Groups change their names—sometimes they split and, amoeba-like, spawn other groups—or they may undergo a change in ideology and discard their old identities, while others give themselves new names in order to disguise their affiliations. Splinter groups with exotic names are sometimes set up to carry out specific operations. For example, the combined PFLP and Baader-Meinhof group led by the Venezuelan Carlos that carried out the raid on the OPEC headquarters in Vienna called itself the Arm of the Arab Revolution. On a more permanent basis, Black September was formed as the terrorist arm of Al Fatah. Its origins were kept secret to prevent political embarrassment of Fatah's leader, Yasser Arafat, and through him the whole of the Palestine Liberation Organization. Those of us who traced this killer group to Al Fatah and showed that it was led by Arafat's deputy, Abu Iyad, were bitterly attacked for denigrating the good name of Fatah.

We have prepared the following "who's who" of the most active of the recent and current international terrorist groups in an attempt to clarify and codify. This section is intended to show how the groups came into being, who runs them, and what their aims are. It also demonstrates their intergroup and international links, as well as their transpolitical and transnational capacity, which is possibly the most dangerous weapon of modern terrorism.

No domestic American terrorist groups are included since those that still exist are moribund, with the possible exception of the FALN, the Armed Forces of Puerto Rican National Liberation, who carried out its last wave of bombings in February 1978. And even they seem to have little or no international significance and virtually no prospects.

# GERMANY

## Baader-Meinhof Gang (Red Army Faction)

*Origins:* This group grew out of the West Berlin student demonstrations of 1967-1968. Given a cause by the shooting of Benno Ohnesorg and a reason by the failure of the demonstrations, various left-wing cells were brought together on the initiative of Horst Mahler, a young lawyer, to form the Red Army Faction, a name adopted from the Japanese Red Army. It came to be known as the Baader-Meinhof gang after two of its leaders, Andreas Baader and Ulrike Meinhof. It would have been more appropriate to name the movement after Gudrun Ensslin, Baader's mistress, for she was the operational commander of the gang, but the honor went to Meinhof because her ability with words enabled her to propagandize the gang's ideology among West Germany's left-wing bourgeoisie.

*Ideology and aims:* Anarchist, anti-bourgeois, anti-American, revolutionary. Its confused philosophy was set in order by Meinhof. She described the group's objective as being "to hit the Establishment in the face, to mobilize the masses, and to maintain international solidarity." Although not overtly communist there is evidence that through Meinhof—whose husband's leftist, soft-porn magazine, *Konkret,* was partly financed by the Russians —it received some loose support from Moscow via East Germany.

*Activities:* The original group pursued a campaign of terror and bank robbery until 1972, when most of the early leaders were arrested. They carried out bombings, attacks on U. S. Army installations, assassinations and arson. They stole arms and grenades from gun shops and armories, and passports and identity documents from town halls. They lived off the proceeds of their bank robberies, grants from the PFLP and money provided for them by their left-wing "respectable" friends. After the arrest of the leaders their campaign was carried on by successor groups, among them the June 2nd Movement and the Holger Heins Commando, which recruited its members from a psychiatric institute at Heidelberg. Their greatest publicity triumph was achieved with the kidnapping of Hans-Martin Schleyer and the back up hijacking of a Lufthansa plane to Mogadishu by a PFLP team. These outrages virtually brought governmental and political life in West Germany to a standstill. But they suffered disaster at this moment of notoriety. Meinhof had already committed suicide in her cell. Now, following the failure of the kidnapping and the hijacking to get them out of jail, Andreas Baader, Gudrun Ensslin and Jan-Carl Raspe took their own lives.

*International links:* Strong connections with the Popular Front for the Liberation of Palestine, and Al Fatah's terror branch, Black September. Baader-Meinhof members have undergone training in terrorist tactics in the Middle East, mainly in Syria and Lebanon. The group also has links with the Italian Red Brigades, the Armed Proletarian Cells (NAP), and Armata Rossa. Its closest link in Western Europe is with the Red Help group in Holland, which is so intimately involved with the German terrorists that it can be described as the Dutch branch of Baader-Meinhof. It has also worked closely with Carlos. Baader-Meinhof members were part of the Carlos group in Paris, where they took part in the attempt to destroy an El Al plane with a rocket; in Vienna, where they formed part of Carlos' team for the assault on the OPEC headquarters; and at Entebbe—which Carlos planned—where two of the hijack team were Baader-Meinhof members and both, Wilfred Bose and Brigitte Kohlmann, were killed by Israeli commandos.

*Achievements:* Red Army Faction activity forced the West German government to pass a harsher law in order to wage war against terrorism, something that the Germans, with their recent Nazi history, were most reluctant to do. It has also forced senior businessmen, politicians and government officials to live tightly guarded lives in homes turned into fortresses.

*Strength:* Some 50 to 60 hard-core members, many of them young women from middle-class homes, and about 2,000 sympathizers, mainly in Berlin (East and West), Munich, Hamburg and Frankfurt. Important members: Verena Becker, Gabriele Krocher-Tiedemann, Jorg Lang, Juliane Plambeck, Ingrid Siepmann, Inge Viett, Susanne Albrecht, Knut Folkerts, Siegfried Haag, Wolfgang Huber, Hanna-Elise Krabbe, Friedericke Krabbe.

*Future prospects:* Not great. The gang still has the capacity to murder, but most of the second-generation leaders have now been arrested along with the lawyers who, while not involved in actual acts of terrorism, acted as liaison officers and planners. Others, now known to the police forces of Europe, are being harried from country to country.


# JAPAN

### The Red Army (Sekigun)

*Origins:* Formed in 1969 during the general upheaval of student demonstrations and turmoil caused by opposition to the war in Vietnam. In 1972 nine of its members joined forces with the 20-member Keihin Ampo Kyoto to form Rengo Sekigun. There have been a number of regroupings, especially following the brutal murder of 14 offenders against Sekigun discipline. The crime of one was to become pregnant. She was tied naked to a tree and left to freeze to death. Three groups are still active in a support role in Japan, but the group that has carried out acts of international terrorism is the "Arab Committee" led by a woman, Fusako Shigenobu, who left Japan for Beirut in early 1971.

*Ideology and aims:* Revolutionary socialistic with strong nihilistic and mystical tendencies, anti-American, pro-Palestinian.

*Activities:* Following a series of robberies and kidnappings and one hijacking in Japan, the Japanese Red Army (JRA) went international when three of its members working for the PFLP murdered 26 people at Lod airport, Israel. The JRA has since been involved in hijackings and seizures of embassies, mainly in efforts to secure the release of imprisoned members and to raise money through ransoms.

*International links:* The JRA outside Japan is completely dependent on the PFLP. These two groups first made contact in 1970, when Sekigun members were lectured by PFLP propagandists and later went to the Middle East to discuss cooperation and to get training. In one of the first acts of cooperation they set up a Japanese medical team to work in Palestinian refugee camps. The JRA has also been helped by Carlos in his role as the PFLP operational commander in Europe.

*Achievements:* Entirely because of the Japanese government's refusal to risk innocent lives threatened by JRA hijackers, who had proved that they would kill without compunction, the JRA has been able to rebuild its organization with members and criminals released from prison. It has also acquired some $6 million as ransom for a hijacked aircraft, though this money was probably handed over to Wadi Hadad of the PFLP for the central treasury.

*Strength:* In Japan, about 70. The international "Arab Committee" numbers about 30. Important members: Fusako Shigenobu, Osamu Maruoka, Jun Nishikawa, Junzo Ukudaira, Haruo Wako, Kazuo Tohira, Kunio Bando.

*Future prospects:* In Japan, apart from sporadic bombings, the JRA is not active, and does not appear to become so. The Japanese police seem to have a firm grip on the situation. The prospects of the Arab Committee depend entirely on what happens politically in the Middle East and how long Wadi Hadad's successors can retain his safe bases in Iraq and South Yemen. Without the PFLP and these bases, the Japanese would find it extremely difficult to operate.

# PALESTINE

## Black September

*Origins:* Formed by Yasser Arafat's Al Fatah organization as a weapon of terror. It was based on Fatah's intelligence branch, Jihaz ar-Razd, and took its name from the September of 1970, when King Hussein destroyed the power of the Palestinian guerilla movement in Jordan. Fatah has always denied its connection with Black September in order to keep Arafat clear of charges of being involved in terrorism, thus enabling him to continue his international political role. But evidence of the connection is now so damning that even Fatah tends not to protest the connection too much. Abu Daoud, one of Fatah's leaders, provided confirmation of the link when he was arrested while on a Black September mission to attack governmental ministries in Amman.

*Ideology and aims:* Nationalistic. It is dedicated to the overthrow of Israel and its replacement by a Palestinian state governed by Al Fatah and led by Arafat.

*Activities:* Black September started its operations with

bombing attacks on commercial installations in Europe that were connected with Israel. When these proved successful, the name of Black September was announced to the world in the most horrific fashion on November 28, 1971 with the murder of the Jordanian Prime Minister Wasfi Tell on the steps of the Sheraton Hotel in Cairo. The Palestinians blamed Tell for their defeat in Jordan, and, apart from King Hussein, he was their number-one target. There followed a series of outrages: the Munich Massacre, the killing of the diplomats at Khartoum, the letterbomb campaign of 1972, the hijacking of a Lufthansa jet to secure the release of the survivors of the Munich gang. Black September also engaged in the war of kill and counterkill that raged throughout Europe in the early 1970s. It ceased operations in 1974, when it became obvious that its terrorist outrages were harming the political image of Al Fatah and the PLO. At a time when Arafat was appearing before the United Nations, and presenting himself as the potential leader of a sovereign state, he could not afford to be linked with terrorism. However, there is an element within Fatah, led by the Black September leader, Abu Iyad, Arafat's second-in-command, that still believes in the use of terror, and this group sometimes breaks the bonds of respectability. It was, for example, Abu Iyad and his Black September followers who tried to kill King Hussein at the Arab summit meeting at Rabat in October 1974. There are other renegade Black September groups, particularly that led by Abu Nidal, which still persevere with terrorism as the principal weapon of Palestinian nationalism.

*International links:* Because of its intimate but clandestine involvement with Al Fatah, Black September is able to use all of Fatah's associations with the Communist world. Arms, training and military support are provided by the Soviet Union, Czechoslovakia and East Germany, and they can legitimately claim that this help was given to Fatah and not to Black September. Funds are channeled from the oil-rich Arab states through Fatah to the terrorists. There are links with the major European terrorist groups and with supporters in France. Black September also used sympathizers among the many Arab students and workers in West Germany. This connection was important to them in setting up the Munich Olympic Games operation.

**Achievements:** Its activities have ensured that the whole world knows about the Palestinian cause. With the massive TV coverage of the Munich games, the Munich operation was transmitted into tens of millions of homes around the world. In the message they left behind, the terrorists wrote: "Why should the whole world be having fun and entertainment while we suffer with all ears deaf to us?" What the rest of the world saw as a terrible act of murder was considered a great triumph by the Arabs. However, Black September's later operations, especially the killing of the three diplomats in Khartoum—which may have been carried out by a splinter group— proved counterproductive. Khartoum was the last operation officially claimed by Black September.

**Strength:** This is impossible to assess, for Black September never existed as a separate entity. It had no organization, no office and no paperwork. When the various leaders of Black September concerned with terrorism decided to mount an operation, they selected personnel from Al Fatah, from other Palestinian groups and from foreign groups to form the strike force just for that particular operation. The men named by Abu Daoud as the warlords of Black September with authority to mount operations were: Sallah Khalef, code-named Abu Iyad, who is Arafat's deputy; Ali Hassan Salameh, thought to have mas-ter-minded the Munich operation and assassinated in January 1979 in Beirut; Fakhri al-Umari, accused of planning the killing of Wasfi Tell; and Khalil al Wazir, code-named Abu Jihad.

**Future prospects:** This concept—it was never an organization—is dormant, but it could be reactivated at any time. At the time of writing the indications are that Abu Iyad, engaged in an attempt to seize power from Yasser Arafat, is prepared to move back into terrorism in an alliance with Abu Nidal in a Rejection Front in opposition to any attempt to make peace with Israel. Black September could start operating again at any time, possibly under a different name and this time in direct opposition to Arafat.

# PALESTINE

## Popular Front for the Liberation of Palestine (PFLP)

*Origins:* Formed in December 1967 following the disaster of the Six Day War by the merger of several small guerilla groups associated with the Arab Nationalist Movement. It is led by the founder of the ANM, Dr. George Habash. The operational commander until his death early in 1978 was Dr. Wadi Hadad.

*Ideology and aims:* Nationalist and Marxist. It is opposed to any settlement with Israel, leads the Rejection Front and insists on the complete liberation of Palestine. This, however, is only the first of its objectives. It aims to bring about the Arab revolution in all the states of the Middle East and then move on to join with other revolutionary groups in establishing world revolution. Its targets are Israel, imperialism and capitalism.

*Activities:* Terrorism of the most ruthless nature. It fought the Israelis on the West Bank and especially in the Gaza Strip after the 1967 war, but the Israelis wiped out the PFLP fighting cells and the group was forced to operate first from Jordan, then from Beirut and now from Aden and Baghdad. Since their defeat by the Israelis, they have concentrated on international terrorism. Many acts of hijacking and murder stemmed from Wadi Hadad: the multiple hijacking to Dawson's Field; the Lod massacre by Japanese Red Army kamikaze killers; the raid on the OPEC headquarters in Vienna; the Entebbe and Mogadishu hijackings. In 1975 it was announced that George Habash had expelled his friend Wadi Hadad because he opposed Hadad's obsession with terrorism, but there is evidence which shows that the expulsion was for propaganda reasons and that Hadad's Foreign Operations Group enjoyed a relationship with the PFLP similar to that of Black September with Al Fatah. Hadad concentrated on building up links with foreign terrorists and his operations almost invariably involved terrorists from other countries. He established training camps for transnational terrorists and built up a truly international gang. After Hadad's death his organization was taken over by Habash, who by that time was moving into a more extreme position. With the help of the Iraqi government, the organization began preparing for further action though there were signs from Baghdad that the new management had come to the conclusion that hijacking operations were no longer the most satisfactory ones.

*International links:* The PFLP is supported by all the "Rejectionist" countries—Libya, Iraq, Algeria and South Yemen—with offices in all these countries. In addition, Habash established close ties with North Korea. He also maintains a love-hate relationship with both China and the Soviet Union. It was Hadad, however, who established close operational links with European, Japanese and South American terrorists. The links become obvious on examination of his operations. Entebbe was undertaken by West Germans and Palestinians; OPEC by West Germans, Palestinians and Carlos; Mogadishu by Palestinians in support of the West German kidnappers of Schleyer; and Lod by the Japanese. Carlos was Hadad's number-one hit man. There are connections with groups in Italy, Holland, France, Turkey, Iran and even with the IRA. The PFLP can truly be described as the framework without which international terrorism could not work.

*Achievements:* PFLP, apart from keeping Palestinians claims in the forefront amidst the turmoil of world affairs, has done little to advance the Palestinian cause. Its actions have been so extreme and so cruel they have occasioned nothing but disgust. The PFLP is truly terrorist, it influences by fear and not by reason.

**Strength:** Active membership is now thought to have declined to about 500. The organization commands an international gang of about 50, but can call on the services of a number of sympathizers throughout Europe.

**Future prospects:** As the world's security services become more efficient in fighting terrorism, this group is becoming less effective. Both its last major operations, Entebbe and Mogadishu, were disasters. Before his death Hadad replenished his core of killers with Japanese released from jail by a hijacking and by Baader-Meinhof members fleeing from West Germany, but the world is closing in on his organization. Much depends on the political situation in the Middle East. The PFLP can only exist in a state of war. If peace comes, it is finished. It remains to be seen what effect the death of Wadi Hadad will have on this group. Carlos, who worked closely with him in many operations, may become even more important. On the other hand, the fact that Carlos is a foreigner may weigh against him, and there were indications in the spring of 1978 that Abu Nidal was improving his position within a new organization known as the Corrective Movement for Al Fatah, and that—from the Baghdad base he shared with the PFLP—he was getting closer to Abu Iyad as both felt that more violent action was needed to upset any new moves toward Egyptian-Israeli rapproachment.


# PALESTINE

### As-Sa'iqa (Thunderbolt)

**Origins:** Came into being in October 1968 as the military wing of the Vanguards of the Popular War for the Liberation of Palestine, which was formed before the Six Day War in 1967 from the Palestinian branch of the Syrian Ba'ath Party and the Palestinian battalion of the Syrian Army. It is a Syrian creation and dependent on Syria.

*Ideology and aims:* Nationalist, but subservient to Syria.

*Activities:* Has been involved in small-scale guerilla warfare in Israel and in the internecine fighting in Lebanon. Its leaders declared themselves opposed to international terrorism, but it was members of this organization, calling themselves Eagles of the Palestine Revolution, who attacked a train in Austria carrying Soviet Jews on their way to Israel in September 1973. By holding hostages they forced Chancellor Bruno Kreisky of Austria to promise to close the Schonau transient camp for Jewish emigrants from Russia. In a similar exercise in September 1975, four Sa'iqa members were arrested in Amsterdam. They had planned to take train passengers hostage to force Holland to stop helping Jewish emigrants.

*International links:* Delegates visit the Soviet Union for talks on political cooperation, but there is no evidence of terrorist links. It is suspected, however, that in the Schonau attack the terrorists were allowed to cross the border fully armed with the knowledge of the Czech authorities.

*Achievements:* The pressure they put on Kreisky and his capitulation produced an unforeseen result. The Israeli government and in particular then-Prime Minister Golda Meir were so enraged that their attention was diverted from the buildup by Egypt and Syria for the launching of the Yom Kippur War.

*Strength:* Believed to have a fighting strength of some 2,000 but very few of these are engaged in terrorism. Leader is Zuheir Muhsin, a former Syrian Army officer who is also head of the Palestine Liberation Organization's Department of Military Affairs.

*Future prospects:* Will do whatever the Syrian government requires. The group has no future without Syrian support.

# PALESTINE

## Democratic Front for the Liberation of Palestine (DFLP)

*Origins:* Formed in 1969 by the breakaway of extreme left wing members from the PFLP. This secession led to bitter fighting in the streets of Beirut by adherents of both groups. A number were killed before Al Fatah intervened to stop the fighting.

*Ideology and aims:* Marxist-Leninist. The only Palestinian guerilla group that subordinates armed struggle to political struggle. It was among the first to support the principle of Jewish national rights inside a liberated Palestine and has called on all "progressive Israelis and Jews" to merge with it in one popular Palestinian front.

*Activities:* Opposed to the PFLP policy of international terrorism and has not been involved in any major operation outside Israel. It qualifies as a terrorist organization by its attacks on a school in the Israeli village of Ma'alot in May 1974 in which 22 children were killed and on an apartment house in Beth Shean in November 1974.

*International links:* Has no international terrorist connections but has political links with left-wing students in Europe and the U.S. Is supported by the Soviet Union and has good relations with China, where some of its members have been trained.

*Achievements:* Political rather than military. Attempts to woo Israeli leftists have had more positive results than the raids on Ma'alot and Beth Shean, which caused only outrage.

*Strength:* About 300. Led by Naif Hawatmeh, a Greek Orthodox Christian who graduated from the University of Beirut with a degree in philosophy and the social sciences.

*Future prospects:* Interesting. Although without military muscle, its policy of appealing to left-wing Israelis could pay off with influence in any political settlement.

# PALESTINE

## Popular Front for the Liberation of Palestine—General Command (PFLP-GC)

*Origins:* Stemmed from a small commando group called the Palestine Liberation Front formed in 1959 by ex-Syrian Army captain Ahmed Jibril. Its aim was to wage a guerilla war inside Israel. After 1967 it joined with other groups, some associated with the Arab Nationalist Movement, to form a branch of the PFLP. But a year later the Jibril faction broke away again, protesting that there was too much emphasis on ideological squabbling in the PFLP and too little fighting.

*Ideology and aims:* A purely military organization, which, as a member of the Rejection Front, opposes a Middle East peace settlement except on Arab terms.

*Activities:* In keeping with its aim of fighting a guerilla war, this group has made a number of forays across the border into Israel with fighting patrols of three to five men. In May 1970 an ambush party fired a rocket at a school bus on a road running along the Lebanese border, killing eight children and four other passengers. In April 1974 a three-man team attacked the Israeli village of Qiryat Shemona, mainly populated by refugees from North Africa, and killed 18 people before it was wiped out. Ahmed Jibril said that this attack was aimed at bringing into existence a "new school of struggle based on the highest degree of revolutionary violence." However there is no record of his group carrying out any attacks since that time. From 1970 to 1972 the PFLP-GC also became involved in international terrorism. It specialized in letter bombs and the blowing up of aircraft. Its aircraft technique became familiar. Agents persuaded naive girls to carry apparently harmless parcels on board aircraft heading to Israel. The packages contained bombs that exploded when the aircraft reached a certain height. On February 21, 1970, one of the group's bombs destroyed a Swissair plane en route from Zurich to Tel Aviv. Forty-seven people were killed.

*International links:* Supported by President Qaddafi of Libya and by Syria.

*Achievements:* None, apart from slaughter.

*Strength:* About 500 active members. The group is commanded by Ahmed Jibril. His second-in-command is believed to be Talal Naji (Abu Jihad Talal) who is the group's representative on the PLO's Executive Committee.

*Future prospects:* Negligible, but as a member of the Rejection Front could cause trouble for the peace makers.

# PALESTINE

## National Arab Youth for the Liberation of Palestine (NAYLP)

*Origins:* President Qaddafi formed this group in 1972 from a mixed bag of Black September and PFLP militants who wanted to carry out acts of terrorism so extreme that even their own organizations turned them down. Qaddafi chose as its leader Ahmed al-Ghaffour, a Lebanese who had been one of Arafat's closest colleagues. Arafat had sent him to Libya to act as his ambassador to Qaddafi. But al-Ghaffour, disappointed by Arafat's adoption of political rather than military methods, deserted to Qaddafi and extremism.

*Ideology and aims:* The use of terror to bring about a total Arab victory and the destruction of Israel.

*Activities:* Some of the most vicious acts of terrorism have been the work of this group. One hit team carried out the Rome massacre, throwing two thermite bombs into a Pan American plane, killing 32 people and wounding 18. When the killers eventually surrendered after hijacking a plane to Kuwait, they told their interrogators that it was Qaddafi himself who had ordered them to carry out the attack. Even so, they said, it was only a secondary target: the Libyan leader had originally wanted them to assassinate then Secretary of State Henry Kissinger to wreck any prospect of a negotiated peace settlement. This group is also believed to have been responsible for the machine-gun attack on passengers waiting to board a TWA flight at Athens airport. Three passengers were killed and 55 wounded. This group concentrated its activities on aircraft and airports.

*International links:* Libya.

*Achievements:* Blackmail release of several members arrested for acts of terrorism.

*Strength:* No longer believed to exist as a terrorist group. It split up and its members drifted to other groups, especially that of Abu Nidal, after al-Ghaffour had been arrested and executed by Al Fatah as a traitor. Fatah had tried him in absentia, but confident in his role as a terrorist leader and certain that Qaddafi would protect him, al-Ghaffour ignored the death sentence Fatah had passed. He went back to Beirut, where he was captured by Fatah's own internal security force—run by the fearsome Abu Iyad, leader of Black September. The Libyans remembered him in a later operation by naming a hijacking the martyr Ahmed al-Ghaffour group. But that was the last that was heard of him.

*Future prospects:* None

# PALESTINE

## Black June (The Corrective Movement for Al Fatah)

*Origins:* Formed by Sabri al-Banna, code-named Abu Nidal, as a renegade Black September group to carry on the fight against Israel by means of terror. Abu Nidal took a number of al-Ghaffour's men into his group, and he has been sentenced to death in absentia by Al Fatah just as al-Ghaffour was. His crime was to attempt to assassinate moderate Fatah leaders. He has been described as the "outstanding practitioner of pure unbridled terrorism."

*Ideology and aims:* In late 1976 Abu Nidal told an interviewer that in his view inter-Arab terrorism, however regrettable, was the price that had to be paid for precipitating the all-embracing Arab revolution that alone could lead to the liberation of Palestine.

*Activities:* Almost completely confined to inter-Arab terrorism. Black June was responsible for the murder of the moderate Said Hammami, Al Fatah's representative in London in January 1978. Hammami was killed because he had established a dialogue with some moderate Israelis. The group is totally dependent on the Iraqis; it has its headquarters in Baghdad and a training camp outside the city by the Euphrates. It undertakes terrorist missions on behalf of the Iraqi government, particularly against the Syrians. Three members of the group were hanged publicly in Damascus in 1977 after attacking a hotel and seizing hostages.

*International links:* Has a considerable following among radical Arab students, especially in London.

*Achievements:* Has terrified those Arabs who are seeking to bring about a peaceful settlement in the Middle East. Al Nidal has made good men frightened of being involved in peace talks and so can claim a measure of success in his aim of preventing any settlement that does not involve the destruction of Israel.

*Future prospects:* Bleak. If Abu Nidal is abandoned by the Iraqis, he will almost certainly be killed by Al Fatah or the Syrians. However, he is not completely without allies. The polarization that occurred among the Arabs following Sadat's peace mission to Jerusalem brought Nidal closer to Wadi Hadad, who also had headquarters in Baghdad, and to Abu Iyad who, early in 1978, was once again showing signs of rebellion against Arafat's political line.

# IRELAND

## Provisional Irish Republican Army (PIRA)

*Origins:* The Provos came into being in 1969 as the military wing of the Provisional Sinn Fein, when they split away from the main body of the IRA, the Officials. In a reverse procedure to most such schisms, this was a breakaway of traditional, religious nationalists from a movement that was becoming more and more Marxist in outlook. The Officials had also "gone soft" and were looking for a political victory rather than a military one. The Provos then embarked on one more round of "the troubles" that have bedeviled Ireland for the last 400 years.

*Ideology and aims:* According to the Provo leader, David O'Connell, their primary objective is to "destroy British rule in Ireland." This is to be achieved by following a formula used in Algeria: "Armed action plus political action equals revolutionary action." There is, however, more than a hint of fascism in their pronouncement and actions.

*Activities:* They have attempted to force the Protestants who form the majority in Northern Ireland to abandon their claim that Ulster is a country in union with the

United Kingdom. To do this they have taken on the British Army and have attempted to bring normal life to a standstill in Northern Ireland. They have murdered, blackmailed, bombed, firebombed and engaged in skirmishes with the army both in the cities and the countryside. They murdered the British ambassador to Dublin and carried their fight to England using Active Service Units, composed of small groups of men and women, to bomb and murder. In the nine years that this present round of fighting has lasted some 1,800 people have met violent deaths in Northern Ireland.

*International links:* Contacts with the Breton and Basque movements and some links with the Palestinians, particularly the PFLP. Some members have trained with the Arabs, and Colonel Qaddafi has given them financial support and a small amount of arms. However, even the Arabs are wary of too close an association with the Provos, who have achieved a reputation for wildness that makes the Palestinians seem tame. Most of the Provos' overseas links are with the large Irish immigrant population in America, although in 1977 there was a noticeable cutback in this support, largely as a result of a campaign by Sen. Edward M. Kennedy, New York Gov. Hugh Carey and other influential Irish Americans to show that the activities of the Provos had done grievous harm to Ireland's cause.

*Achievements:* In a strictly military sense the small core of Provo guerillas have fought with skill and no small measure of success against a British Army that for political reasons has not been able to use its full power. At the height of its success, the Provos held part of Londonderry as a "liberated area" and reduced the local police to impotence. There were also areas of the border country, especially in Armagh, which was classified as a "bandit country," where the army itself was at risk. In London, when the Balcombe Street gang was bombing seemingly at will in Mayfair, routine police activity was brought to a halt and the West End of London was swamped with policemen. But those days now seem over in London and in

Northern Ireland itself. The Royal Ulster Constabulary is back on the streets and even making arrests for crimes committed five and six years ago. Many of the Provos' best people are dead or in jail. The British Special Air Services unit has cleared up Armagh. The Provos are on the defensive throughout the province. They can still mount attacks, they can still destroy businesses. But their strength is ebbing. Politically, they may have achieved more than they yet realize. Certainly the Roman Catholic population will benefit both politically and socially once this round of "the troubles" is over. There can be no going back to a status of second-class citizens for them. But the Provos have failed to achieve their main objective: the incorporation of Northern Ireland into the Irish Republic in a federation of the country's historic provinces. Although the British people are thoroughly sick of the Irish problem, the British government has no wish to face another bout of fighting in a few years' time, and the British Army has no liking for fighting with one hand tied behind its back, it is extremely improbable that after nine years of war and the expenditure of millions of pounds the British government would throw the Irish Protestants to the wolves.

*Strength:* The hard-core membership is estimated at 300 to 400. But the "godfathers," the leaders who never appear on the streets, can summon stone-throwing gangs of youths at a moment's notice and a demonstration of women and children can be organized almost as quickly. They would be useless, however, if it were not for the 20 or 30 real professionals who can organize a "snipe" or a sophisticated bomb with built-in booby traps. Leading members are: David O'Connell, Seamus Twomey, Martin McGuinness, Joseph Cahill, Gerry Adams, Billy McKee, J.B. O'Hagan, Eamon Doherty.

*Future prospects:* As the British Army gradually closes in on the Provos and curtails their activities, it is likely that more and more of the militants will fall away, give up the fight for the time being or turn to political work. But the history of Ireland shows that even if one violent branch of the nationalist movement is defeated, there is always another ready to take its place in a few years' time.

# ARGENTINA

## Ejercito Revolucionario del Pueblo (ERP)

*Origins:* Founded in 1969 by Roberto Santucho as the armed branch of the Revolutionary Workers' Party. It started operations in 1970, three years after the death of Che Guevara, who had rejected Argentina as the most suitable place to set up a revolutionary *foco* in favor of Bolivia, a choice that was to lead to his death.

*Ideology and aims:* Marxist-Leninist, with a strong vein of Trotskyism. The group is dedicated to the overthrow of the capitalist system in Argentina and other South American countries.

*Activities:* Has carried out a unique combined program of urban terrorism and rural guerilla warfare. In the towns it has concentrated on raising money through the kidnapping of foreign businessmen and diplomats, the murder of officials and of members of right-wing assassination teams, and a general assault on the structure of society. In the countryside large forces of combined ERP and Montoneros fighters, sometimes in battalion strength, have taken on the army in pitched battles. The bloodiest of these actions took place on December 22, 1975 when an estimated 500 ERP guerillas tried to storm the barracks at Monte Chingolo, only a few miles south of Buenos Aires. The garrison seems to have been forewarned and was ready for the attacking party. The fighting went on all night and in the end six civilians, nine soldiers, and 85 guerillas lay dead. It was a devastating blow and followed a series of defeats in the guerillas' attempts to occupy a "liberated area" in the rugged mountains and jungle of Tucuman. They lost an estimated 600 men in this campaign, including Santucho's brother, Asdrubal. These losses forced a change in tactics. Fewer large-scale operations were mounted and none of them involved more than 50 men and women. The group turned increasingly to urban warfare and selective assassination. In July 1976, however, ERP was dealt a blow that may prove fatal. Roberto Santucho, his second-in-command, Jose Urteaga, and several other leaders were killed when the police raided their hideout in a Buenos Aires apartment. Since then the scale of activity has dropped dramatically.

*International links:* The ERP cooperates with most of the other South American groups through an organization called the Junta de Co-ordinacion Revolucionaria (JCR). Established in 1974 to facilitate joint planning, funding and support, the JCR was dependent financially on the ERP. Since the authorities in South America began to inflict heavy casualties on the revolutionaries in the mid-1970s, the JCR's overseas headquarters in Paris has become increasingly important. Assassinations of South American ambassadors in Europe have been carried out under the auspices of the JCR, terrorist cells have been set up in a number of countries and links have been established with European and Palestinian groups. Other members of the JCR are Bolivia's National Liberation Army (ELN), Chile's Movement of the Revolutionary Left (MIR), Paraguay's National Liberation Front (Frepalina) and Uruguay's Tupamaros (MLN).

*Achievements:* The ERP has become rich and has caused the deaths of many people. But it has failed in its aim of bringing about revolution in Argentina. It is one of the ideological touchstones of terrorists that if they can succeed in provoking a right-wing coup or the enforcement of extremely repressive measures, a countermovement will inevitably arise to destroy the government and bring about the revolution. But in both Uruguay and Argentina exactly the opposite has happened. The right-wing governments brought to power because of revolutionary terrorism have crippled the terrorist movements in both countries. ERP activities also caused the formation of right-wing terrorist groups, notably the Alianza Anticomunista Argentina, better known as the Triple A. This organization, which operated with some official support and included policemen and soldiers in its ranks, killed anyone suspected of supporting the ERP or the Montoneros. They tortured, then shot their victims and left them lying literally in heaps around Buenos Aires. They fought a war of kill and counterkill even more ruthless than that fought between the Arabs and the Israelis after Munich. However, with the decrease in the ERP's activities and the strong line taken by the military government of General Jorge Videla, this organization, too, has become less active.

**Strength:** Despite the losses among the fighters, there is still considerable support for the aims of the ERP, especially among intellectuals, radical priests of the Roman Catholic Church and left-wing trade unionists.

**Future prospects:** As its strength is being whittled away, the ERP is likely to turn more and more to classic urban terrorism, operating in small units. It remains in existence but is hard pressed and could only return to its days of glory if there was a major political upheaval in Argentina.

# ARGENTINA

## Montoneros

**Origins:** Formed by left-wing supporters of Peron, it has strong affiliations with the trade union movement. Disappointed with Peron's performance and that of his widow, who succeeded him, the Montoneros emerged in 1975 as the guerilla wing of the Authentic Peronist Party.

**Ideology and aims:** It was reported in February 1976 that this group saw itself engaged in a "war of liberation" involving a socialist revolution and the defeat of the "imperalism" of foreign capital. Its aims in fact recall the original ideals of Peronism with their glorification of the *descamisados* (the shirtless ones).

*Activities:* Has carried out assassinations, bombings and kidnappings, and has made an attempt to seize control of the trade unions through an underground amalgamation of unions called the Confederation General de Trabajo en Resistencia (the General Confederation of Workers for Resistance). Also took part in the rural guerilla campaign with ERP and armed itself by setting up weapons factories—with expert help from the trade unions—to produce its own arms.

*International links:* None are known; the Montoneros is essentially an Argentinian group.

*Achievements:* Has had considerable success in its trade union activities, provoking strikes and engaging in industrial sabotage. But is under increasing pressure from the security forces.

*Strength:* At one stage the group was estimated to have a well-organized military force of some 7,500—this has now been whittled down to less than 2,000. Roberto Quieto, one of its founder-leaders, was captured in December 1975, and the leadership is now in the hands of Mario Firmenich. It still has extensive support in the factories and, like ERP, among radical priests, though less so among the intellectuals.

*Future prospects:* In the latter part of 1976 and 1977 the Montoneros became less effective due to pressure from the military government, but through working-class support it could still pose a threat to Argentina's stability, although this would stem more from industrial action than terrorism.

# URUGUAY

### Tupamaros—Movimiento de Liberacion Nacional (MLN)

*Origins:* This group takes its name from the Inca chief Tupac Amaru, who rebelled against the Spaniards and was burned at the stake. It is a Marxist group, which began operations in the early 1960s as a rural guerilla force but soon changed to urban operations in the capital, Montevideo.

*Ideology and aims:* Marxist and revolutionary.

*Activities:* Has virtually ceased to exist since 1972, but we include the Tupamaros because it was the prototype for the other urban guerilla movements in South America. It specialized in the kidnapping of diplomats; it was this group which held the British Ambassador Sir Geoffrey Jackson prisoner in a "people's prison" for eight months in 1971 and had previously murdered the American police adviser Daniel Mitrione. It also carried out a series of attacks on foreign establishments in Uruguay.

*International links:* Some connection with the PFLP, but its strongest links are with the Argentinian ERP and the consortium of South American movements, JCR, in Paris. The group also has links with the Basques.

*Achievements:* Provided the other South American movements with a blueprint for organization and action. It was also the first of the modern movements to be destroyed by repressive measures forced on a traditionally democratic country. Most of the Tupamaros are dead or in prison, but the repressive measures that the military government took are so harsh that ordinary democratic life has ceased in Uruguay. Freedom of the press and all political trade union rights have been suspended. Perhaps the Tupamaros may have a posthumous success, the one that terrorists always argue should be achieved: a revolution provoked by the repressive measures taken to contain terrorism. But there is no sign of this at present.

*Strength:* Those members who are not dead or in prison have fled abroad. Some are fighting with the ERP in Argentina, while others are carrying on their struggle in Europe.

*Future prospects:* None. If any future organization becomes powerful in Uruguay, it is likely to be on pure communist lines with the backing of the Soviet Union.

# FRANCE

### Front de Liberation de la Bretagne—Armee Revolutionnaire Bretonne (FLB-ARB)

*Origins:* Emerged from a number of Breton nationalist and cultural groups, undertaking its first violent action in June 1966. It is a member of the Comite National de la Bretagne Libre, whose secretary-general is Yann Goulet, a veteran Breton activist convicted of wartime collaboration with the Germans, now living in Ireland.

*Ideology and aims:* Liberation of Brittany from French rule. It demands "a free Brittany, the Bretons their own masters, a Breton Assembly and Government." Another group, the Front de Liberation de la Bretagne—Pour la Liberation Nationale et le Socialisme (FLB-LNS) accuses it of representing the "Breton right-wing" and having "fascist overtones."

*Activities:* Responsible for a wave of bomb attacks in the late 1960s that were ended when 60 members were arrested in 1969. However, the 60 received amnesty and the bombings resumed in 1971–1972. They were stopped for a time when 11 members were arrested in 1972, but started again the following year and have continued sporadically. The group has so far not carried out any hijackings or assassinations.

*International links:* In October 1972 Saor Eire (Free Ireland) said that 16 FLB members had received arms training in secret camps in Ireland, and there were reports in the same year of contacts between the Basque Euzkadi Ta Azkatasuna, the IRA and the FLB, resulting in agreement on political aims and cooperation, including joint arms supplies. The group appears to be outside the mainstream of transnational terrorism and does not have much in common with radical left-wing groups.

*Achievements:* Apart from drawing attention to its claims for Breton autonomy, it has achieved nothing.

*Strength:* No more than 150 to 200 activists.

*Future prospects:* Negligible. The Free Breton movement is fragmented, thoroughly penetrated by the French police, and while many Bretons would like to achieve autonomy, the group's terrorist activities command little support or respect.

# FRANCE (CORSICA)

## Action pour la Renaissance de la Corse (ARC)

*Origins:* Founded in 1967 to promote the regional identity of Corsica. In particular, it protests against the concentration of the island's economic resources (essentially vineyards and tourism) in the hands of non-Corsicans—especially "pieds noirs" French settlers forced to leave Algeria—while many native islanders have to emigrate to mainland France to earn a living. ARC set out to be nonviolent but has become increasingly radical and militant. It is the largest of half a dozen Corsican groups of varying political allegiances.

*Ideology and aims:* Nationalistic. The group wants an autonomous assembly and executive within the framework of the French Republic.

*Activities:* Mainly bomb attacks. Its most spectacular exploit was the occupation in August 1975 of wine vaults owned by a French repatriate from Algeria. Some 50 armed farmers led by Dr. Edmond Simeoni carried out the occupation and killed two policemen before they surrendered. Simeoni was sentenced to five years imprisonment, two years of which were suspended. Bomb attacks have been mainly directed against targets on the island, but some have been exploded on the mainland.

*International links:* None, though it has been claimed that Colonel Qaddafi of Libya offered money.

*Achievements:* Has forced the replacement of some high officials by men of Corsican origin and the removal of the 3,000 French Legionnaires who traditionally trained on the island.

*Strength:* Has a large following on the island and draws on its tradition of banditry to provide bombers whenever needed. A crowd of 10,000 demonstrated for Simeoni's release. Important members: Dr. Simeoni and his brother, Max, who is the group's secretary.

*Future prospects:* Could well win the measure of autonomy that it demands. If autonomy is achieved, the ARC would then cease to exist as a terrorist group because it seems to have come to terror by default rather than design, and is not involved in transnational terrorism.

# HOLLAND

## Republik Malaku Selatan—Independent Republic of the South Moluccas

*Origins:* Sprang from the desire of South Moluccan exiles living in Holland to return to an independent state of South Molucca. These exiles, former soldiers of the Dutch East Indies colonial army in Indonesia, came to Holland after Indonesia won its independence in 1949 and the South Moluccan nationalist movement was crushed by the Indonesian Army. Originally some 12,500 Moluccans arrived in Holland. Their numbers have grown to 40,000. The movement was political among the original exiles but has turned to terrorism among the young—who have spent all their lives in Holland and have never seen the islands for whose independence they now conduct terrorist operations.

*Ideology and aims:* Independence from Indonesia and

the right to set up their own nation on islands that have been internationally recognized as part of Indonesia since 1949.

*Activities:* Campaign of bombings and occupation of Indonesian offices in Holland started in 1970. It was disclosed in April 1975 that the Dutch police had discovered a plot by an extreme faction, the Tamaela group, to kidnap Queen Juliana. On December 2, 1975 seven South Moluccans belonging to the radical Free Young South Moluccans Movement hijacked a train near Beilen and held it for 12 days. They murdered three of its 23 occupants. Two days later seven more terrorists stormed the Indonesian Consulate-General in Amsterdam and took 43 hostages. They surrendered after 15 days. Both groups were tried and imprisoned. This led to the hijacking of another train at Assen and the occupation of a nearby school in May 1977. After 20 days Dutch commandos stormed the train and killed six of the terrorists. Two of the 85 hostages also died. The terrorists in the school surrendered.

*International links:* Some of the South Moluccans have established a link with Arab groups and have received training at Palestinian guerilla camps. A few have been to Moscow. Both these links are tenuous, and there is little real transnational interest in their cause, which is generally deemed hopeless. Their only real support comes from members of the Dutch Red Help movement.

*Achievements:* Because of their two train hijackings they have ensured that the world knows about their cause when, previously, most people had never heard of or had forgotten the South Moluccans. They have also forced the Dutch government to take a closer look at this community growing in size and militancy in the heart of Holland. But apart from making life easier for the South Moluccans, there is little the Dutch can do for them. Most of this group's achievements are negative. They have aroused a great deal of bitterness among the Dutch, who assimilated the other populations from the former Dutch empire. And they have harmed Holland's relations with Indonesia.

**Strength:** The militants have a great deal of support among the South Moluccan community and although Johannes Manusama, President of the self-styled South Moluccan Government in exile, does not condone violence, many do. Activists probably number about 250.

**Future prospects:** There seems no chance whatsoever that they will achieve any of their aims. With growing bitterness in their towns and among the Dutch, it seems certain that there will be more trouble.

# SPAIN

## Euzkadi Ta Askatasuna—Basque Homeland and Liberty (ETA)

**Origins:** This group stems from the struggle for nationhood waged by the Basques, a struggle that has gone on for hundreds of years. ETA dates from 1959, having grown out of a radical group that split from the Basque National Party. It draws its strength from the Basque people, who are spread over the border between France and Spain, around San Sebastian.

**Ideology and aims:** The liberation of Euzkadi from Spanish and French rule and the establishment of an independent Basque Socialist State. The group is heavily influenced by Marxist-Leninist beliefs.

**Activities:** ETA acts of sabotage led to the proclamation of a state of emergency in Spain in 1968. The group has pursued a campaign of bombing, kidnapping and assassination ever since, and murdered Spanish Prime Minister Luis Carrero Blanco in December 1973, justifying their act by claiming it was in revenge for the killing of nine Basque militants by the government. ETA has carried on its activities despite concessions by the government of King Juan Carlos to Basque nationalism, an amnesty and an easing of the anti-terrorist legislation and reform of the security forces.

*International links:* There has been contact with the Provisional IRA, including an exchange of revolvers and training in explosives by IRA experts. The government claims that IRA explosives were used in the murder of Prime Minister Carrero Blanco, but ETA denies this. Contacts with the Breton Liberation Front, Kurdish nationalists and Palestinian groups have also been reported. There is also some loose cooperation with South American groups, particularly the Tupamaros who, forced out of Uruguay, have been looking for other pastures.

*Achievements:* ETA could claim to have forced concessions on the Spanish government through its campaign of murder and bombing. The government of King Juan Carlos has lifted the formal penalty imposed on two Basque provinces for opposing the Crown during the Civil War; the Basque language has been officially recognized; and the Basque flag is allowed to fly alongside the flag of Spain. It is likely, however, that the King in his search for an "authentic consensus of national harmony" would have moved in this direction without the killing. Certainly ETA has lost much support by continuing its campaign after these concessions were made.

*Strength:* Like other nationalistic groups it can draw on a pool of fervent supporters. The Basques have always been hard men and courageous fighters. They take easily to terrorism. But for the reasons set out above, support is beginning to erode.

*Future prospects:* There seems little chance that the Basques will give up their struggle to achieve independence. After all, they can date their exploits back to the Battle of Roncevalles, where they ambushed Roland. The question is: given that the Spanish government is prepared to make concessions, at what stage would it become unprofitable for the Basques to continue to use the bomb. That time may be approaching, for on January 18, 1978, the government legalized the political arm of the ETA movement and two days later ruled that all 14 suspects arrested for the assassination of Premier Carrero Blanco would be granted full amnesty.

# SPAIN

## Frente Revolucionario Antifascista Patriotica (FRAP)

*Origins:* First reported in 1971, but was not formally constituted until January 1974. It is an umbrella organization for numerous extreme left-wing groups.

*Ideology and aims:* Members of this group have killed policemen and members of the security forces often for no apparent reason other than that they were "fascist pigs." Three members were executed in September 1975.

*International links:* Tenuous connections with the Basque ETA and even more tenuous links with the IRA.

*Strength:* Small with little popular support. Relying on the ever-changing loyalties of volatile left-wing groups, FRAP finds it hard to retain a core of activists.

*Future prospects:* None, unless there is a dramatic change in the political situation in Spain. The left-wing groups are now totally involved in a guerilla war with their opponents on the right. They have little influence with the population in general.

# SPAIN

## Grupo de Resistencia Antifascista Primo de Octubre— First of October Anti-Fascist Resistance Group (GRAPO)

*Origins:* The name of this group refers to the day in 1975 when four Madrid policemen were assassinated in retaliation for the execution of five convicted urban guerillas.

*Ideology and aims:* A senior police official said the group is "the armed wing of a radical breakaway group of the Spanish Communist Party." It has Maoist tendencies.

*Activities:* Kidnappings, murder of policemen, bank robberies and bombings. GRAPO is suspected of being responsible for a bomb attempt on the life of King Juan Carlos in Majorca. Among its bombings were that of a Madrid radio station and the offices of the newspaper *Diario 16.* According to Elvira Dieguez Silveira, who admitted to the police that she had bombed the newspaper, the publication had particularly incensed the terrorists because it claimed that GRAPO was being manipulated by the CIA.

*International links:* None discernible.

*Achievements:* None except to heighten the tension in post-Franco Spain.

*Strength:* Small and severely eroded by police raids in 1977. Fifteen members of its "executive commission" including its operational commander were arrested in an apartment in Benidorm. The police also seized 100 pounds of explosives, 419 detonators, 19 shotguns, three revolvers, and scores of false identity cards and number plates. Police arrested Fernando Hierro, said to be the group's leader in a series of raids in Madrid.

*Future prospects:* Seems to be taking on anarchistic tendencies similar to Baader-Meinhof and could be a threat if new militant members take over the roles of those arrested. No real political future.

# SPAIN

### Guerrilleros Del Cristo Rey—Warriors of Christ the King

*Origins:* First appeared as a right-wing religious group opposed to liberal and left-wing priests. In the past two years this group has extended its activities to general opposition to all things left of center.

*Ideology and aims:* Its leaders would like to see a Fascist International set up to fight both capitalism and communism. It has connections with the Partido Espanol Nacional Sindicalista, a neofascist syndicalist party. Other extreme right-wing groups that appear to have some identity of ideology are: the Apostolic Anti-Communist Alliance, which is modeled on the Argentine Triple A group and which claimed responsibility for the slaughter of five communist lawyers in a Madrid law office in 1977; and the Adolf Hitler Commando, which has carried out minor operations of destruction.

*Activities:* Members like to dress up in Nazi uniforms and beat up bishops, journalists and others who disagree with them. Its leader, Mariano Sanchez Covisa, was arrested in February 1977 when the police uncovered a clandestine arms-assembly factory in an apartment he had rented in Madrid.

*International links:* With fascist groups in South America and Italy.

*Achievements:* None, except to heighten tension in post-Franco Spain.

*Strength:* Considerable among extreme right-wing religious supporters of the old regime who believe the new regime is drifting towards communism.

**Future prospects:** In direct ratio to left-wing terrorist groups. The growth of one form of fanaticism inevitably leads to the growth of an opposition group.

# YUGOSLAVIA

### Hrvatsko Revolucionarno Bratstvo—Croatian Revolutionary Brotherhood (HRB)—Ustashe (literally Insurgents)

**Origins:** Long-standing Croatian nationalist dissidence within Yugoslavia feeding upon hostility to Serbian dominance in the government of the country. Ustashe agents organized the murder of King Alexander of Yugoslavia in Marseilles on October 9, 1934.

**Ideology and aims:** Nationalist with fascist tendencies. The Ustashe collaborated with the German Army during World War II and carried out massacres of the Serbs, who mainly supported the Communist partisans of Tito.

**Activities:** They have carried on a campaign of bombing, assassination and hijacking against the Yugoslav government at home and abroad. The Yugoslavs have responded by sending out their own hit teams to kill members of these groups in a small-scale version of the Arab-Israeli war of secret agents. On September 10, 1976, Croatians hijacked a TWA jet on a flight from New York to Canada and forced it to fly to Europe where it made "bombing runs" over London and Paris, dropping leaflets expounding the Croatian cause. They left a bomb behind in New York to show they meant business. It exploded and killed a policeman, but when the hijackers finally surrendered in Paris, it was found that the bomb with which they threatened to blow up the plane had been assembled on board from an empty cooking pot, paste and putty, all of which had escaped the vigilance of the security personnel at the airport.

*International links:* None of the usual links, but Croatian immigrant communities, particularly in Australia, form the basis of HRB activities outside Yugoslavia. There are also active communities in the United States, Canada, Argentina, Venezuela, West Germany, Spain and Sweden. Soviet-inspired provocateurs are said to be active among Yugoslav workers and students in some European countries.

*Achievements:* None, except to make the world aware that it has one more problem to face.

*Strength:* The number actually engaged in terrorist operations is small, probably about 30. But there is considerable sympathy for them among Croatian communities around the world, thus providing HRB with the potential of setting up a widespread web of bases.

*Future prospects:* Will carry on with their intermittent campaign of terror but seem unlikely to achieve any of their goals as long as a Communist government is in power in Yugoslavia.


# TURKEY

## Turkish People's Liberation Army (TPLA)

*Origins:* Emerged in the early 1970s as one of a series of violent offshoots of Dev Genc—the Turkish Revolutionary Youth Federation—which itself sprang from the student riots in France and West Germany in 1968. It has since become the most militant. While most of Turkey's left-wing students engage in campus confrontation with right-wing students and the police, the TPLA uses terror as its weapon.

*Ideology and aims:* Marxist-Maoist, it has not announced its aims, but the intention is clear: the overthrow of the Turkish government by revolutionary violence and the establishment of an ultraleftist regime.

*Activities:* The usual mixture of murder, bombing and hijacking. On July 27, 1976, the TPLA attempted to kill opposition leader and former Prime Minister Bulent Ecevit during his visit to the United States. The most bloodthirsty of their actions was the murder of the Israeli consul general in Istanbul in 1971 and the kidnapping and murder of three radar technicians, two British and one Canadian. Ten TPLA terrorists were killed in the subsequent shoot-out.

*International links:* Strong, especially with the Palestinian movements. Members of the TPLA have been trained by the Palestinians; they killed the Israeli consul general in Istanbul at the request of the Palestinians; and the French police discovered a close alliance between a foreign cell of the organization and Carlos when they raided a villa at Villiers-sur-Marne, south of Paris. The group also has links with Communist states, particularly East Germany and North Korea, and is believed to get financial aid and guidance from East Germany.

*Achievements:* Internationally, none. But inside Turkey the TPLA has contributed to the instability of the political situation.

*Strength:* Estimated at 300 activists. The group has suffered losses at the hands of the security authorities—its founder, Mahir Gayan, and several other leaders have been executed or killed in gun battles. It is likely, however, that the fury of the student conflict has produced more than enough militants to replace the lost leaders.

*Future prospects:* The present political situation in Turkey with a failing economy, a weak coalition government, and a fierce conflict between the right and left provides an ideal working atmosphere for terrorism. It would seem that apart from fulfilling its international commitments, this group will concentrate on trying to overthrow the government from inside the country. It may well have some success.

# ITALY

**Brigate Rosse—Red Brigades.**

*Origins:* Emerged as an extreme left-wing organization in the early 1970s. The Red Brigades had much the same early history as Baader-Meinhof, springing from the 1968 riots and drawing its members from disillusioned middle-class students.

*Ideology and aims:* The official view, given at the end of a three year inquiry by public prosecutor Dr. Guido Viola is that this group seeks to establish communism through armed struggle. It is doubtful, however, that classic communism is its true aim. It is both more Maoist and more militant.

*Activities:* Arson, murder, kidnapping and bombing. This group has all the talents of terrorism. It wages war on the extreme right wing and anybody else who opposes its views. Journalists are its particular targets. At first the offending writers were shot in the legs. But in November 1977, Carlo Casalegno, deputy editor of the Turin newspaper *La Stampa*, was shot three times and died a lingering death. A telephone call to a news agency gave the message: "The servant of the State has been brought to justice by the Red Brigades." In December 1977 a member of the extreme right wing, Angelo Pistolesi, was similarly shot down in Rome. In addition to these assassinations, this group wounded 37 people during 1977. They were mostly employees of state agencies or large private industrial concerns. The Red Brigades also specialize in sabotage at industrial works, particularly by arson. In 1976 the Fiat company in Turin—headquarters of the Red Brigades—suffered four arson fires that caused extensive damage. This group also publishes a clandestine newspaper with the title of *Mai piu Senza Fucile (Never Without a Gun)*. Care must be taken to differentiate between political kidnappings carried out by the Red Brigades and similar groups and the purely criminal kidnappings in Italy, which are proving so profitable at the present time.

The "historic leaders" under Renato Curcio began their campaign by "arresting" those they designated "enemies of the people," such as managers and executives in the industrial north, who were beaten up and then released. From such beginnings they graduated to murder and ransom demands. After the arrest of Curcio and 15 other leaders in 1974, new and more efficient commanders launched a sustained campaign to prevent the trial of the original leaders from taking place. They murdered judges, anti-terrorist squad officers and journalists. This violent campaign culminated in March 1978 as the big trial began in Turin, during which the Red Brigades kidnapped and murdered former Prime Minister Aldo Moro.

*International links:* Some contact with the Palestinians but because of geographical and ideological links, its closest foreign contacts are with Baader-Meinhof and its successors. One link was through Petra Krause, who was both a West German and Italian national; she was arrested in Switzerland in April 1975 on suspicion of directing a gang accused of stealing guns for distribution to both groups. There are many remarkable similarities between the Red Brigades and the West German Red Army Faction. At the time of the Moro kidnapping, it was reported that one of the terrorist raiders gave orders in German. As early as 1972 Holger Meins of the Red Army Faction (RAF), who later died on a hunger strike in prison, had killed an Italian police inspector "as a favor" to the Red Brigades. Weapons acquired by Petra

Krause in Switzerland went to Siegfried Haag, the West German lawyer believed to be a second-generation Red Army Faction leader. At one stage it was claimed that the Red Army Faction and the Red Brigades were almost branches of the same organization.

**Achievements:** This group has contributed substantially to the terrorism that plagues Italy and has brought the country to the brink of anarchy. It can claim to be approaching the classic terrorist aim of causing the downfall of the established government. It has had, however, a great deal of help from nearly a score of other left-wing groups and half a dozen right-wing groups contributing to the turmoil in Italy's political and industrial life.

**Strength:** No reliable figure for the number of activists, but a reasonable estimate would be around 100, for the group has shown the ability to mount operations involving a number of squads in action at the same time. In the aftermath of the Moro affair, it began to look as though the Red Brigades had more militants than had been thought. Its leader, Renato Curcio, was arrested but freed from prison by armed supporters in February 1975, and then recaptured in January 1976 to face charges of kidnapping, multiple theft and arms offenses.

**Future prospects:** Italy's new anti-terrorist inspectorate is conducting a vigorous campaign against the Red Brigades and has made a number of arrests. These do not seem to have affected the group's ability to cause trouble. Far more of a threat to the group are the continuing forces of fission that plague Italy's terrorist bands as much as they disrupt the country's political parties. One split that has hurt the Red Brigades was the break away of a group of hardliners, who have formed another organization called the Communist Frontline. It is believed that these professional terrorists have built up their new group by recruiting radical high school students and other young people, who, in their eagerness to prove themselves, have become ultraviolent.

# ITALY

## Nuclei Armati Proletari—Armed Proletarian Cells (NAP)

*Origins:* Based largely in Naples, this group emerged as a significant force in late 1974. It is believed to bring together a mixed bag of students, criminals and dissidents from Lotta Continua (an extreme left-wing group that promotes strikes and aims at infiltration of prisons). NAP linked with the Red Brigades in 1976 to carry out joint attacks.

*Ideology and aims:* A spokesman described members as "revolutionaries . . . not Marxists; neither Leninists nor Stalinists. We are burying the corpses of the old ideologies." (*L'Europa*, May 23, 1975).

*Activities:* Specializes in attacks on prisons and in 1975 launched a simultaneous attack on three prisons, incited a riot in Viterbo prison and abducted a Roman magistrate, Giuseppe di Gennaro. When two women leaders, Maria Pia Vianale and Franca Salerno, were sentenced to four years' imprisonment for taking part in a gun battle with the police in which their comrade, Antonio Lo Muscio, was killed, they shouted that he "did not fall in vain, thousands of proletarians hold guns in their hands."

*International links:* Baader-Meinhof through Petra Krause.

*Achievements:* None, except to contribute to anarchy in Italy.

*Strength:* Membership was considerably reduced in July 1977 when 20 were sent to prison after being found guilty of "forming an armed band against the state." The group is still capable of mounting attacks in cooperation with the Red Brigades, even though the Red Brigades continue to look down on them, "as proles," describing them as "not the right cadres."

# ITALY

### Right-Wing Extremist Groups

A number of right-wing extremist groups, some of them committed to terrorism, have also been spawned in Italy over the past few years. Some came into being through a revival of old-fashioned fascism and others as a direct reaction to the activities of the left-wing groups. There has also been a growth of right-wing extremism among individual members of the armed forces and the security authorities. The thinking of these men was expressed in an article in *Corriere dell' Aviatore*, October 1975, which said a *coup d'etat* might be seriously considered as a "therapeutic measure" to resolve a "gangrenous" political situation. As a result of this article a group of high-ranking officers were charged with incitement to subversion.

None of the right-wing groups seems to possess much power. Among the better-known organizations are: La Fenice, Mussolini Action Squads, Revolutionary Action Movement, Rosa Dei Venti, Ordine Nero, which has now combined with Ordine Nuovo, and Avanguardia Nazionale. In January 1978, the trial in Rome of 132 members of Ordine Nuovo ended with all but 15 of the defendants being found not guilty. The remaining 15 had their trials suspended until additional evidence could be produced. The trial was held under a postwar law that makes it a crime to promote or reorganize the old Fascist Party, which it defines as "a movement with anti-democratic aims, given over to the exultation of and to the use of violence as a means of political change, and denegatory of democracy and its institutions"—not a bad definition of terrorism.

# 10

# The Chronology of Terror

It is possible to chronicle every known act of terrorism in modern times, but the result would be a thick volume devoted to nothing else and of value only to those readers seeking specialized knowledge. So what we have set out to do is to list those acts of terrorism which, over the last 10 years, have actually affected the course of national and world affairs. It would be pointless to list every bomb exploded in Belfast, or the murder of every policeman in Argentina or even every hijacking. But where those acts generated an importance outside their own immediate impact and demonstrated the way in which terrorism and counterterrorism have developed, we have included them.

We chose 1968 to start our list because it is the watershed year of terrorism. It was the year in which Arab terrorists became active following the defeat of the Arab armies in the Six Day War of 1967. At that time the Palestinian guerillas were the only forces in the Arab world able to carry the war to the Israelis. This they did by launching small-scale raids inside Israel – which were quickly stamped out – and then turning to international terrorism. 1968 was also the year of the student uprising in Europe, which failed in its objective of overturning governments but which led, through the frustration of the militants, to the formation of groups prepared to use terrorism to achieve the upheaval that the riots had failed to bring about. In addition, it was the year that saw the emergence of the Provisional IRA and the start of the present round of "the troubles" in Ireland. Finally, it was the year in which the first tentative moves were made towards international cooperation among the terrorists.

## Glossary of abbreviations used

| | |
|---|---|
| PFLP | Popular Front for the Liberation of Palestine *(Palestine)* |
| ALN | Action for National Liberation *(Brazil)* |
| MR-8 | Revolutionary Movement of the Eighth *(Brazil)* |
| ECLP | Executive Committee for the Liberation of Palestine *(Palestine)* |
| PFLP-GC | Popular Front for the Liberation of Palestine -General Command *(Palestine)* |
| JRA | Japanese Red Army *(Japan)* |
| FLQ | Quebec Liberation Front *(Canada)* |
| ETA | Basque Nation and Liberty *(Spain)* |
| TPLA | Turkish People's Liberation Army *(Turkey)* |
| JDL | Jewish Defense League *(United States)* |
| ERP | People's Revolutionary Army *(Argentina)* |
| NAYLP | National Arab Youth for the Liberation of Palestine *(Palestine–Libya)* |
| PIRA | Provisional Irish Republican Army *(Ireland)* |
| FALN | Armed Forces of the Puerto Rican National Liberation *(United States)* |
| SLA | Symbionese Liberation Army *(United States)* |
| UDA | Ulster Defense Association *(Ireland)* |
| RB | Red Brigades *(Italy)* |

| DATE | PLACE | INCIDENT | GROUP |
|---|---|---|---|
| **1968** | | | |
| July 22 | Rome | First Palestinian hijackings. El Al airliner flying from Rome to Tel Aviv hijacked to Algeria. | PFLP |
| December 26 | Athens | Two men attack El Al plane with light arms and grenades at airport. One passenger is killed. Two Palestinians | PFLP |

| DATE | PLACE | INCIDENT | GROUP |
|---|---|---|---|
| | | are captured and imprisoned but released after hijacking of Greek airliner to Cairo on July 22, 1970. | |
| December 28 | Beirut | First Israeli retaliatory attack on Beirut. Commandos landed by helicopter take over Beirut airport and destroy or damage 13 aircraft. | Israeli Army |
| **1969** February 18 | Zurich | Arab terrorists machine-gun El Al airliner preparing to take off for Tel Aviv. Copilot is killed, five passengers wounded, one attacker killed by Israeli flight guard. Surviving three terrorists are sentenced to prison but released after hijacking of Swissair plane to Jordan on September 6, 1970. | PFLP |
| July 18 | London | Marks & Spencers' stores are firebombed. George Habbash threatens more Jewish-owned stores in all parts of the world. | PFLP |
| August 29 | Rome– Tel Aviv | TWA Boeing 707 is hijacked to Damascus. All passengers are released except two Israelis, who are exchanged for two Syrian pilots held by Israel. Plane destroyed. | PFLP |
| September 4 | Rio de Janeiro | The first of the diplomatic kidnappings. Charles Elbrick, U.S. ambassador to Brazil, is held until 15 prisoners released and flown to Mexico. Leads to arrest of 4,000 leftists and harsh repressive measures. | MR-8 and ALN |
| September 8 | Brussels, Hague, Bonn | Hand grenade attacks on Israeli offices. | PFLP |
| October 6 | Cordoba (Argentina) | Bombs damage offices of U.S. companies: First National City Bank, Pepsi Cola, Squibb and Dunlop Tires. Start of three-day campaign of bombing U.S. institutions. | Unknown |
| December 12 | West Berlin | Explosive charges are found and defused near the El Al office and America House office block. Third bomb explodes in U.S. Army officers' club. | Baader-Meinhof |
| **1970** February 10 | Munich | Hand grenade attack on bus at airport kills one El Al passenger and wounds 11, including Hannah Marron, well-loved Israeli actress. One terrorist is wounded and three others | ECLP |

| DATE | PLACE | INCIDENT | GROUP |
|------|-------|----------|-------|
| | | are arrested but freed following the September 1970 hijackings. | |
| February 21 | Zurich | Swiss airliner is destroyed by mid-air explosion; 47 people killed. Bomb explodes in Austrian airliner carrying mail to Tel Aviv without causing casualties. | PFLP-GC |
| March 6 | New York | Greenwich Village townhouse is destroyed in series of explosions, killing three persons who were apparently engaged in manufacturing bombs. | Weathermen |
| March 31 | Tokyo | First of Japanese Red Army's international incidents. Armed with samurai swords hijackers force a Japanese airliner to fly to North Korea. | JRA |
| June 24 | Ottawa | Woman clerk is killed in a bomb blast at the Canadian Defense Department building. | FLQ |
| July 31 | Uruguay | A spectacular day of kidnappings (the frequency of which has increased since the abduction of Charles Elbrick): two diplomats are taken hostage—Daniel Mitrione, U.S. police adviser in Uruguay, and Aloisio Gomide, Brazilian consul in Uruguay. Mitrione is murdered when Uruguayans refuse to negotiate on demands for freeing of 150 prisoners; Gomide is released on February 21, 1971. On same day attempts are made to kidnap Gordon Jones, second secretary at the U.S. Embassy in Montevideo, and Nathan Rosenfeld, the cultural attache. Both escape. | Tupamaros |
| August 24 | Madison, Wisconsin | Bomb destroys University of Wisconsin Army Mathematics Research Center, killing a physics researcher. | Unaffiliated terrorist group |
| September 6 | Dawson's Field, Jordan | In a spectacular operation two aircraft are hijacked over Europe and flown to a wartime airfield, Dawson's Field, in Jordan. A third is taken to Cairo and destroyed, but a fourth, an El Al Boeing 707 en route from London to Amsterdam, escapes when Israeli sky marshals shoot dead Patrick Arguello, a Nicaraguan working for | PFLP |

| DATE | PLACE | INCIDENT | GROUP |
|------|-------|----------|-------|
| | | the PFLP, and capture Leila Khaled. A fifth plane, a BOAC VC-10, is hijacked on September 9 and flown to Dawson's Field to provide hostages for Leila Khaled. The 300 hostages at the field are eventually released in exchange for Palestinian terrorists imprisoned in Switzerland, the United Kingdom and West Germany. This incident leads King Hussein to drive the Palestinian terrorist groups out of Jordan, to the formation of Black September, and, because the strain of making peace between Yasser Arafat and King Hussein is so great, to the death of President Nasser. | |
| October 5 | Quebec | James Cross, British trade commissioner for Quebec, is kidnapped by French-Canadian separatists and held in ransom for the release of prisoners, publication of political manifesto and payment of $500,000 in gold. Canadian government rejects demands, and on December 3 the kidnappers release him in return for safe conduct to Cuba. | FLQ |
| October 10 | Quebec | Pierre LaPorte, minister of labor in the Quebec Government, is kidnapped and killed because demands made by James Cross' kidnappers were not met. Prime Minister Pierre Elliot Trudeau invokes emergency powers and breaks the FLQ. LaPorte's kidnappers are sentenced to life imprisonment. | FLQ |
| December 1 | San Sebastian | Basque nationalists kidnap Eugene Beihl, honorary West German consul, and force the Franco government to commute death sentences passed on six Basques accused of murdering a head of the provincial police. | ETA |
| 1971 January 8 | Montevideo | Geoffrey Jackson, British ambassador to Uruguay, is kidnapped and held for eight months in a "people's prison." Kidnappers demand release of 150 prisoners but government refuses to negotiate. 106 of the prisoners escape and Jackson— | Tupamaros |

| DATE | PLACE | INCIDENT | GROUP |
|------|-------|----------|-------|
| | | later knighted for his courageous behavior—is released. | |
| March 1 | Washington | Bomb explodes in Senate wing of U.S. Capitol causing extensive damage. | Weather Underground |
| March 4 | Ankara | Four U.S. servicemen stationed near Ankara are kidnapped and held in exchange for money and publication of political manifesto attacking American imperialism in Turkey. Police capture one of the gang, who talks, and 45,000 soldiers and police mount a search. The hostages are released unharmed on March 8. The kidnappers are caught—three are hanged, one imprisoned and one killed in a gunfight. | TPLA |
| March 14 | Rotterdam | Palestinian and French sympathizers blow up fuel tanks—the first co-ordinated attack mounted from Paris by Yasser Arafat's organization. | Fatah |
| May 17 | Istanbul | Ephraim Elrom, Israeli consul general, is kidnapped and murdered by gang who demand release of all guerillas detained by Turkish government. | TPLA |
| June 11 | Bab el Mandeb, Israel | Israeli tanker *Coral Sea* is damaged by four men who fire rockets at the tanker from a small boat and then escape to South Yemen. | PFLP |
| July 20 | Rome | First of series of attacks are mounted by Fatah on Jordanian offices and aircraft in revenge for Black September. Attack is made on the office of Alia, the Jordanian airline. | Fatah |
| July 24 | Cairo | Attack on Alia plane at airport. Plane is slightly damaged. | Fatah |
| July 27 | Paris | Several explosive charges are thrown at Jordanian Embassy. | Fatah |
| July 28 | Tel Aviv | Attempt to blow up El Al plane in mid-air by terrorist who gives suitcase bomb to innocent Dutch girl. This is the first in a series of such attempts. | PFLP-GC |
| September 1 | London-Tel Aviv | Attempt to blow up El Al plane in mid-air by terrorist who gives suitcase to innocent Peruvian girl. | PFLP-GC |
| October 20 | New York | Jewish extremists fire rifle shots into apartment occupied by members of | JDL |

| DATE | PLACE | INCIDENT | GROUP |
|------|-------|----------|-------|
| | | Soviet delegation to the United Nations. | |
| November 28 | Cairo | Jordan's prime minister is assassinated on the steps of the Sheraton Hotel by a team of Black September gunmen. This is the first acknowledged operation by Black September and is carried out against the man they blame for their disaster in Jordan in September 1970. Black September was set up after initial operations mounted by Fatah proved successful. | Black September |
| December 15 | London | Zaid Rifai, Jordanian ambassador to London, is wounded when his car is fired upon by a Black September gunman. | Black September |
| 1972 January 26 | New York | Offices of the late Sol Hurok, the impresario who managed American tours by Soviet performers, are firebombed. | JDL |
| January 27 | New York | Two police officers are assassinated by black extremists. | Black Liberation Army |
| February 6 | Rotterdam | Two gas-processing plants are blown up. | Black September |
| February 6 | Cologne | Five Jordanian workers—allegedly Israeli spies—are shot to death. | Black September |
| February 8 | Hamburg | Factory making electric generators for Israeli aircraft is heavily damaged. | Black September |
| February 22 | Aldershot | Bomb at Parachute Regiment headquarters at Aldershot, England kills nine soldiers and civilians. | Provisional IRA |
| February 22 | New Delhi-Athens | Lufthansa airliner is hijacked to Aden by five terrorists claiming membership of Organization for Victims of Zionist Occupation. They are in fact members of PFLP. Plane and passengers are released after airline pays $5 million ransom. South Yemen government exacts $1 million for "landing rights." | PFLP |
| March 21 | Buenos Aires | Oberdan Sallustro, president of Fiat of Argentina, is kidnapped. Fiat agrees to pay $1 million ransom and reinstate 250 workers fired in industrial dispute. Government refuses to release | ERP |

| DATE | PLACE | INCIDENT | GROUP |
|------|-------|----------|-------|
| | | 50 prisoners, launches a hunt for the kidnappers' hideout, finds and surrounds it. Just before soldiers attack, the terrorists carry out their threat and murder Sallustro. | |
| March 27 | Ankara | Three NATO radar technicians, two British and one Canadian, are kidnapped by terrorists who demand the release of three terrorists sentenced to death. Like Sallustro, the three technicians are murdered when the police surround the terrorists' hideout. In the subsequent battle the police kill 10 terrorists. | TPLA |
| April | Tel Aviv | Israeli police arrest the "Easter Commando," a group of Westerners led by Evelyne Barge, who had taken part in the attack on the Rotterdam fuel tanks and had been sent to Israel to attack tourist hotels. | Black September/ PFLP |
| May 8 | Tel Aviv | Two men and two women hijack Sabena airliner and force it to land at Tel Aviv, where they demand the release of 317 Palestinian guerillas. In first successful assault on a hijacked plane, Israeli paratroopers disguised as mechanics burst into plane, kill the two men and capture the women. One passenger dies in the shooting. | Black September |
| May 11 | Frankfurt | Series of bombs explodes at the Fifth U.S. Army Corps Headquarters killing Colonel Paul Bloomquist and wounding 13 others. Bombing is said to be in retaliation for American bombing of North Vietnam. | Baader-Meinhof |
| May 31 | Tel Aviv | Three Japanese kamikaze killers, members of the Japanese Red Army recruited by Wadi Hadad's PFLP, attack passengers at Lod airport with grenades and assault rifles, killing 26 people and wounding 76. Two terrorists are killed, the other sentenced to life imprisonment. This is the first of the Japanese "Arab" operations and the first of the transnational murder attacks. | JRA-PFLP |
| June 1 | Frankfurt | Andreas Baader and Holger Meins are captured after firefight in which both men are wounded. | Baader-Meinhof |

| DATE | PLACE | INCIDENT | GROUP |
|------|-------|----------|-------|
| June 15 | Hanover | Ulricke Meinhof is betrayed and arrested. | Baader-Meinhof |
| September 5 | Munich | The Munich massacre. Seven terrorists take control of the dormitory of the Israeli athletes in the Olympic village, killing two athletes and taking nine as hostages. Israel rejects the gang's demands for release of 200 imprisoned Palestinians, but West German government agrees to give the gang and their hostages safe passage to Egypt. At Furstenfeld-bruck airport West German sharpshooters open fire. In the ensuing gunfight all hostages, five terrorists and one policeman are killed. The incident focuses attention on the Palestinian cause. | Black September |
| September 9 | London | Dr. Ami Shachori, agricultural consul at the Israeli Embassy, is killed by a letter bomb, the first casualty of the letter bomb "war." In the next few days some 50 letter bombs sent to Israelis are intercepted —all posted in Amsterdam. Soon after a second batch posted in Malaysia start to arrive. These are followed in November by a batch posted in India. | Black September |
| October 24 | Belgrade | The Israelis retaliate. A series of letter bombs posted in Belgrade arrive on the desks of Palestinian resistance leaders in Lebanon, Egypt, Libya and Algeria. | Mossad |
| October 29 | Beirut-Ankara | Lufthansa plane is hijacked by two terrorists who threaten to blow it up in mid-air if the three Munich massacre terrorists are not released. They are. | Black September |
| December 8 | Paris | Mahmoud Hamshari, the Palestine Liberation Organization's representative in Paris, is killed by an electronically triggered bomb attached to his telephone. Along with Wael Zwaiter—Fatah's representative in Rome who was shot outside his apartment—Hamshari is the first victim of the Munich revenge killings. | Mossad |

| DATE | PLACE | INCIDENT | GROUP |
|------|-------|----------|-------|
| December 10 | Buenos Aires | Donald Grove, managing director of the British Vestey industrial group, is kidnapped, but released unharmed nine days later after Vestey's pays a $1 million ransom. | ERP |
| 1973 | | This is the most destructive year of the Provisional IRA's campaign — 467 die in acts of political violence. | |
| January 26 | Madrid | Israeli intelligence officer, Baruch Cohen, is shot down in cafe on the Grand Via. Palestinians claim he had taken part in killing of Hamshari and Zwaiter. | Black September |
| February 9 | Amman | Jordanians arrest team of 17 Palestinians led by Abu Daoud, a leader of Fatah, who had been sent to attack the U.S. Embassy and Jordanian government officials. Abu Daoud talks freely under questioning and makes first public admission that Black September was part of Fatah. | Black September |
| February 21 | Sinai | Israelis shoot down Libyan airliner that had strayed over Sinai, fearing it had been taken over and would be used as a flying bomb against Tel Aviv. | |
| March 1 | Khartoum | Eight Black September terrorists take over the Saudi Arabian Embassy during a party for American diplomat George Curtis Moore. Terrorists seize Moore and a number of other diplomats and demand the release of Palestinian and Baader-Meinhof prisoners, Sirhan Sirhan (the murderer of Robert Kennedy) and Kozo Okomato, surviving member of the Lod killers. President Nixon refuses. The terrorists shoot Moore; U.S. ambassador, Cleo Noel; and the Belgian charge d'affairs, Guy Eid. The terrorists are arrested and tried, but eventually released. President Gaafar Mohamed Numayri of the Sudan blames Libyan leader Colonel Qaddafi for instigating the attack. | Black September |
| April 10 | Beirut | Israeli commandos attack apartments of leading Palestinian guerillas and kill 17 people, among them three | Mossad |

| DATE | PLACE | INCIDENT | GROUP |
|------|-------|----------|-------|
| | | high-ranking guerillas, spreading panic through Palestinian ranks. Some Palestinian leaders withdraw to Cairo and Baghdad for safety. | |
| June 6 | Buenos Aires | Charles Lockwood, a British businessman, is kidnapped and held for 53 days until he is ransomed for $2 million. Lockwood is later kidnapped by another group. He tells them that it is unfair to expect a "second suck at the orange." | ERP Splinter Group |
| June 28 | Paris | Mohammed Boudia, the leading Arab terrorist in Europe—organizer of the Rotterdam attacks, the raids on factories in West Germany and the Easter Commando—is killed by a bomb placed under his car seat. His death clears the way for Carlos, the Venezuelan assassin, to be called from London to take over the European operations of the Palestinians and to build a truly transnational terrorism network incorporating West Germans, Dutch, Japanese and French terrorists. | Mossad |
| July 1 | Washington, D.C. | Colonel Yosef Alon, the Israeli military attache, is shot to death by an unknown assailant outside his home. A Voice of Palestine broadcast says he had been executed in retaliation for the murder of Boudia. | Unknown |
| July 20 | Amsterdam— Tokyo | A group of three Arabs and one Japanese, led by an unidentified woman, hijack a Japan Air Lines Boeing 747. The woman kills herself accidentally when she drops the grenade she is carrying. The aircraft flies around the Middle East for four days until it arrives at Benghazi, where passengers are released and the plane is blown up. The hijackers are arrested and some of them spend a year in jail before being released. | PFLP-JRA |
| July 21 | Lillehammer, Norway | A Moroccan waiter is killed in error by a Wrath of God team who thought they were on the trail of Ali Hassan Salameh, one of the leaders of Black September and a planner of Munich. Several of the hit team are arrested | Mossad |

| DATE | PLACE | INCIDENT | GROUP |
|------|-------|----------|-------|
| | | and jailed. This is the last operation carried out by the Israeli assassination teams in Europe. | |
| August 5 | Athens | Five passengers are killed and 55 wounded in machine-gun and grenade attack on passengers from TWA plane that had just landed in flight from Tel Aviv. Two Arabs sentenced to death are released as ransom in subsequent hijacking on February 2, 1974. Killers claim to be members of Black September but are disavowed. Later identified as members of breakaway National Arab Youth for the Liberation of Palestine. | NAYLP |
| August 18 | United Kingdom | Fire and letter bomb campaign is launched in London, Birmingham and Manchester. In six weeks some 30 people are injured by 40 bombs. Many other bombs are safely defused. | Provisional IRA |
| September 5 | Paris | Saudi Arabian Embassy is seized by by five Palestinians—members of of a Black September Splinter Group, the Punishment Squad—who demanded the release of Abu Daoud. Hostages are released and terrorists surrender in Kuwait three days later. | Black September Splinter Group |
| September 5 | Rome | Terrorism adopts electronic aerial warfare. The Italian police arrest five Arabs armed with two Soviet Strela heat-seeking, ground-to-air rockets (SAM 7s). The terrorists had rented an apartment in a house on the flight path to Rome airport and were planning to shoot down an El Al airliner. | Black September |
| September 28 | Vienna | Two Palestinians claiming to be members of yet another splinter group, the Eagles of the Palestinian Revolution, seize a train and take hostage three Jewish emigrants from Russia. They are released after Austrian Chancellor Bruno Kreisky promises to close the transient camp for Jewish emigrants at Schonau Castle. The terrorists are later shown to be members of Saika, the Syrian-backed group. | Saika |
| November 6 | Oakland, California | Marcus Forter, black superintendent of city's schools, is assassinated. | SLA |

| DATE | PLACE | INCIDENT | GROUP |
|------|-------|----------|-------|
| December 6 | Buenos Aires | Victor Samuelson, American executive of Exxon, is kidnapped and ransomed for the huge sum of $14.2 million. Released on April 29, 1974. | ERP |
| December 17 | Rome | Five armed terrorists set fire to a Pan Am plane with thermite bombs, burning 32 passengers to death and injuring 40. They then hijack a Lufthansa plane, murder an airline worker, and fly to Damascus and Kuwait with hostages. They surrender at Kuwait and are arrested by the PLO, which says that they will be tried by a revolutionary court for carrying out an "unauthorized operation" detrimental to the Palestinian cause. Said to be carried out by the National Arab Youth for the Liberation of Palestine, the operation marks the emergence of Abu Nidal, a renegade from Fatah and Black September, as the most ferocious leader of the splinter group. | NAYLP |
| December 18 | London | Bombs in two cars and a parcel bomb injure 60 people in reprisal for jailing of IRA terrorists who exploded car bomb outside the Old Bailey in March 1973. | IRA |
| December 20 | Paris | Sabotage headquarters is discovered in a villa outside Paris. Used by international group comprising members of PFLP, Algerian and Turkish terrorist groups. Cache of arms, propaganda and bomb making equipment found. Discovery is setback to Carlos' attempts to rebuild Boudia network, but confirms international nature of terrorism in France. | PFLP |
| December 20 | Madrid | Prime Minister Luis Carrero Blanco assassinated by explosion that blows his car over a church. Basque militants claim responsibility saying it was in revenge for the killing of nine of their comrades. | ETA |
| December 31 | London | Leading British Zionist Teddy Sieff, | Carlos |

| DATE | PLACE | INCIDENT | GROUP |
|------|-------|----------|-------|
| | | president of Marks & Spencer department store, is shot by an intruder later identified as Carlos, but survives owing to malfunction of assailant's gun. | |
| **1974** January 24 | London | In his second act of terrorism, Carlos throws a bomb, based on a Russian grenade, into the Israeli Bank Hapoalim in London and wounds a woman. | Carlos |
| January 31 | Singapore | Two Palestinians and two Japanese attack Shell Oil Co. fuel installations; later they seize a boat and five hostages, holding out for a week until five more terrorists take over Japanese Embassy in Kuwait. All nine are picked up by Japanese Air Lines plane and flown to South Yemen. | PFLP-JRA |
| February 3 | England | A 50-pound suitcase bomb hidden in the luggage compartment of a bus carrying soldiers and their families back from leave explodes and kills 11 people. | Provisional IRA |
| February 5 | Berkeley, California | Heiress Patricia Hearst is kidnapped. | SLA |
| March 3 | Amsterdam | British VC-10 hijacked en route from Bombay to London is blown up in Amsterdam, in another operation by Abu Nidal's splinter group. | NAYLP |
| April 11 | Qiryat Shemona, Israel | Three guerillas storm a residential building in northern Israeli town, killing 18 and wounding 16. Attackers are killed in battle with Israeli troops. Next day the Israelis mount a series of revenge raids across the Lebanese border. This is the first major ground attack carried out by the splinter group Popular Front for the Liberation of Palestine-General Command. | PFLP-GC |
| April 26 | Dublin | Rose Dugdale is arrested for the theft of Sir Alfred Beit's art collection, which she threatened to destroy unless four convicted IRA terrorists are transferred from English to Irish jails. Dugdale is later sentenced to nine years in prison. The paintings are recovered unharmed. | IRA |
| May 17 | Los Angeles | Six Symbionese Liberation | SLA |

| DATE | PLACE | INCIDENT | GROUP |
|------|-------|----------|-------|
| | | Army suspects in Hearst kidnapping die in gun battle with police. | |
| July 26 | Paris | Yoshiaka Yamada is arrested at Orly airport carrying Japanese Red Army treasury—$10,000. Most of the money is counterfeit. | JRA |
| August 3 | Paris | Car bombs explode outside the offices of *L'Aurore, Minute* and *L'Arche.* A fourth unexploded car bomb is discovered near the French radio and TV offices. | Carlos-PFLP |
| September 13 | Hague | In an operation partly planned and financed by Carlos, three Japanese take over the French Embassy and successfully demand the release of Yoshiaka Yamada, their currency courier. | JRA-Carlos |
| September 15 | Paris | Carlos throws hand grenade into Le Drugstore, killing two and wounding 12, in support of the demands of the Japanese occupying the French Embassy in the Hague. | Carlos-PFLP-JRA |
| October 8 | Greece | TWA airliner that had arrived in Greece from Israel is blown up in flight over the Aegean. All 88 on board are killed. | NAYLP |
| October 11 | Rabat | Attempted assassination (led by Abu Iyad, Black September leader and Arafat's second-in-command) of King Hussein and possibly other moderate Arab leaders gathered at the Rabat summit is foiled by Moroccan authorities, who arrest 15 after Israeli tip-off. | Black September |
| November 22 | Dubai | British Airways airliner is hijacked to Tunis by members of Abu Nidal's group. In exchange for the release of passengers, two terrorists imprisoned in Holland for a previous hijacking of a British plane and the prisoners from Rabat are freed. | NAYLP |
| **1975** | | | |
| January 13 | Paris | Members of Carlos' gang try to destroy an El Al plane at Orly using hand-held rocket missiles. They miss, but hit a Yugoslav plane and one of the airport buildings. | Carlos-PFLP |

| DATE | PLACE | INCIDENT | GROUP |
|---|---|---|---|
| January 19 | Paris | Carlos' men make another attempt with hand-held rocket missiles at Orly but are spotted before they can fire and in ensuing gunfight seize hostages and bargain their way onto a flight to Iraq. | Carlos-PFLP |
| January 24 | New York | A bomb explosion at Fraunces Tavern in the Wall Street area kills four and injures 53. | FALN |
| January 29 | Washington, D.C. | Bomb explosion causes extensive damage to U.S. State Department building but causes no casualties. | Weather Underground |
| February 27 | Berlin | German politician Peter Lorenz is kidnapped and ransomed for the freedom of five Baader-Meinhof terrorists. The West German government capitulates, freeing the five and giving the terrorists 20,000 deutsche marks each. | Baader-Meinhof |
| April 24 | Stockholm | Six West German terrorists, former patients of the Neurological-Psychiatric Clinic of Heidelberg—the "crazy brigade"—occupy the West German Embassy and murder two diplomats when their demands are not met for the freeing of 26 Baader-Meinhof members. The embassy is blown up as police prepare to attack. One of the terrorists is killed, another dies later and the other four are arrested and deported to West Germany. | Baader-Meinhof |
| May 21 | Stammheim, West Germany | Trial of the Baader-Meinhof leaders begins. | |
| June 27 | Paris | Carlos' identity is revealed when French police are led to his flat on the Rue Toullier by Michel Moukharbel, his liasion officer with the PFLP. Carlos kills Moukharbel and two of the police officers and wounds a third before escaping to Algeria. Until now no one had known of his existence or his involvement in terrorism in London and Paris. From now on he boasts, "I am the famous Carlos." | Carlos-PFLP |
| August 4 | Kuala Lumpur | U.S. Consulate and Swedish Embassy are seized to secure the release of seven imprisoned terrorists. Two | JRA |

| DATE | PLACE | INCIDENT | GROUP |
|------|-------|----------|-------|
| | | refuse to go. Remainder flown to Libya. | |
| September 18 | San Francisco | Patty Hearst and three members of Symbionese Liberation Army are arrested and held on bank robbery charges. | SLA |
| December 21 | Vienna | OPEC's headquarters is seized by Carlos and a mixed gang of Palestinian and Baader-Meinhof terrorists. Three men are shot and 11 oil ministers kidnapped and held hostage, among them Sheik Yamani of Saudi Arabia and Dr. Jamshid Amouzegar of Iran. The Palestinians and Germans want to kill them both, but Carlos holds out for ransom—and gets it. The hostages are released in Algeria. Up to the time of writing, this is the last known operation in which Carlos has been involved "in the field." | Carlos-PFLP-Baader-Meinhof |
| December | Holland | South Moluccans seize a train at Beilen and the Indonesian Embassy in the Hague in pursuance of their hopeless cause to wrest an independent republic from Indonesia. They kill three and are given heavy prison sentences. | South Moluccans |
| 1976 January 8 | Ireland | Detachment of British Strategic Air Services is delayed in Armagh. They effectively wrest control of what was "bandit country" from the Provos. | Provisional IRA |
| March 11 | Dublin | Eddie Gallagher is jailed for 20 years and Marian Coyle for 15 for kidnapping Dutch industrialist Tiede Herrema in an attempt to force the freeing of Gallagher's mistress, Rose Dugdale. | Provisional IRA |
| May 4 | Stammheim | Gudrun Ensslin admits the Baader-Meinhof gang's responsibility for three of the lethal bombings with which they were charged. | Baader-Meinhof |
| May 8 | Stammheim | Ulricke Meinhof hangs herself from the bars of her cell window. | Baader-Meinhof |
| May 23 | Assen | South Moluccans seize a train at | South |

| DATE | PLACE | INCIDENT | GROUP |
|------|-------|----------|-------|
|  |  | Assen and children's school at Bovinsmilde. The school children are released after four days when they fall ill with a stomach virus; the train is captured in a dawn assault by Dutch Marines after a seige that lasts 20 days. Two hostages and six terrorists die in the assault. | Moluccans |
| June 18 | Buenos Aires | General Cesareo Cardozo, chief of Federal Police, is killed by bomb exploding under his bed. The bomb was believed to have been placed there by a friend of his daughter. He is the second police chief killed in less than two years. | ERP |
| June 27 | Entebbe | A mixed group of West German and Palestinian terrorists hijack an Air France airbus to Entebbe, where they separate the Jews from other passengers and threaten to kill them unless their demands for the release of imprisoned terrorists are met. At least three governments are involved on the terrorist side, those of Uganda, Somalia and Libya. The hijacking is brought to an end by the spectacular assault on Entebbe airport by Israeli paratroops. It is the first great defeat of international terrorism. The Israelis kill the two West German terrorists involved—one of them Wilfred Bose, one of Carlos' Paris gang—and five members of the PFLP. | Baader-Meinhof-PFLP |
| July 19 | Argentina | Robert Santucho, overall leader of the ERP, is killed in battle with the authorities. His death is a severe blow to the movement. | ERP |
| July 31 | Dublin | British ambassador to Ireland, Christopher Ewart-Biggs, is assassinated by a culvert bomb. | Provisional IRA |
| October 28 | Belfast | Maire Drumm, violently anti-British Provisional IRA leader, shot to death in hospital while recovering from an operation. | UDA Splinter Group |
| 1977 January 24 | Madrid | Five communist lawyers are killed when two men with submachine guns attack left wingers meeting in Madrid lawyer's office. | Warriors of Christ the King |

| DATE | PLACE | INCIDENT | GROUP |
|---|---|---|---|
| February 9 | London | Balcombe Street gang terrorists are found guilty of multiple murders and sentenced to life imprisonment. Up to time of writing, no further Active Service Units of the Provisional IRA have gone into action in London. | Provisional IRA |
| March 9 | Washington, D.C. | Gunmen seize three buildings and hold 134 hostages for 39 hours before surrendering. | Hanafi Muslims |
| April 7 | Karlsruhe | Siegfried Buback, West Germany's chief public prosecutor, is shot to death in revenge for Ulricke Meinhof's suicide. | Baader-Meinhof |
| April 10 | London | Former Yemeni Prime Minister Abdullah al-Hejiri, his wife and the minister at the Yemeni Embassy are assassinated by Palestinian hit man. Killer later commands Mogadishu hijacking. The murder was committed because Hejiri was working for the Saudis to form a Western-orientated alliance of Arab countries in southern Arabia and the Horn of Africa. | PFLP |
| July 31 | Frankfurt | Juergen Ponto, one of Germany's most influential bankers, is murdered by terrorists who are led into his heavily protected home by his god-daughter, Susanne Albrecht. | Baader-Meinhof |
| August 3 | New York | Two office buildings are bombed resulting in one death and seven injuries. | FALN |
| September 5 | Cologne | Hans-Martin Schleyer, a powerful West German businessman, is ambushed by a terrorist gang who kill his driver and three bodyguards and kidnap him. In return for his life they demand the release of 11 Baader-Meinhof prisoners, who are to be given about $50,000 each and flown to the country of their choice. This kidnapping virtually brings governmental life to a standstill in West Germany. | Baader-Meinhof |
| September 28 | Bombay | Japanese Red Army hijacks Japanese Air Lines plane and demands release of six Red Army prisoners and a $6 million ransom. Japanese government capitulates. The Japanese hijackers | JRA |

| DATE | PLACE | INCIDENT | GROUP |
|------|-------|----------|-------|
| | | make their way to Baghdad to join the international group being built up by Wadi Hadad and Carlos. | |
| October 13 | Majorca-Frankfurt | Lufthansa airliner with 79 passengers is hijacked by Palestinians—two men, two women—who demand the release of Baader-Meinhof leaders and an $18 million ransom. Terrorists threaten to kill Schleyer and passengers and crew on board airliner. After wild flight around the Middle East and the Horn of Africa, during which the terrorist leader, "Captain Mahmoud," shoots the pilot, Jugen Schumann, the plane lands at Mogadishu, Somalia. There, the plane is assaulted by members of the West German GSG9 commando unit and all the passengers are released. Two British Strategic Air Services soldiers take part in the assault using special "stun" grenades. Three of the terrorists are killed and the fourth, a woman is wounded. The terrorist leader is identified as one of Wadi Hadad's professional killers, Zohair Akache, who had murdered the three Yemenis in London six months previously. | PFLP on behalf of Baader-Meinhof |
| October 19 | Mulhouse, France | The body of Schleyer is found in the trunk of a car. He has been shot through the head. | Baader–Meinhof |
| October 20 | Stammheim | Andreas Baader, Gudrun Ensslin and Jan-Carl Raspe, who had expected to be freed through the Schleyer kidnapping and Mogadishu hijacking, commit suicide in their cells. | Baader–Meinhof |
| December 7 | Cairo | David Holden, London *Sunday Times* Middle East expert, is murdered. | Unknown |
| December 31 | London | Two Syrian diplomats are killed by a car bomb in Mayfiar. Victims are members of Syrian Intelligence and it is thought that they are killed by scoring an "own goal" with a bomb they are taking to plant. | Syrian Intelligence |
| 1978 January 4 | London | Said Hammami, the PLO's representative in London, is shot dead in his office. Killing causes | PFLP or Black June |

| DATE | PLACE | INCIDENT | GROUP |
|---|---|---|---|
| | | furor in the Arab world: Hammami, a moderate, was being used by Yasser Arafat to conduct negotiations with the Israelis. Killer is thought to be a member of one of the rejectionist groups, either Wadi Hadad's PFLP or, more likely, Abu Nidal's Black June. | |
| February 18 | Nicosia | Two Palestinian gunmen murder Egyptian editor Yusuf Sebai then hijack Cyprus airliner. Jet returns to Nicosia, where Egyptian commando mission to seize terrorists tragically misfires and 15 men die in fight with Cyprus National Guard. | PFLP |
| March 9 | Turin | Trial of Red Brigades leader Renato Curcio and 47 members begins. They appear caged and manacled in court. | |
| March 10 | Rome | In reprisal action Red Brigades murder Judge Rosario Berardi and prison official. | Red Brigades |
| March 16 | Rome | Aldo Moro is kidnapped and five bodyguards are slaughtered. | Red Brigades |
| March 25 | Rome | Communique announces Moro is to be tried by "people's court." | Red Brigades |
| March 30 | Rome | Italian Communist Party joins Christian Democrats in refusing to negotiate or to free prisoners. | Red Brigades |
| April 1 | East Berlin | Wadi Hadad, operational commander of PFLP and allies, dies of cancer. He is buried in Baghdad. | |
| April 7 | Vatican | Pope appeals to terrorists to spare Moro's life. | |
| April 13 | New York | David Graiver, Argentine terrorists' banker, is indicted in absentia. "He may still be alive." | |
| April 15 | Rome | Red Brigades announce that Moro has been condemned to death. | Red Brigades |
| April 18 | Rome | False announcement is issued that Moro has been "executed by suicide." | |
| April 24 | Cairo | Egyptians smash terrorist ring they claim is masterminded by Abu Nidal and the Corrective Movement of Al Fatah. Twenty-four are arrested including a German woman and three Swiss said to be linked with Italian Red Brigades. | |

| DATE | PLACE | INCIDENT | GROUP |
|---|---|---|---|
| May 10 | Rome | The body of Aldo Moro is found in the back of a car in Rome. He has been murdered. | Red Brigades |
| June 15 | Kuwait | PLO representative Aly Yasin is assassinated. | Black June |
| June 23 | Turin | Renato Curcio is sentenced to 15 years' imprisonment. Another founding member of Red Brigades, Pietro Bassi, is also sentenced to 15 years. Of the 47 on trial, 16 are acquitted. | Red Brigades |
| June 24 | Brussels | Iraq embassy is bombed, but there are no casualties. Bombing signals start of miniwar between Iraqi Rejectionists, spearheaded by Abu Nidal's Black June group, and Yasser Arafat's PLO. | PLO |
| July 9 | London | General al-Naif, former Iraqi prime minister, is assassinated outside Intercontinental Hotel. | Iraqi Secret Service: Al Mukhabara |
| July 26 | Britain | Britain expels 11 Iraqi diplomats because of their involvement in acts of terrorism. Iraqi Embassy has become center of terrorism. | |
| July 28 | London | Grenade is thrown at Iraqi ambassador's car. No casualties. | PLO |
| July 31 | Beirut | Unsuccessful machine-gun attack on Iraqi ambassador. | PLO |
| July 31 | Paris | Gunmen invade Iraqi Embassy and take eight hostages. Gunmen surrender but are ambushed by Iraqi secret servicemen as they are taken from the building. Fire-fight ensues between Iraqis and French police. French police inspector and Iraqi diplomat are killed. | PLO |
| August 2 | Karachi | Two gunmen attack Iraqi Consulate. One of them is bayoneted to death by a police guard despite the guard's four bullet wounds. One diplomat is wounded. | PLO |
| August 3 | Paris | PLO representative, Ezzedine Kalak, is assassinated. | Black June |
| August 5 | Islamabad | Three PLO men and police guard are killed when four gunmen attack PLO office. | Black June |

| DATE | PLACE | INCIDENT | GROUP |
|------|-------|----------|-------|
| August 7 | Lebanon | Fierce inter-Arab battles break out in refugee camps between PLO and Iraqi-backed groups. | |
| August 20 | London | El Al aircrew bus is attacked outside Europa Hotel. One Israeli stewardess is killed and another wounded. | Black June |
| September 6 | Dusseldorf | Peter Stoll, believed to have played major part in kidnapping and murder of Hanns-Martin Schleyer, is killed by West German police attempting to arrest him in restaurant. | Baader-Meinhof |
| September 13 | Milan | Corrado Alunni, prime suspect in the murder of Aldo Moro, is arrested in apartment filled with guns, explosives and false documents. | Red Brigades |
| September 15 | London | Astrid Proll is arrested at garage where she had been working for 10 months. West German government asks for her extradition on charges of attempted murder of two policemen. She is believed to have links with Carlos. | Baader-Meinhof |
| September 24 | Dortmund | Angelika Speitel and Michael Knoll are wounded and arrested after shoot-out with West German police while target shooting in a forest. Speitel was wanted in connection with murders of Siegfried Buback, Jurgen Ponto and Hans-Martin Schleyer. | Baader-Meinhof |
| 1979 January 22 | Beirut | Ali Hassan Salameh, also known as Abu Hassan, is killed by car bomb. Al Fatah blames Israeli intelligence. Hassan had allegedly planned the 1972 Munich massacre. | Mossad |

As the year ended the West German security forces were bringing more and more pressure to bear on the remnants of the Baader-Meinhof gang and Red Army Factions, while Red Brigade terrorists in Italy and ETA terrorists in Spain continued their assassination campaigns. At the same time, the new liberal regime in Spain was threatened with terrorist action from an extreme right-wing Patriotic Justice Committee, composed of the Anti-Communist Apostolic Alliance, the Warriors of Christ the King, and ATE, the anti-ETA organization.

# Bibliography

Becker, Jillian. *Hitler's Children*, Philadelphia: J. B. Lippincott, 1977.

Begin, Menachem. *The Revolt*, Plainview: Nash Publishing Corporation, 1977.

Bianco, Mirella. *Gadaffi, Voice from the Desert*, London: Longman, 1975.

Burns, Alan. *The Angry Brigade*, London: Quartet, 1974.

Clutterback, Richard. *Living With Terrorism*, New Rochelle: Arlington House, 1976.

Conrad, Joseph. *The Secret Agent*, New York: Doubleday, 1953.

Cozier, Brian. *Annual of Power and Conflict 1976, 1977, 1978*, London: Institute for Study of Conflict.

Debray, Regis. *Revolution in the Revolution*, New York: Grove Press, 1967.

Debray, Regis. *Strategy for a Revolution: Essays on Latin America*, New York: Monthly Review, 1970.

Dobson, Christopher. *Black September: Its Short, Violent History*, New York: Macmillan, 1974.

_____ and Ronald Payne. *The Carlos Complex: A Study in Terror*, New York: Putnam, 1977.

Fanon, Frantz. *The Wretched of the Earth*, New York: Grove Press, 1965.

Gott, Richard. *Guerrilla Movements in Latin America*, London: Nelson, 1976.

Guevera, Che. *Guerrilla Warfare*, New York: Random House, 1968.

Hidalgo, O. C. *Spy for Fidel*, Miami: Seeman, 1971.

Horchem, H. J. *West Germany's Red Army Anarchists*, London: Conflict Studies No. 46, 1974.

Jackson, Geoffrey. *Surviving the Long Night: An Autobiographical Account of a Political Kidnapping*, New York: Vanguard Press, 1974.

Johnson, K. *Guatemala: From Terrorism to Terror*, London: Institute for Study of Conflict, 1972.

Kitson, Frank. *Low Intensity Operations: Subversion, Insurgency, Peace-Keeping*, Hamden: The Shoe String Press, 1974.

Laqueur, Walter. *Terrorism*, Boston: Little Brown & Co., 1977.

Marcuse, Herbert. *Five Lectures*, Boston: Beacon Press, 1970.

_____. *One Dimensional Man*, Boston: Beacon Press, 1964.

Marighella, Carlos. *For the Liberation of Brazil*, Harmondsworth: Penguin, 1971.

Masters, Anthony. *Bakunin*, London: Sidgwick and Jackson, 1974.

O'Brien, C. C. *Herod, Reflections on Political Violence*, London: Hutchinson, 1978.

Phillips, David. *Skyjack*, London: Harrap, 1973.

Stevenson, William. *90 Minutes at Entebbe*, New York: Bantam Books, 1976.

Tabbora, Lina. *Suvivre dans Beyrouth*, Paris: Olivier Orban, 1977.

Thadden, Adolf von. *Die Schreibtischtater, Das geistige Umfled des Terrorism*, Hanover: Greiffen-Verlag, 1977.

Thomas, Hugh. *Cuba: The Pursuit of Freedom, 1762-1969*, New York: Harper & Row, 1971.

Tophoven, Rolf. *Fedayin, Guerrilla ohne Grenzen*, Municho: Bernard und Graefe Verlag fur Wehrwesen.

Trotsky, Leon. *The Defense of Terrorism*, London: Allen and Unwin, 1921.

Wilkinson, Paul. *Political Terrorism*, New York: Halsted Press, 1976.

_____. *Terrorism and the Liberal State*, New York: Halsted Press, 1978.

# A

# B